THE BELEAGUERED COLLEGE

THE BELEAGUERED COLLEGE:
Essays on Educational Reform

Joseph Tussman

Institute of Governmental Studies Press
University of California
1997

Library of Congress Cataloging-In-Publication Data

Tussman, Joseph.
    The beleaguered college : essays on educational reform / Joseph Tussman.
        p. cm.
    ISBN 0-87772-373-7
    1. Education, Higher—Aims and objectives—United States. 2. Education, Humanistic
—United States. 3. Educational change—United States. 4. Education—United
States—Experimental methods—Case studies. 5. Academic freedom—United States. I.
Title.
LA227.4.T87 1997
378.73—dc21   978303
                                                                           CIP

CONTENTS

PREFACE

These essays, written at different times without planned coherence are, nevertheless, unified by a cherished conception of liberal education. The basic story of the attempt to give that conception concrete form is told in "Experiment at Berkeley" and "A Venture in Educational Reform." The other essays contribute to the theoretical and even personal context of an attempt to reform "liberal education," or at least to demonstrate a possible alternative to the virtually universal form of lower-division college education in America.

There are a few persistent themes: First, I see a fateful conflict between the university and the college, between the graduate school and the undergraduate college. This is a conflict not sufficiently grasped or appreciated. Somewhere, in an apocalyptic mood, I sum it all up by saying that the university, merely by being what it is, has killed the college. I don't know if the reader will come to share this academically unpalatable view, but I hold it with unflagging conviction.

Second, I argue that "liberal" education is, like so much of education, "vocational," that the vocation is, in a fundamental sense, "politics," that it is concerned with initiation into one of the greatest of arts, the art of governing the body politic, and that, in a democratic society, it is an education needed by everyone. This seems to me to be obvious, but I am no longer surprised at how widely it is rejected and even detested—especially by respectable scholars and humanists.

And third, I am haunted by the sheer pedagogic sterility of the undergraduate college. Curricular incoherence and a fragmentary course structure are largely responsible, but the situation is now made worse by the tendency to see the student not as an apprentice to be initiated and developed—that is, as a *student*—but as a customer seeking freedom from educational constraint under the banner of "choice."

These are among the main themes and, I think, they are sufficiently developed here. Or, at least, I am not inclined to supplement the argument with belated additional inspiration. The question is not whether I have said all that I think should have been said, but why I bother to say or re-say it all now. This is, I am reliably informed, the '90s , not the '60s. Surely, someone must have re-invented college education, rendering inherited practices and ideas obsolete—especially anything that might be tainted by respect for a Euro-centric tradition? Surely we have outgrown earlier

vii

ailments, have cured the defects of recent pre-enlightened misconceptions? Surely, our problems are all new ones, requiring new analysis and new forms of treatment?

"Surely," my answer is, "not!" With respect to "liberal education" there has only been further deterioration. It is in worse shape than ever and its victims are hardly even aware of the fact. The world of higher education is dominated by an establishment that is utterly unimaginative, conventional, safe, and hopeless. A conveniently thoughtless "pluralism" supports the faculty reluctance to engage in serious curricular thought and leaves the college helpless in the face of strident consumer and transient ideological demands. The uncreative complacency of the establishment is challenged by an anti-establishment "critique" of a shallowness and fruitlessness unmatched in living memory. In these depressing circumstances these essays may remind us of the fundamental problems that must be addressed if the college is to regain a sense of identity and mission and do for society what badly needs doing.

"A Venture in Educational Reform" is an attempt at recollection in tranquility. For 20 years after the closing down of the Experimental Program I had been sporadically troubled by the need to explain and evaluate—and to defend—the short-lived institution that embodied some utopian hopes for undergraduate education. But I had trouble with the shape of the funeral oration. I remained convinced about its educational virtues, but it did not seem right for me to try to prove the case. I had no desire to try to marshal an objective assessment in support of my unshaken intuitions, no desire to commit research. Telling the story seemed more attractive, especially the thought of finally "telling all." In the end I settle for merely telling quite a lot, but, I think, enough.

"Experiment at Berkeley," written while the program was in progress, is, unfortunately, out of print. I present it here in a shortened version, purged of some of what I consider of only transient significance and of some repetition.

"Why We Should Read the Greeks" is a bow in the direction of the "canon" controversy, or rather, my way of avoiding a rather sterile debate while making the obvious point about tradition and identity—a point that underlies the curriculum of the Experimental Program.

"Remembering Alexander Meikljohn" is a tribute to my teacher, whose Experimental College at Wisconsin in the late '20s was the inspiration for my own venture. His life was a joyous merging of thinking and teaching in a way that overshadows conventional academic concerns about teaching and "research." He understood teaching as a great art, but not a performing or histrionic art.

"Government and the Teaching Power," a chapter from my book, *Government and the Mind,* is an attempt to remedy the shocking failure to understand the theoretical or constitutional basis of the great tutelary power, inherent in any polity, and, consequently, to understand the nature, scope, and limitations of "academic freedom." The undeniable existence of the teaching power is a standing refutation of the absurd view that government has no authority in the realm of the mind. What is dangerous about this view is not the view itself but our reluctance to think about it.

CHAPTER 1

A VENTURE IN EDUCATIONAL REFORM: A PARTIAL VIEW

I pass the house every day. It stands at the edge of the campus, looking very much as it looked a quarter of a century ago. It had once been a fraternity house, but when I first got involved with it, in the early sixties, it had been standing vacant, almost derelict, not yet assigned to its university use. It became the home of the Experimental Program and the center of my life for four years—a slowly fading scar for a lot longer. It now, more sedately, houses a graduate program. The last time I stepped inside, almost a decade ago, I noted the familiar mellow wooden panels in the great hall, now without a defacing collection of student poems protesting my behavior, and I saw, still in use, the enormous round wooden table that had taken up most of the room in my office—the table I had found in the university warehouse, around which the fabled Teggart had once conducted his seminar.

There was a time when the sight of the house in the early morning produced a surge of anxiety, a deep reluctance to approach the door, to open it and step into whatever it held for the day. And for some years after I had ceased to enter, the mere sight of the building as I drove past evoked a vague sense of apprehension that dissipated slowly as I moved through the paces of a normal academic day—as a disturbing dream lingers and fades through an uneventful morning. But now when I pass the house nothing happens. It may be possible at last, "all passion spent," to recollect in tranquility.

The question most difficult for me to deal with is "why did the program fail?" I usually rush to explain that as an educational venture it did not fail; that it "failed" only in not establishing itself as a permanent part of the university. But there is something unsatisfactory about that answer. Why,

---

This was originally written December 21, 1988.

1

if it was educationally valid or even significant, did it disappear without a trace?

I have never really told the whole story of the program. In the middle of its third year I wrote "Experiment at Berkeley," giving an account of the rationale and of some of the problems we were facing. It was essentially a progress report. I have never completed the report nor written anything about the problems of educational reform or about the state of college education generally, or joined very seriously in our local educational controversies. When the Experimental Program had run its trial four-year life I returned to writing and to departmental teaching for the dozen years until retirement. I did not turn away from the program as a sad experience best buried in oblivion, but, obviously, I put off writing about it. "Experiment at Berkeley" does give a good idea of what it was all about, so some of the things I would want to say have already been said—although without the benefit or disadvantage of several decades of reflection. There are things to add and things that deserve emphasis and amplification, but apparently not urgently enough to have overcome my reluctance to plunge back into the depressing world of educational controversy to reargue tattered issues.

Since this is reflection on educational reform let me say that I am not concerned with "normal" educational improvement. Reasonably good teachers improve with experience, although they may grow out of the stage of energetic novice enthusiasm whose glow may be mistaken for the aura of Socratic genius. The teaching of good teachers tends to grow better; the teaching of poor teachers tends not to improve, or not to improve enough to make up for the belatedly discovered mistake in hiring. Improving the educational system by improving teaching is obviously a good thing. But American higher education is not in danger of being destroyed by bad teaching, nor, if it needs salvation, is it going to be saved by an outburst of great teaching or by the improvement of its normal teaching. The state of the art of teaching is not, for the college or university, a life-threatening problem.

And, of course, in a good or, as we are in the habit of saying at UC Berkeley, a "great" university, the level of conventional teaching is bound to be rather high. There are always complaints, some even legitimate. Classes too large or too hard to get into, confusing advice, preoccupied or unsympathetic faculty. But the place is undeniably full of vigorous minds engaged in research and in teaching, full of bright students doing what bright students are supposed to do. Most consider themselves lucky to be where they are, not awaiting reform.

Why then, at such a place, in the early sixties, did I think that a drastically different educational model should be tried. And not tried merely as one does an experiment to prove a point or a theory, but as an effort to bring about a significant change in our educational way of life. To work out the conception of an alternative pattern, to show that it worked, in practice, much better than the conventional pattern—much better, since if it was only as good as or a slight improvement over what we had, it would not be worth the trouble—and then to keep it alive as a regular and even growing part of the university and a model for adoption by colleges and universities everywhere. That was the idea, the dream, the project.

The program was not a response to particular events or pressures. Students had not yet discovered the delights of hurling themselves upon the cushioned cogs of the machine demanding institutional change, and, in any case, student educational demands, as they came to be made, were utterly at odds with the spirit of the program. There was deep irony in the fact that the student movement on the educational front fought under the banners of the system it thought it hated. That is, it demanded "decontrol," the abolition of "requirements," consumer sovereignty, an elective system ad absurdum—the marketplace, in short. Whereas, alas, I considered "marketplace" applied to education or to the mind as bizarrely oxymoronic. But I am getting ahead of myself. . . .

The program, I repeat, was not a response to pressure. No one was demanding it or anything like it. So far as I am aware, I did not need it. I had recently returned to Berkeley after a half dozen or so years in the East. I was delighted to be back. I was a professor in the philosophy department. I had tenure. I had written a book. My classes were going well. I had a backlog of writing projects. I was not even on a Committee to Foster Educational Innovation. Why, then, an unsolicited venture in educational reform?

I suppose that a purely analytic treatment of the educational issues posed and faced by the Experimental Program could avoid that question. The account of genesis is more historical and biographical than analytical; the order of creation and development is not the same as the order of justification. But this is a sort of apologia and an apologia, if we can judge by its great models, is a complex mixture of the two orders. At any rate, I will say something about the genesis of the program, not so much out of

3

autobiographical concerns as for its relevance to the problem of introducing significant change into the educational system. Significant or at least drastic change—if that is, in the end, what one wants.

There is a kind of ameliorative change that is rather easy to achieve. A professor can usually fiddle with his course as he pleases. He can change its substance and its methods as he thinks best without anyone's permission. With little trouble he can substitute new courses for old ones and keep his teaching in line with his interests and educational convictions. This sort of change is generally so easy that there is seldom an accumulation of frustration calling for drastic measures. From the faculty point of view, being able to teach what one wishes, as one thinks best, without external interference, is, short of teaching less and in the extreme case not at all, to enjoy the good life. To change, modify, improve the courses one teaches does not require one to be an educational reformer.

There is also a familiar class of educational changes beyond these that, generally, do not interfere very much with the established way of life. Should a requirement be added or dropped for all or for a special group of students? More math or writing or a foreign language or American or western or world history? Should all students be required to achieve computer-literacy or ethnic-consciousness? Should a new or an interdisciplinary "major" be established or the requirements for a particular major changed? Should grading be tougher, more revealing than tactful, or forced on a curve, and should students grade their teachers? Should we divide the year into quarters or semesters? Should we have small courses or seminars for freshmen? . . . Questions of this sort have popped up on the academic agenda for as long as I can remember, staple items in the politics of education, normally requiring collective faculty and administrative action. Faculty members differ in their degree of concern with such matters taken as general educational questions. They will, however, be alert to proposals that effect their own teaching, resistant to those that might require them to handle their own courses differently, and supportive of the claims of colleagues to teaching autonomy.

It is obvious, of course, that all this is about courses, about their inner life and their external ordering. The course is the familiar, the inevitable unit of our educational life. To teach is to give a course; to study is to take a course or a mildly ordered collection of courses; to administer is to arrange that the takers and the givers are properly brought together. The fate of the

Experimental Program can be foreshadowed in a simple statement: In a world of course-givers and course-takers it tried to abolish "the course."

I need here to account for two things: The shaping of the alternate conception of lower-division liberal education, and the motivation to try to bring it into existence.

I forget who it was who first said "nothing is ever said for the first time" —broadened for this occasion into "or thought." Discovering what you believe is discovering the tradition into which you fall. My deepest educational conviction is certainly not original. It is that what we call "liberal education" is essentially the education of the Ruler. It is not primarily aesthetic—for the heightening of "enjoyment," the enriching of leisure. It is not the education of the human being as human being. It is not education for scholarship or research or the professorate. It is not primarily spectatorial. It is vocational, and the vocation is governing or ruling—in a broad sense, politics. It is the forbidden fruit so deeply associated with our aspirations for participation in the ruling function. To say this is to raise all sorts of specters and to summon hostile spirits from the vasty deep—worthy opponents, decent, well-motivated, cultured, humane, skeptical, tolerant, anti-authoritarian opponents—all honorable, although tending to archo-phobia and to regarding this "merely" political emphasis as a disparagement of the mind that is to be valued for its own sake. Nevertheless, it was, for me, the conception at the very heart of the Experimental Program, without which I would not have tried to launch it and without which, therefore, it would not have come into existence at all. It was, although I am resigned to the probability that this will seem at least paradoxical, the educational vision of a rabid democrat.

I consider myself indebted for this view to my teacher, Alexander Meiklejohn, and I have been dominated by it for as long as I can remember, and long before the program took shape. I need to acknowledge, although I do so reluctantly, a fundamental disposition expressing itself in a drift into political and legal philosophy, manifesting an intellectual provincialism giving its special character to the curricular core of the program. Reluctantly, because I would like to think of the program as based on something more than a temperamental devotion to the "political" as against other claims. At any rate, I start with the conception of the wonderfully baffling idea of liberal education as education for the ruling function and the companion conviction that since everyone in a democracy is to share in the ruling function, everyone needed to share in the education reserved, in elitist societies, to the ruling class.

To this must be added the perception that the college was not providing it and, rather fortuitously, that there was a vacuum where it should or might be. The freshman and sophomore years, the lower division, is generally the wasteland of American higher education. That is, in part, because we still tend to protect those years against the vocationalism or professionalism dominating the graduate schools and even the upper-division majors, without having a very clear idea of what we are protecting them *for*. The lower-division student is not yet under the aegis of a particular department, has not made his fateful choice, and is considered to be engaged in remedial or preparatory or exploratory or even "general" education. From the point of view of the dominant power structures—graduate and research-oriented departments—the lower division is someone else's responsibility, a holding area in which some grazing is done before, fleshed out a bit, the creature can be put to serious work. If anyone is responsible for the lower-division student it is probably a powerless dean trying to marshal some educational energy not elsewhere engaged (and therefore a bit suspect), for a venture professional scholars seldom find professionally interesting or important—except, perhaps, as an exercise in recruiting. But this is an old and hackneyed tale and I will not linger over it. The program idea was to take the conception of liberal education as broadly politically vocational and insert it into the spiritually empty lower-division years—thus filling a deep but unfelt need while at the same time giving a significant point to an otherwise pointless phase of American college education.

The curricular embodiment of this conception needs to be spelled out, but it might appear to be something that could be done in the usual way by stringing courses together and, if necessary, creating some special courses—by creating, in effect, a lower-division variant of an upper-division disciplinary or interdisciplinary major. Why, then, did the program abandon the course structure and propose instead a single massive highly organized two-year program? Since this was the distinctive feature of the program most responsible for its unique quality and for its special problems, I suppose I should explain. But I may do so slowly and in bits and pieces.

Imagine, if you can, that you are a freshman newly enrolled in the program. You will be introduced to the idea that, unlike what you have been used to, you will, during the life of the program, be doing—be thinking about—only one thing at a time. And you are told that for the next two weeks or so you are to spend all of your time, *all* of your time (well, almost all, since you will be allowed to take one course, a language course, for example, in addition to the program. "Comic relief," I heard it called.) reading or studying Homer's *Iliad.* You are advised not to bother reading *about* Homer or *Iliad,* not to consult secondary or scholarly or "critical" material—just to read *Iliad* itself. You will not be aware of the blood that had been shed in support of those instructions, of the academic proprieties being trampled on, but you might consider it a strange beginning to a college career. You had expected more formidable assignments but, accepting unexpected gifts, you decide to go along—not without the shadow of a worry that you may not be going to get a real college education after all. ("All the guys in my dorm are already taking quizzes in three subjects and I'm still just fooling around with the *Iliad*!")

What we are trying to do, and probably without much initial success, is to lead the student into the experience of relaxed, enjoyable immersion, a sustained involvement of mind, in a great work whose significance is far from obvious and about whose significance nothing, at this stage of the game, should be said. Many people will go through college—through a lifetime—without such an experience. Two whole weeks out of your life in which your job is to soak yourself in *Iliad* or something like it. But this is not to be an exercise in solitary reading. Everyone in the program will be doing the same thing, including the faculty. And during those two weeks there will be some scheduled program activity. Informal lectures or panel discussions, seminar meetings, a short paper to be discussed in a private tutorial session. And all, during that two-week period, on *Iliad.* Intensive, undistracted, essentially enjoyment-directed. Clearly, all our resources are marshaled to encourage the having of a particular kind of intellectual and emotional experience. It is very difficult to describe, but we have gone to a great deal of trouble to try to make it possible. We have cleared the decks, provided the time, gotten rid of a distracting multiplicity of intellectual tasks, tried to discourage the desire for information of a scholarly, historical, literary, sociological sort, to restrain the tendency to find out what others have said, from doing "research." But what, you may well ask, is there left to do? And why do that? This is, I am afraid, one of those familiar situations in which it is futile to try to explain to someone why he should do something until after he has done it. Of course, freeing up time, telling students to relax and wallow in a book and try to enjoy it, doesn't do very much. If you have been taught to read rapidly you will have forgotten how to read slowly; You will simply read rapidly and wonder what to do with all the spare time on your hands. And no one will enjoy something because a teacher tells him to. And what, by the way, —if it is difficult to explain what the student was supposed to do—was the faculty supposed to do?

I am almost afraid to confess that the faculty was not supposed to do what it was supposed to be good at, what it had been chosen by the university to spend its life doing. We were not to practice the "disciplines" with which we, as faculty members, were identified. There were five of us. I was a member of the philosophy department, usually teaching courses in political or legal philosophy. I had recruited as colleagues in this venture: a political theorist with a great reputation as a charismatic teacher; a talented poet, a bit Byronic, who later created some havoc as the academic vice-president of a private university and died gloriously hang-gliding; a radical youngish civil-liberties lawyer, a bulldog in argument, reputedly a strong "Socratic" teacher; a mathematician-engineer, a well-known maverick, politician, golfer, and a man of broad culture. None of us had grappled professionally with *Iliad*. What or how were we to "teach"?

But I should explain first (I see I may have problems with Shandyesque tendencies) how this odd crew came to be gathered around the large table contemplating such a strange problem. I need to make a rather delicate decision. Or rather, explain it, since I have obviously made it. I am going to talk about faculty colleagues. I need to, or I can't explain why the odds are so stacked against the success of such a program. There is really very little written about the college teacher at work. I used to read every academic novel I could get my hands on, and it is surprising how little is revealed about teaching. Compared to the surgeon working in the glare of the operating room the professor's teaching is normally a private affair, largely shielded from peer scrutiny. Of the several dozen colleagues from a variety of departments with whom I have gossiped at lunch for several decades, labored on committees, and manned the academic barricades, I cannot think of one whose class I have ever visited or who has visited one of mine. We assume, I suppose, that we can infer from a person's ordinary behavior how he would behave as a teacher. Apart from ordinary risks in inference I have discovered belatedly that, adding to predictive risks, there are actually teachers who think of teaching as a performing art, and who, when they enter a classroom, become strangely transformed. Ordinarily, it may not matter. As long as each is enclosed in his own watertight compartment the great ship of learning can stay afloat even if some compartments collapse or shelter weird side-shows. But if you put to sea in a single ark. . . .

Between conception and fruition lay a great many obstacles. The first step I took, before I discussed my plan with anyone else, was to drop in on President Clark Kerr. As university president, he was not directly in charge of the Berkeley campus, but I thought his support would be useful. I told him I wanted to try to establish a variant of Meiklejohn's Experimental College and wanted to know whether, if I got through the campus obstacles, there would be difficulties at a higher level. I remember his pleased smile. "Ah," he said, "the Revolution from below!" Of course he was all for it. He believed in education and, as president, there was little he could do; education was in the hands of the faculty. I told him I'd be back if I got far enough to need his help, and we parted cheerfully.

There were a number of decisive points at which, if I did nothing, if I sat still, peace, like a frightened kitten, would return, but if I did something, took the contemplated step, wrote the letter, asked to appear before the committee, I would have to face the next problem, more deeply and inextricably involved. And eventually, retreat would no longer be an option. The visit to Kerr was a first tentative step; I had indulged an impulse but had not yet assumed a commitment. I cannot explain the movement from having an idea about how things might be, to actually trying to do something about it without evoking the compelling powers of discipleship, of hero-worship, of sheer stubbornness and pride. I was driven by the desire to vindicate the educational vision of Alexander Meiklejohn. Of course, I got no encouragement or support in this venture from Meiklejohn himself, although he was still living in Berkeley when I made the opening moves. I now think that I was obtuse not to realize that he must have had deep reservations about my project and that, had I asked him, he might have advised against it. But it never occurred to me to ask, and he died before the program came into being. I mention all this to acknowledge that, as is so often the case, behind the public proposal lurked a private passion.

I would need to do three things to bring the program into existence. First, I would need to draw up an educational proposal that could win the approval of the appropriate faculty authorities. There had to be something on paper a committee or a faculty could consider and judge academically legitimate or respectable or desirable. This would pose some problems since I was asking approval not for the usual single course in a traditional departmental subject, but for a nondepartmental offering worth the equivalent in academic credit of about 16 out of the 20 semester courses normally taken in the first two years. Beyond the enormity of that, I was unable and unwilling to do more than offer a brief sketch of the plan. I did not propose to spend time working up a detailed syllabus to offer to a committee for its approval, not only because I found the task uncongenial, or because I shuddered at the thought of opening myself to the scrutiny of what I felt, correctly, to be the hostile academic mind of which, in educational matters, I had a rather deep distrust, but because, for reasons I now turn to, it was impossible. What was needed was a formulation clear enough to give a fair idea of the plan and vague enough to allow for a wide range of discretion as we went along.

I needed—this was the second of my three tasks—to find or recruit colleagues. In the intuitive groping for form I had settled on about 125 to 150 students as a good number. And since I did not want an experiment that, if successful, could be dismissed as "too expensive," I thought we needed a faculty of five or six—something like a ridiculous 25-1 ratio. So I began to look for four or five colleagues. Who?

It was clear, to begin with, that it would be foolish to consider anyone without tenure. We needed regular tenured Berkeley faculty members whose respectability would do something to fill the gap left by the sketchiness of the proposal. On the other hand, we needed teachers who were bold or reckless enough to step out into a wilderness unmarked by reassuring disciplinary signs. Respectable adventurous teachers are not people to whom you can hand a syllabus someone else has worked out. Normally they are the masters of their own courses. If they enter into cooperative ventures at all, they do so as "colleagues."

My problem, then, was to find colleagues, and that turned out to be extremely difficult. I could not simply approach someone as if with a tabula rasa. Should we make up an educational program? I wanted people who liked the general idea and were willing to work out the details together as we went along. But acceptance of the general idea, as I described it, was a primary necessity; there were some curricular and pedagogic givens—or I would not have bothered with the whole business. And this created a situation about which I was quite uneasy. I was clearly the prime mover and conception guardian, but I was trying to find full colleagues—I was quite romantic about collegiality—who would be happy to implement the plan. It was to be *our* program even though it was really my idea. As you can see, I was a bit naive.

Most of the people I approached were not interested or available. They were fully occupied with their work, had all sorts of plans and commitments, wouldn't think of taking two years off to go slumming outside their own fields, were vaguely puzzled that I would, but no, thanks. I hasten to say that I do not criticize them. They *were* fully occupied with research and teaching and university service, they were doing good, distinguished work and there was no reason for them to stop in order to do something they didn't believe in doing or didn't think they could do well. Nor do I really object to the fact that the UC Berkeley faculty is what it is—a group of hard working, self directed, high powered, research and graduate school-oriented professors—clearly reflecting its primary function. But there *is* a lower-division, and I thought we could afford, there, a daring attempt at a different form of significance—staffed by its regular faculty, not by a group of lower-division teachers not up to regular or peculiarly Berkeley standards.

I had great difficulty recruiting, and might well have had to give up. But in the end I found two who could come in, but only for a single year, and two who could come in for two years—enough for the launching. We decided to settle for a group of graduate student teaching assistants instead of trying to find a sixth faculty member. The process was even more complicated than it sounds. It was a sort of juggling act. I couldn't really push for program approval until I could point to a faculty. I couldn't tie down a faculty member, get him to change his plans and arrange leave from his regular duties in his department, unless the program was given an academic green light, and that was far from a sure thing—in fact it was downright unlikely. And finally, nothing could be done without a budget—salaries, space, staff support, and all that. And it was hard to arrange that without having done the other things first—which could not be done first without budgetary assurances. And I was in a hurry; I did not intend to get bogged down in "planning"; it was "next year or not at all."

In the end, budgetary and other matters depending on the administration turned out to present no problems at all. The administration was invariably and ungrudgingly helpful, granting every request (of course I made only reasonable requests) and easing every difficulty. Academic approval was, I think, the greatest hurdle. I won't trace the complicated process, but one scene persists in fond memory.

It was a meeting of the College of Letters and Science at which I was to present the plan for approval. I had distributed a couple of pages explaining the program curriculum. Sketchy, of course, and not very deeply analyzed.

I elaborated a bit and took questions. Then up rose a stalwart old-timer, an old-world social democrat whom I greatly admired for his stentorian defense of freedom and virtue in past academic battles. "I see," he boomed "that you start with the Greeks. Very Good. Then you jump to Seventeenth Century England. Also very good. Then you go to early America and then to present day America. Good! Good! So it is a historical program, is it not?"

It wasn't, but I hadn't figured out quite how to describe it. I began something like "not exactly" or "well, sort of, but. . . ." But he would not be denied. "A historical program! But look at the gaps. Full of gaps. For a historical program too many gaps!" He smiled at me, pitying, benign. "Too many gaps. I will vote against it!"

Someone came to my aid. "Isn't it really just a study of periods of crisis, of revolution—that's it, a study of Revolution?"

"I suppose so," I mumbled gratefully—a mumble I would pay for later.

Then rose a very bright young professor, greatly admired for having introduced the phrase "academic oatmeal" into our deliberations, to ask whether I was open to suggestions. "If I started considering all your good suggestions," I said tactfully, "I'd end up where we are now. So I guess it's take it or leave it."

Naturally, after that brilliant defense, it was approved. I'll skip further harrowing details; in a relatively short time we were all ready to go. But before I get back to *Iliad* I want to take up several things that combined, as it turned out, to make my life miserable, taking all the joy out of the first two years.

There was the house. It was obvious that some sort of physical center was needed. If students were to interact in a common program there had to be someplace for them to meet. Space was scarce and we considered, as a last resort, taking over a student dorm. Apart from whether that would have been possible, we were not sure it was a good idea to add the problems of residential separateness to those of distinctive curricular eccentricity. In the end we considered ourselves lucky to be able to capture an abandoned fraternity house on the edge of the campus, and it was patched up and sparsely furnished for our use. Rooms were fixed up as offices for the faculty, a few as seminar rooms. There was a program office, a large reading room, a great hall. Not lavish, but adequate. I suppose it was because I began with such high hopes that I came to detest the very sight of it. I had dreamed that it would be the lively center of our life, a place you could drop in to at any time and find students and faculty working and talking. . . . Well,

I am not, a quarter of a century later, going to allow myself to feel again the disgust at the ugly culture that came to dominate and to mock the university conception of civilization. What should have been part of an adult university became a juvenile counter-culture hangout. I felt responsible for the existence of the house and felt guilty at my betrayal of my university colleagues who had trusted me to conduct, in their name, an experiment in liberal education. For the first two years, the sight of the house made me sick.

Contributing to the discord was a decision we had taken, about which the faculty had had its first disagreement. When it appeared that we could not find a sixth faculty member we decided, as I said, to take on five graduate student teaching assistants. There was to be a great deal of writing, and we thought we would need help in reading and discussing student papers. There was never any thought—we explicitly rejected the thought—that the T.A.s would assume full or general faculty roles. We were seeking assistants, not colleagues. We invited applications. There was a complication. Usually a T.A. is a graduate student working for a Ph.D. degree in a department, assisting in an area, a discipline, in which he is working, getting experience in his own field. That was not possible in our nondisciplinary program, and we worried about diverting a graduate student from his primary work in his home department, but we concluded that if the T.A. was kept narrowly to reading papers and discussing them with the students, the experience would be a good one and not too distracting. In the process of selection it became clear that a graduate student very active in the student movement had virtually managed to wring an utterly unauthorized promise from our poet. Trying to forestall this, I had, in turn, gotten the assurance that no commitment would be made. I did not want him because I had seen enough of him to conclude that he was a pretentious militant who would not accept an assistant role and would dedicate himself to bringing the revolution to the program. I thought he would be uncontrollable and destructive and that we would have enough problems without this one. So I explained why I was against taking him on. His faculty sponsor admitted the danger, but said he had indeed promised and that he would undertake to control him. I knew he would be unable to do that and I was adamant. What to do?

Since this was a rather fateful turning point, I must explain that we had no formal structure of authority. We had no chairman, no director, no head, no CEO. I happened to still be chairman of the philosophy department, but that had absolutely nothing to do with the program. I never had a program title but had drifted, not unnaturally, into being the one who had to sign things. Whatever I may have thought, I religiously refused to let the words "my program" cross my lips or even emerge from between clenched teeth. I was, as I have said, romantic about collegial equality. But a decision needed to be made and, oddly enough, we had no way of doing so. I felt strongly enough about this matter to brood, over a weekend, about simply asserting a veto power, but I didn't think the program would survive such an act and, against my better and bitter judgment agreed to abide by a majority vote. I lost, of course, 2-3. I never forgave the triumphant three—two of whom knew they were only to stay in the program for one year but still had no qualms about violating the obviously appropriate principle of consensus. Needless to say, my worst fears were quickly realized, and in a few short months the entire faculty agreed that we would have to work without T.A.s, although the damage had been done and the first program was in something of a sullen, alienated shambles.

But while the problem of authority manifested itself first over an administrative question, it underlay the program more fundamentally and, because of its intrinsic nature, in ways not generally present in the College at large. The program attempted to establish an intellectual community, a college, and it conceived of such a community not as a collection of persons living in the same place, or rooting for the same team, or, as Clark Kerr once said, united by a common grievance over parking, but as a group of persons studying the same thing. We had a required curriculum that lasted for two years and we were all to go through it together—reading, writing, thinking about the same works at the same time. So to begin with, there had to be some curricular-determining authority. Obviously, the "faculty." The program did not share in the increasingly popular view that a student's human right to participate in the decisions that effected his life extended to his voting on the reading list or deciding whether, indeed, he would write an assigned paper. But usually, where the course is the unit of educational life, the individual professor is in authority, determines course content and method, and works out a *modus vivendi* with his students. In the program, no single professor was in authority, could not do as he pleased about those things normally subject to his pleasure, was not free to exercise his discretion, let us say, in modifying or changing assignments. Faculty and students alike subjected the program to centrifugal forces that could all too easily have destroyed its unity, its character, its very excuse for existing. If, for example, we had decided to raise the problem of obedience to law by reading *Antigone*, it was not up to one of us to decide to read *Billy Budd* instead, or even in addition. We might entertain an argument that *Billy Budd* was better than *Antigone* and that we should all read it instead, but we wanted all students to be studying the same thing. If faculty members are free chose their own variations they will do so in preference to arguing about the best common decision, avoiding the most fruitful kind of educational discussion—apart from destroying what is common in a supposedly common enterprise.

Or, if a student, living at his own unique rhythm, wanted extra time to complete a paper due, for good arbitrary reasons, on Friday, he needed to be told to get it in on time, that we did not want a better paper later, that we wanted the best he could do by Friday, that there was no such thing as a late paper, that he was, after Friday, to be starting on the next assignment, not to be alone and palely loitering with the old.

Or again, a student will announce, after the *Iliad* (which the student may have been reluctant to read in the first place) that he now wants to devote his life to the study of the epic, and would like to be excused from Thucydides and all that in order to work on Beowulf and Burnt Njal and Gilgamesh and Aeneid and Morte d'Arthur, etc.—and is stunned when he is told that if he wants to stay in the program he will do the program work and that if he wants to write his own ticket he can leave.

I need hardly point out that all these—and other—tendencies to fly apart, to take our separate amiable ways to salvation, come clothed in attractive educational or metaphysical garb. The enemy is not the power of brute anti-intellectual inertia; it is the romantic, individualistic, consumer-oriented view of reality with which we have perforce become well acquainted. Under some circumstances it carries the day—"nothing," I used to say, "is as irresistible as an error whose time has come"—and it was sweeping the American Campus even as we tried to establish a small island of sanity. But to protect the program required the systematic and constant assertion of authority. Its common character had to be protected against the tendency to fly apart. Someone had to say "no."

Oddly enough, after my defeat in our one and only vote, as if by general consent, without comment, I was left in charge. I made a few unsuccessful attempts to develop a genuinely cooperative way of life. An attempt to establish a faculty dinner meeting once a week was abandoned after a single farcical meeting. The assembly meetings, because, I think, of faculty reluctance to perform without shining, fell apart. A small student faction took over the house and drove most students away. Some faculty members became "cult" or coterie figures, subtly shielding students from my tyranny. And I sank more deeply into the dictatorial or authoritarian role. Anguish at a distance is, I find, essentially comic, and I am now faintly amused at what once tormented and enraged me. I remember lying awake nights reviewing the twisting path from Clark Kerr's office to yesterday's ordeal at the house, resolving that I would not, after everything I had gone through, abandon the program to the irresponsible views or impulses of those who would turn the program into a caricature of the elective system that had reduced American college education to the mediocre joke against which the program was to stand as a fruitful alternative. If the program had been my idea, the mess was my fault; I would fight it through, and, after the first two-year run—I could see no way of salvaging it—try again with a different faculty. In the meantime I, who was still a card-carrying member of the American Civil Liberties Union, a veteran of the Loyalty Oath fight, a Meiklejohnian extremist in defense of the First Amendment and, for that matter, a deep rebel against the practices of the educational establishment, slipped without a murmur into the role of wielder and defender of authority.

It was, of course, necessary. For example, when even those who had voted for my T.A. bane had had enough of being undermined and agreed unanimously (the last straw for the sponsoring poet was overhearing the advice given to a student who had emerged from a tutorial session. The poet had requested the rewriting of a short paper along certain lines. "Don't do it" we heard the T.A. urging, "don't do what he says. Just do what you want.") that the T.A.s should all be allowed to finish the year but not be reappointed, I said that they should be informed in time to apply for appointments in their own departments. All agreed. As the deadline approached, worried that if they were not notified they would have a legitimate complaint, a claim to reappointment, I kept reminding the faculty. But weeks passed, and they were not notified by their strangely reluctant supervisors. Finally, I told the secretary to hand each T.A. a letter, by me, informing them that they would not be reemployed. Naturally, at the next Assembly I was handed a petition by students requesting that the T.A.s be reappointed, and naturally I said "no." (I admit it may have been tactless of me, standing at the podium, to do what I usually do when presented with a bit of student writing—reach for a pencil and start correcting.) I did not bother to embarrass anyone by stressing that it was a unanimous faculty decision, and no one came to my support. There was an uproar, but I did not budge. Nor explain. What was there to explain? That this was a counter-revolutionary putsch? Or that in a program that did not allow students to determine the curriculum students had no role in choosing their teachers? I had to go East for a conference on Education—ironically, to explain the program—and when I returned I found that all the furniture in the great hall had been piled into a pyramid that reached the ceiling. The deserted house echoed to my steps. I did nothing, and the pyramid gradually eroded.

We staggered through the year. For the second year I was able to get some faculty replacements, and we managed a sort of weary truce. Quite a few students dropped out and into the regular university across the street, many unwilling to put up with the turmoil. Most of the most active of the rebellious students stayed on, naturally, manifesting their own deep loyalty to the program. I should say, lest this general complaint misleads you, that on the whole the students were intelligent, energetic, imaginative, and had a strong sense of integrity. Also, in spite of everything, full of charm and promise. I really remember them with pleasure. I owed it to them to have chosen a faculty less beset by vanity and insecurity. And I owe it to the T.A.s, also, to acknowledge that, on the whole, they were well-motivated and helpful. After the first year we worked without them, and the decision to do so was a wise one. But not because of ideological or personality clashes or because they were poorly chosen but because of something deeper. Bright graduate students are at the stage of their careers at which they are most technically involved in their disciplines. If they teach, that is what they should be teaching. They should not be thrown into a nondisciplinary arena where they cannot use what they are in the process of mastering. It is no reflection on their intelligence or teaching talent to say that they are not, at that stage of their careers, ideally suited for ventures in liberal education, however attracted to it they may be.

This has been a longer excursion than I had expected into the institutional background of the program. It is time to return to a consideration of what would justify all the trouble. What were we to do with, to make of, *Iliad*? We had all read it during the previous summer (or rather, reread it, since I learned that you do not ask a professor if he has read one of the obvious classics, you ask if he has reread it recently). Obviously, we did not expect our engineer to focus on the fortifications of Troy and the defenses of the beached fleet, the poet to focus on the Homeric art or do an Auden on the Shield of Achilles, the political scientist to lecture on government on the

17

Plains of Troy, the lawyer to enlighten us about Agamemnon v. Achilles in re Briseis, the philosopher to pontificate about Zeus, fate, and freedom. But what? We were rather nervous. I remember the lawyer complaining privately to me with a hopeless shrug, "What's there to teach? There are no arguments to analyze!" He cheered up when I suggested that the Thersites episode could be seen as a free-speech class-struggle case. Well, it's really a wonderful book and you might want to reread it if you haven't done so lately. But teach it?

Years later I was a guest at a gathering of St. John's faculty—a highly accomplished group of teachers—and strolling to lunch I listened to a senior member fondly extolling his own old teacher. "My life changed forever when he walked into a class on Homer and asked his first question!" I broke in eagerly, afraid he might not explain, to ask what the question was. "Oh," he said, surprised, as if the answer was obvious, "What was Achilles like?" I remember my surge of pleasure at his reply. Of course! Nothing about the profound significance of the Homeric World View and all that. What was Achilles like, and Hector, and Helen, and Agamemnon . . . and off we go.

By instinct or by some happy accident we decided that at the first assembly—"lecture"—each of the five faculty members would simply read out the passage in *Iliad* that appealed to him most, with perhaps a brief remark. It should make an interesting, revealing, provocative opening exercise, encouraging students in a similar venture, sharpening the intensity of their reading. I still, after 20 years, remember it vividly. The engineer who was also an elected city official, a practicing politician, focused on the futile attempt of some Greek leaders to lure Achilles who was, as we know, sulking in his tent, back into the struggle, and marveled that here was a man with a grievance who, unlike most political leaders he knew, simply couldn't be bought, wouldn't compromise, had no price. . . . The poet movingly deployed the scene in which the aged King Priam was reduced to pleading with his son's killer for the return of his son's body. The lawyer, of course, read the Thersites bit with great passion, his voice ringing with indignation over the fact that Odysseus would simply strike the only man who dared to question the value of the war at a public meeting while fellow soldiers laughed and applauded Odysseus, ridiculing their own spokesman, as blood trickled down Thersites' back and a tear ran down his cheek. I read the long passage in which Hector, awaiting the furious approach of Achilles and almost certain death, toyed with the possibility of avoiding battle, yearning for the bygone days of peace, resigning himself to his doom in a soliloquy unmatched, I think, except for Satan's on Niphates in *Paradise Lost*.

Well, the *Iliad* is full of great things, and we did our best reading, our Rorschach bits. Except for the political scientist. He stood up, opened his book to the first page, read the opening sentence, turned to the back of the book, read the last sentence, opened it somewhere near the middle and read a random sentence. Then he said "It's an organism. Wherever you cut it, it bleeds." And resumed his seat. Point, set, match. A sharp collective intake of breath from the assembled students. Hail the victor! While I thought: "The S.O.B. He's staked out his position. The program Rebel. Not for him to do what we had agreed to do. Even in a program itself in rebellion he is more rebellious still. Pompous drivel, but appealing. Impressive. He is going to play the Pied Piper and steal the children. . . ."

I am quite aware that by even mentioning this episode I invite you to think me over-sensitive, jealous, unbalanced, disturbed by what I should have merely smiled at. I did, in fact, merely smile. I did not say what I thought. But what I thought was utterly correct, prophetic. I saw a subtle breaking of faculty discipline, an "individualistic" act, an invitation to the battle of vanities. The political scientist had clearly gotten off to a good start and was never headed. The radical lawyer, thenceforth, played the even more radical lawyer, the romantic poet the even more romantic poet. Only the mathematician was unaffected, full of down-to-earth common sense and aware that there was no place for him in the dance of prima donnas. As for me, my role was unmistakable. I was the symbol of authority, of the establishment, the doomed defender of the flawed system (Aha! Hector!). I must have found the role congenial, since I sank into it easily and seem to have been playing it ever since.

I will let this odd episode stand for the many ways, subtle and not so subtle, in which the conflict between the tendency to fly apart into autonomous journeys and the insistence on a common path found expression. Obviously, the easier course is to abandon resistance to entropy or the death-wish and allow everyone—faculty, and perhaps even students—to go their own ways, pursuing their own interests. But the whole point of the program was its commitment to a special kind of common intellectual life that by its very commonality nourished a deeper individuality. There was no reason for our existence if we were going to recreate the free market that generally prevailed in the university—autonomy for professors, elective options for students. It took

19

a constant and active assertion of authority to counter the tendency to degenerate into chaos.

In a jointly taught program, the unity of the faculty on certain questions is crucial. *On certain questions.* I want to make it clear that vigorous faculty disagreement, open, prolonged, heated, is essential to the vigor and success of the enterprise. I used to say that we must agree on "constitutional" questions in order to disagree on "legislative" ones. Perhaps I should say that we must agree on procedural matters in order to be able to disagree fruitfully about substantive questions. To agree to read a book is the necessary prelude to significant disagreement about it.

But the distinction between procedural and substantive is not always clear, and I will refer to a controversy that seems to have made an indelible impression on those who witnessed it. We had agreed to read Hobbes's *Leviathan.* The reason for doing so—although there are many reasons—is that Hobbes makes the fundamental case for respect for political authority as the alternative to a life that is, as everyone has heard, "solitary, poor, nasty, brutish and short." You can quarrel with this formulation, but it is close enough to remind you of what the general question is and, I need hardly remind you, of its special appropriateness for the world in the mid-sixties and of the opportunity it offers to bring the discussion of urgent questions from the street to the classroom. Whether you agree with him or not, Hobbes is formidable and worth, educationally, grappling with.

The political scientist was to do the introduction. Imagine my feelings as I heard him say that Hobbes was very powerful, an overpowering writer, but that his doctrine was pernicious. If you followed the first step, you would be trapped by the argument (not true, by the way). So you should not pay attention to what Hobbes says, but only notice his rhetorical artistry, read it as a literary critic would. But pay no attention to his argument; don't try to grapple with that. Instruction, in short, about how not to read a book we were supposed to read.

I, of course, rose to make an unplanned rejoinder, to the effect that the reason we were to read Hobbes was so that we would have to deal with an argument—a desperate message sent across three centuries from the midst of a terrible civil war—not to enjoy, unmoved, a literary and rhetorical gift. I may have lost my temper and revealed a small fraction of my contempt for the mind of an educator capable of making such a statement. I refrain, even now, from saying what I think. Well, the moment passed, but from that moment working in harness was impossible and we could, at best, barely tolerate each other's presence.

There are some lessons to be drawn from this episode. I begin with the reminder of the very oddity of the possibility of its occurrence. In the ordinary course of events he would be teaching his own course in the political science department and he might or might not, at his discretion, include *Leviathan* and deal with it as he thought best. I would be teaching a course in the philosophy department, might choose to use *Leviathan*, and would deal with it as I thought best. We would neither know about nor be in a position to interfere with each other's conception of what to teach and how to teach it. It could even be argued that with each free to follow his own professional judgment the best teaching would result. Certainly, there would be less conflict.

But in a program, as distinct from a single-teacher course, certain problems force themselves on to the agenda. I can no longer continue to use, or use in a special way, the books that I, for some reason or other, find congenial or fruitful or simply reassuringly familiar. I must propose something to colleagues who have their own preferred lists. *We* must make a case for what we do; we will argue, sometimes bitterly, since the stakes are, in spite of superficial appearances, quite high. And we will have to decide, if we are to continue together and not settle for each going his separate way, about a significant range of educational problems that may seldom, in other circumstances, come in for serious consideration at all.

Once the "private" course is abandoned the teacher finds himself in a transformed and problematic world, without familiar landmarks and accustomed usages, naked to his colleagues, forced to justify his conception of the teaching art and even to change his practice. The common program is a cauldron for the brewing of educational insight, and I use this image fully aware of its evocation of Medea—some promise of rejuvenation, some destructive dissection, lots of heat. The difficulty is this: On the one hand, involvement in a common program is the great device for forcing attention to the essential and neglected problems of education. On the other hand, collegial life in such a program can be so searing and demanding that one must doubt whether, except for a short time and by a happy accident, such a program can be institutionalized—except by heroic efforts and unusual commitment to a mode of educational life whose very point an outside observer is hardly likely to discern.

But I must turn to other matters—although there is more to be said about the virtues and difficulties peculiar to "programs" as against "courses." Curriculum! In my missionary years I used to point out that the program had two distinguishable aspects: its noncourse pedagogic structure and its completely required curriculum. I would make the point that the structure had its own virtues and could be adapted to a variety of situations and was not tied peculiarly to our curriculum. I thought, especially, that it would be easy and useful to try it for an upper-division departmental major, unplagued by our special personnel and nondisciplinary features. And, of course, I had to grant that even for purposes of lower-division liberal education the world did not have to begin with Iliad and proceed through Greeks, Jews, and Englishmen to Henry Adams and Malcolm X as we were doing. The form did not entail any particular content. It did mandate a common required curriculum, but it did not require *this* particular one.

Nevertheless, I did and do have a special attachment to this particular one, although my defense of it has tended to be a bit diffident. In my eagerness to convince others of the virtues of the program I might stress the structural pedagogic features and might even push my view that a liberal education required a broadly "political" curriculum—the cultivation of the sovereign mind. And although I would offer our curriculum as an example, I shied away from defending it as anything more than a contingent option. I was doing, in short, what we tend to do in academic life—avoiding argument about curriculum.

I tend to think (mistakenly) that "required," applied to "curriculum," is redundant; but in the world of the contemporary American college it is merely anomalous. If we must have requirements—as from time to time we are shocked into saying—we try to have as few as possible. To the assertion that all students need this the rejoinder may be that they also need that and the other. You can't require too much so you must decide which. Everyone should certainly have a basic course in American history! Yes, and for that matter, in world history too. After all! It's terrible how we are turning out monoglot English language chauvinists. Everyone should be required to master a second language! And how about math? It's the language of science, and look at the Japanese! And our scientific illiteracy! And our computer illiteracy! And our literary illiteracy! And our ethnic ignorance! And our sexism! And can we really give anyone our degree without teaching him some economics? And isn't there something about philosophy, or ethics or values . . . ah, yes, almost forgot that.

Obviously, we can't have everything, and we can't easily agree about what to require, so we end up about where we are. We agree, shaking our heads sadly, that high schools should have prepared our students better, but now that they are here, apart from a bit of remedial work, we offer freedom and pluralism. That is, we offer our students "freedom" to choose, and justify our own irresponsible reluctance to impose requirements as "pluralism." A feeling of weariness steals over me as I face the prospect of arguing about that most dubious of freedoms, student elective freedom, about treating the student as a customer or a consumer who, presented with a rich catalogue containing a myriad of courses, is supposed to know what he wants or know what he needs. "Elective" should be a vacation, not a way of life.

Suppose we consider the tension, the interplay, between what a student chooses to do and what he is required to do in the course of his undergraduate college education—a more pervasive problem than is suggested by electives and requirements. We may begin with the recognition that his very presence is an ambiguous mixture of freedom and necessity—of wanting to be there and having to be there if he wants to have a certain kind of life. It is important to recognize, that the normal American student is in college because it is the normal place to be at that time of life, not because he is driven by a thirst for the higher learning, by a desire to be a professor, to spend his life within earshot of the bells of the ivory tower. His presence is voluntary, but in a Pickwickian sense. Let us say then, that the student presents himself, enrolls in, chooses to enroll in, the College of Letters and Science still undecided, as he is permitted to be, about his or her major and subsequent career. What shall he study? Or rather, what courses should he take? What can he take? What must he take? What does he want to take?

The burden of choice is mercifully relieved by the existence of *some* requirements. If he has not already satisfied our minimal demands in language or mathematics he is encouraged to attend to such matters promptly, and to take the required course in reading and composition at once. But beyond this, dim visions of the future begin to make their demands. The decision about the major (even about career and life) looms. Students will have to choose by the third year, and will discover that there are prerequisites. That is, before they can be admitted to a particular major they will be expected to have taken some lower-division courses in preparation. By this device, some departments have come, with dubious legitimacy, to preempt almost half of a student's lower-division premajor course life. And the danger of not knowing what you are going to major in is that when you do decide you may be delayed or prevented by lack of foresight about prerequisites. So, in addition to general requirements there are prerequisites to worry about—courses you must take first if you want to take something else. And it is often the case that if there is something you *want* to do there is also something you are required to do along with, in addition to, what you want to do. If you decide to major in philosophy because you are interested in moral problems you will find that you have to struggle with logic, which you may not be interested in at all. In fact, every major, in addition to the goodies that attract you, is likely to involve you in doing things you don't want to do, or at least think you don't want to do. (It is surprising how often we find that what we think we want to do turns out not to interest us after all, while what we think we are not interested in turns out to be very interesting). And not only the major, or the career for that matter, but any particular course will be a mixture of the chosen and the given, the wanted and the required. You chose a course because it involves X and find yourself willy nilly also involved with Y.

All this is to induce some confusion about the chosen and the given, the elected and the required, in the realm of education. I do this in the hope of making what I want to say more palatable to readers for whom freedom of choice is a primary value. That is, that the significance of one's education depends less on the operation of student choice at every point than on the involvement of the student in coherent sequential activity imposed by the situation—a coherent sequencing that the student, by virtue of his status and condition—not by virtue of his sinfulness or folly—is generally unable to provide for himself, even aided by the misconceptions of his peers. The question, then, is not how much choice the student has—he will always have some—but what we provide in the way of coherent sequenced intellectual life within the framework of choice—within the structure of a single course or a loosely related sequence of courses, the structure of the upper-division major, the structure of a graduate or professional school program. Obviously, only the first of these is available for the lower-division orphan. He has only courses. I used to say, when I was saying things like that, that a collection of coherent courses is still an incoherent collection of courses, and I would still defend my early description of the life of the lower-division student as, perforce, that of a distracted intellectual juggler.

So it was partly to remedy the fragmentation of attention and energy, especially in the lower-division, that I developed the conception of a two-year program, that operated not by stringing unrelated or loosely related courses together but by abandoning the very conception of the course and claiming and directing the bulk of the student's attention for the first two years. From the faculty point of view, this shift in unit involved the difference between planning a course—which every faculty member does routinely—and planning an education—which a faculty member is seldom if ever called upon to do. A program makes such planning both possible and necessary and imposes a frightening responsibility on a faculty more accustomed to assuming responsibility for a course and letting the invisible hand take care of education.

The very conception of the program as the significant educational unit called for a common required curriculum. And since, as I have said, the point of the enterprise was to provide something in the way of liberal education, the content was to be broadly and thematically "political." But thematic concentration, the determination to do a single thing at a time, had a price—the omission of many important things, and we were always worried by the price and, apart from our own doubts, had to defend ourselves against the charge that we were leaving out too many important things—especially science and mathematics. My own response was to grant the importance, regret the omission, insist that we were not going to do a number of different things in the program, and invite the challenger to show us how science and mathematics could be integrated into the program. I had, in fact, hoped that our mathematician would solve the problem and suggest appropriate changes. But his response to repeated prodding was something like "no, not now. . . ." I got a card from him during a later summer, from Greece where he had just enjoyed a performance of the Bacchae. A p.s. on his card excited me: "Have solved program science problem!" When he returned, I was waiting. "What's the answer?" He seemed for a moment not to remember. Then to my baffled disgust "Oh. Just add *Prometheus Bound* to the reading list."

No one else accepted the invitation, and I am convinced that it cannot be done. The categories of "science" and of the "humanities" are radically different and irreducible to each other; they are simply different enterprises, both important, and you cannot do both at the same time without doing two different things at the same time. Of course mathematicians and scientists have a great capacity to make you feel guilty if you neglect them, were not

25

inclined to worry about integrating important nonscientific matters into *their* teaching ("students should get that stuff elsewhere") and were prone, in those days, to throw C.P. Snow at you, who, having spoken of two cultures, liked to point out that whereas scientists were familiar with Hamlet, humanists were not equally at home with the second law of thermodynamics (alas! no movie yet about the second law). We hardly argue this issue anymore, partly because no one seems to be worrying about "integrating" anything into a coherent educational scheme.

But in those days I marshaled some sort of diffident defense, hardly convincing myself. All sorts of people, including students, were sure we should be doing something else. I will not attempt a defense now. If you want me to, I'm in the phone book. I might say that it took me a long time to lose my sense of guilt about science and math—after all they have "become death, destroyers of worlds"—clearly important. But a few years ago, drawn into recalling the past and giving an account of the program to a convocation of professors, I was approached over a second drink by someone who introduced himself as a professor of mathematics. "Why," he asked—not asked, really, but accused—"did you leave out mathematics?" "Mathematics?" I tried to raise my eyebrows. "Why not?" I replied. "It's not that important. They can take it somewhere else." He stared at me in shocked disbelief. I felt liberated.

So we had, for students who "voluntarily" entered the program, a completely required curriculum spanning two years—a relatively brief respite from a lifetime of discrete courses—relieving students of the problems of choice, imposing on the faculty the burden of creation. The starting point was the Athens-America conception that Meiklejohn had developed in the '20s at Wisconsin, but beyond that inspiration we went our own way, adding, as Matthew Arnold might say, the Hebraic to the Hellenic strain by dividing the first year between the Greeks and Seventeenth (more or less) century England—the King James Bible, some Shakespeare, Hobbes, Milton, and on through Burke and beyond. The second year was to carry us into America—presenting interesting curricular challenges of greater difficulty. My own inclination was to focus on the Constitution, on constitutional law—a sort of Gentile variety of Talmudic studies—(since we are, more than most, a people of the law book and since most of our problems are transformed, sooner or later, into judicial questions), and literature as the path to the understanding of the American situation, and if I had to do the program again I would want to try to do that again, but better.

26

I do not want, in this account, to re-argue the curriculum, but only to say how it seems now upon reflection. What can you say about the Greeks except that we are forever in debt to whoever brings our mind, with or without our consent, into engagement with Herodotus and Thucydides, Homer and Hesiod, Sophocles and Aeschylus, Plato. Greece seems almost to have been created for our enlightenment, and the Hellenic Testament, the story of its glory, its mind, and its self-destruction, the sad long day's dying, pervades any fortunate Western consciousness. Still, there are some things very close to us that are quite alien to the Greeks. I cannot imagine a Greek Job, and Job, with his anguished cry for justice, is a pervasive echo in our lives. To study the Bible, Milton, and Hobbes is to take a second step towards self-knowledge. There are lots of things we didn't do, but what we did in the first year alone justifies the entire enterprise. Each new reading joined the thickening context of understanding, remaining permanently on the table, a permanent part of the mind. What I said in a daring moment in *Experiment at Berkeley* is quite true—that we had discovered a version of the basic moral curriculum of the West. I seem to be still studying it. I note, with some surprise, that the manuscript I am now completing, that I call *The Burden of Office* and think of more informally as *Agamemnon and Other Losers*, consists entirely of studies of some program readings.

Neither the form nor the content of the program was perfectly grasped at the outset. We learned as we went along. While the basic pattern was the same, there was significant difference between the first and the second run. I have made no attempt here to be accurate about what happened when, to keep the two versions distinct. But we did have two attempts, two versions. It would be a bit misleading to say that the first program did not work the way I had intended and the second program did—although that is true enough. I shy away from saying that it didn't work the first time and did the second, as if we had one failure and one success. Some of the most interesting things happened the first time, and it may be that turmoil has its own special lessons. I have come to think of the two runs, as it seems convenient to call them, in terms of two of the novels of C. S. Lewis. *Out of the Silent Planet* tells of Tellus, our planet, where the great plan was frustrated by the rebellion in Eden. *Perelandra* tells of the planet on which the temptation was resisted and the great plan worked out as intended. Lewis allows us, invites us, to infer that wonderful as the great plan was where it worked in all its docile beauty, the story about where it didn't work as planned was perhaps even more wonderful still. At any rate, I think of the first run as Tellus, the second as Perelandra. I suffered through the first and I enjoyed the second, which was, in fact, wonderful as planned.

Two runs. If I had thought that the second would be like the first I would simply have written it off, called it off, not taken the necessary steps for a renewed attempt. But at the end of the second year of the first run the original faculty—those who had stayed on for the second year—returned to their normal pursuits. Two, as I mentioned, had signed on only for a single year. It was generally a happy parting, much relief on all sides at seeing the last of each other. But I was badly shaken. I had expected that the faculty, masters of their own classes, would have some problems working together, all teaching "our" students instead of each his own. I had expected a range of differing insights, a range of skills and backgrounds. What I had not expected was the raging vanity of the charismatic teacher. The competition of scholars, the thirst for distinction, was a familiar and almost comical fact of academic life. But we encounter it, the vanity of *scholars* at a distance. You published your stuff; he published his; and when he excitedly waved the telegram announcing his award you would say (a famous episode) "What? You?" The scholarly community is diffused through the world, and you usually appeal to it in writing. Its vanity, although sometimes flagrant, is generally tolerable and not too greatly obstructive.

But the teacher, the aspiring great teacher, is, in a perverted version, the seducer, the enchanter working his magic on a concrete local group. He must capture it, or he is nothing. He does not like to share the limelight; the presence of fellow professionals is intrusive and distracting; he is best at a one-man show; he worries about being upstaged or outshone. I think the conception of teaching as a performing art is deeply mistaken, but it is quite popular. And it makes cooperative teaching almost impossible.

Teaching is a subtle quasi-therapeutic art, not a performing art. It is very difficult to observe; it is not spectacular. There is really nothing much to see when you see a great teacher at work. Oh, well, it is a commonplace at the university that we do not know how to really evaluate teaching—which may be why we rely so much on consumer reports. And, like other professions, we tend to close ranks at this point. Policemen are reluctant to condemn a colleague for unprofessional conduct; Lawyers hate to disbar lawyers; Doctors don't like to disqualify doctors. As for teachers—we may say someone is a fine or great teacher, or a competent teacher, or a good teacher for small classes. But we don't seem to even recognize a category of harmful teacher, of teachers who damage minds entrusted to their care. At this point we close ranks. Except, of course, when a common program destroys the isolation of the separate classroom and makes "harming your students" also a case of harming "ours" and impossible to ignore. Life in the isolated classroom is obviously simpler.

I blamed the troubles of the first run on my ineptitude in assembling its faculty. I may have been angry and nursed grudges, but I do not feel greatly justified in blaming my colleagues. They had, after all, merely accepted or succumbed to my invitation and were only doing what apparently came naturally. And I even felt guilty about knowing things about them that I would not have known accept for the special circumstances of the program, as if I had violated the privacy I had invited them to give up. Except for the program, I would still, no doubt, consider some to be the strong teachers I thought they were when I recruited them, and it is unfair of me to first lure them out of their happy niches and then blame them for my disappointed expectations. I am slightly contrite.

But I was determined to give the program another trial, and I tried a different approach to staffing. I went outside the Berkeley faculty and called on friends, most of whom I had known since they were graduate students and I was an assistant professor. They were teaching elsewhere, but were able to get leaves to come to Berkeley for two years—to my rescue, to my delight.

This move, of course, raised some disturbing questions Why could I not find regular Berkeley faculty willing and able to take part? Was I trying to establish a Berkeley Junior college below the dignity of what a now-defunct local paper referred to as the "U.C. Savant"? Did the program, in that case, really belong on the Berkeley Campus? I was troubled by these questions, but I did not look very hard for another Berkeley staff. A perfunctory look turned up a few who were not uninterested, "but not just now." And I was not really interested in searching beyond the circle of those I knew, or thought I knew. I was quite exhausted and bruised and unwilling to spend the next two years re-arguing basic principles and fighting centrifugal tendencies. I wanted colleagues who shared the vision, who understood the whole conception, who did not have local charismatic status to defend, whose educational background I had confidence in, who I thought I would enjoy working with, and who I considered to be first rate minds and good teachers. Of those who came to my rescue, some had Berkeley tenure-equivalent credentials, a few were not in that particular race but had significant intellectual and pedagogic virtues.

The difference was striking. What made the difference? First, I suppose, I now had some experience and was aware of some of the things we needed to avoid. The importance of constitutional agreement was clear from the start—although I had thought it implicit even in the first run. The underlying rationale was more clearly formulated and was accepted as a constitutive condition of participation. But to say that is really to miss the main point: we were friends, and not in a competitive situation. This is really an embarrassing point: I had thought the five of us in the first group were friends; so what was the difference? The most obvious was this: I had been a teacher of the core of the second group. They were in no sense "disciples" or even continuing students, but we had been through the mill together, and knew each other as only those who had been through that sort of mill together can know each other. Our essential mode was cooperative, not competitive. We argued—even quarreled—a lot, but we worked well together.

But the fact that I had surrounded myself with friends of this sort raises obvious questions. Could I not work in harness with contemporaries, only with those a generation younger? Was I taking advantage of the deference of former students? Was the whole search for collegiality really a self-centered hoax? I am, of course, bothered by the possibility, and it would be unseemly and futile to protest too much, but let me at least say something. The basic agreement on fundamentals in the second group made possible a vigorous running disagreement on almost everything else. I was not treated gently about anything—especially about the ideas that ran like persistent threads through the two-year program. And since I did not have to assume the role of program defender I found myself dramatically less "central" to its life. I had, so to speak, specialized in defending the program, and now that was a function shared by colleagues. I felt, for the first time, that I was one of a band of teachers and, when it came to that, I was not an especially good one. The others had, I thought, a better sense of the minds of our students, more devoted patience, better particular diagnostic flair and curative ingenuity and, oddly enough, a more single-minded devotion to the task. For the first time I had the feeling that I was not necessary, that the program could get along without me, that I could relax and enjoy what we were doing. I was still, as the only regular Berkeley faculty member, responsible for whatever administration there was, and I was allowing myself to be drawn, marginally, into the turmoil distracting the campus (a turmoil that had surprisingly little effect on the program). But the actual day-to-day life and work of the program no longer depended on me.

What stands out in my mind when I now think of the program is the habit we, the faculty, fell into of having dinner together every Thursday night in a private room at the Faculty Club. I have mentioned that the attempt to do this on the first run collapsed after a single meeting. But for the two years of the second run we assembled every week over wine and dinner and argued for four or five hours. We had some fairly firm rules. We would not bring up any administrative matters. We simply had a discussion of the material we were reading in the program, explaining, interpreting, arguing about the significance of this or that and, as the evening drew to a close, saying something like "You two seem to be disagreeing about the central point, so why don't you each take 20 minutes or so to say what you think and get everyone launched at the Assembly next Tuesday, and we'll go on from there." Volunteering was frowned on; we were drafted for this or that service and found it very relaxing.

Often it seemed that the entire program was a spill-over from this long-running seminar. We not only discussed the material substantively, we argued about how to use it. Looking back at the first run I would wonder how we could possibly have managed without the faculty seminar. The truth is, of course, that we didn't manage at all, and it is only by virtue of the uncanny unspoilability of the basic material, the inherent fruitfulness of a dimly emerging pedagogic form and, perhaps, the notorious Hawthorne Effect that anything educationally useful emerged in spite of everything. But it was not Perelandra.

I remember the second run seminar as the most exciting, the most significant intellectual and moral experience of my whole life, unmatched, unapproached by anything I experienced in four decades of interesting university life, mostly at UC Berkeley which is, in many ways (was, perhaps) an academic heaven. The seminar *made* the program, and I am sure this judgement would be shared by everyone who took part in it.

I note that I have written far more about the first run and its traumas than about the second run and its triumphs. Obviously, the first shook me; the second renewed my faith. All my joy in recollection is focused on the second, all my anguish on the first. And yet I find myself writing nothing revealing about the quality of the triumph. It is easier to describe pain than health; easier, as Milton demonstrates, to write of hell than of the joys of heaven. Still, I am a bit startled to find how much the first run dominates this

31

account, how little I do to communicate the quality of the second run. I do not intend to try to remedy that imbalance now, but only to acknowledge it.

I emerged after four years reassured that education could still be thought of as the initiation of the new generation into a great continuing and deeply rooted civilization. But this, I suppose calls for some comment.

It was Berkeley in the middle and late sixties, one of the great centers of the generational uprising. The wave of baby boomers had broken over the college, a large cohort especially horizontally or peer-group oriented. The times were stirring and troubled—the civil rights movement, sexual revolutions, the shocking end of Camelot, the war in Viet Nam loomed heavily on the horizon of those who, to the chagrined surprise of their elders, did not remember the great war that had shaped and tempered the minds of parents and teachers. They did not *remember* Munich or Hitler or Pearl Harbor or D Day or reading the headlines the day after Hiroshima, the surge of relief at calling off the million-corpsed invasion, the homecomings to triumphant and shattered worlds. They could not remember what their parents could not forget, their minds could never really meet—the one proud of the triumphant American expedition against the grim Rome-Berlin-Tokyo Axis, the other ashamed of the muddled, ambiguous American expedition to a strange periphery of Asia. But the parents saw them off to college, and they arrived full of contempt for the world they never made, for racial and sexual injustice and hypocrisy, angry at having had to hide from the radiant fruit of science under schoolroom desks, enraged at the "unjust war" that had been doled out to them, without a confident religion, without a glowing political ideology. The scene was littered with fragments, with its own irreverent music, with the temptations of a shortcut to the expansion of consciousness, and armed somehow (god knows who taught them that!) with the powerful philosophical conviction that no one knew better than you what was right or good or even true "for you."

Only a vigorous imagination can begin to grasp the enormity of trying to initiate the class of sixty-something into an ongoing American branch of Western civilization. They gave us a house to try it in. It was the battle-ground, but I'm not sure everyone recognized what the battle was all about. It was to see whether our traditional cultural resources were powerful enough to withstand the contemptuous challenge of a despairing countercul-ture. I suppose that sounds grandiose. I think back to the house in its seedy disarray, half deserted, a handful of disgruntled students arriving for a dispirited seminar, or, again, to an argumentative throng, unexpectedly cheerful about something or other—a confusing sequence of disordered scenes. I am reminded of the scene in which Stendhal's hero, galloping away from a trivial bit of confusion, pauses and wonders "Was *that* the battle of Waterloo?" So, I ask myself, having crept away, was that really a battle in the war over the American soul? Without banners? Without a band? Yes, it was. Sometimes it seemed as if the world was struggling to turn itself into illustrative material to accompany the core curriculum of the Experimental Program. We were dealing, of course, with the themes that swirled about one of our greatest achievements—the creation and development of the great art of politics. To begin with the *Iliad* is to begin in medias res, in the midst of the perpetual war between the Human Expedition and the Human City, between the Quest and the Home. The tale is echoed or mimicked in the masterful account of the war to the death between Athens and Sparta, the paradigmatic cultures of the marketplace and the barracks, of freedom and of discipline. Against that background we grapple with the conflicting claims of Olympian rationality and Dionysian passion, with the elevation of law over fury, with the defiance of law in the name of the higher law, with the great Platonic depiction of the parallel between psyche and polity ranging from the achievement of wisdom to the reign of anarchy and tyranny in each. And then in the other of our great moods we contemplate the covenant in the wilderness on the road from slavery to dreams of freedom, and ring a different set of changes on the problems of authority, obedience, rebellion, war and peace, justice, laws and courts. And in the end, we come to see ourselves, to find ourselves, to know ourselves, as the present act in an ancient and perpetual drama.

So, in spite of everything, I emerged convinced that the traditional spiritual resources of the culture, far from being obsolete or exhausted, were, in fact, if we used them properly, the key to our salvation.

If we use them properly! And who, alas, is doing that? The natural university guardians of the great tradition are, of course the departments of the humanities. But, with a few honorable exceptions, they guard the treasure as Fafnir guarded his—they breathe fire if anyone tries to steal it, to use it, that is, without a license. Simply put, departments in the humanities believe in and practice scholarship. That is to say, they are not interested in what the people they study are interested in. They are interested in what scholars are interested in and, generally, the people they study were not scholars. ("Lord what would they say/ Did their Catullus walk that way?"). I respect what they know, appreciate what they do. I, who know not Greek, live on their scholarly translations. I read Dante and Virgil in translation; Tolstoy and Dostoyevsky in translation; Ibsen, even Goethe. I am parasitic on translators and scholars. I say a heartfelt "Thank you." But they—"Humanists"—are obstacles to the nonscholarly human use of their work. They almost always vote against efforts like the Experimental Program. They usually consider people like me to be ignoramuses and dilettantes. They scare me, (something easy to do to an emeritus professor who still thinks he was hired by mistake) but they kill significant liberal education. Fafnir! I would sooner turn the fate of liberal education over to scientists who don't know what it is, but at least want it, than to "humanists" who should know what it is, but are afraid of it. I am a bit surprised to find myself so bitter against such nice people, but I'll let it stand. . . . They, more than anyone, are responsible for the feeble state of liberal education in America.

But now I turn from the central curricular problem—I had intended to attempt an extended eloquent exposition of the curriculum but on reflection, I don't see why I should—to another pervasive aspect of the program. Even as we were reading and arguing about freedom and authority we were also involved in an aspect of that problem as it colored the daily style of life in the program. Let me begin with an anecdote. A few years ago, long after the program had gone out of existence, I was invited to a reunion of graduates of Meiklejohn's Experimental College on the Madison campus. Meiklejohn had died, but the faithful still gathered. I was invited although I had not been one of them as a student, and I spoke to them about Meiklejohn's later years in Berkeley. At one general session a half dozen of the alumni (it seems strange to call them that) spoke in turn, reminiscing about life in the good old days in the Experimental College. At the end, the chairman asked me, sitting enthralled in the audience, if I had any questions or wanted to say anything. Yes, I said, I have one question: "Did you do your work?" Someone, a bit taken aback, launched a conventional affirmative reply but was interrupted by a tumult of denials. No! No! Not a lick of work for two years! Too young! Too much freedom! . . . It was a rather bitter outburst, a pent up moment of truth, a half-century old complaint. I actually do not remember whether I really said or only wish I had said what I do remember thinking. "Here we are honoring the memory of a man fired as president after bringing Amherst back to life, summoned to Wisconsin to create an educational utopia. He struggled against enormous odds, gathered a faculty, fought with the establishment, forged a novel curricular conception, investing a great mind and soul in the effort. And then you arrive, saunter off to taverns, and have the unmitigated gall to not do your work!"

Long before this episode, at one of the program Thursday night final dinners devoted to a review of our problems, one of us launched into something like a complaint about how we were breaking our backs in our efforts while many students were just loafing. We were taping these review sessions (I still have the transcript). I am recorded as replying "Doctors always work harder than patients." The transcriber unexpectedly notes "Silence. And then laughter." Silence, and then laughter. What else?

There is a problem about freedom and coercion, impulse and habit, autonomy and shared ritual, in education as elsewhere. If we can state our objectives as the cultivation of certain habits of mind—whether stated grandiosely as the habit of rational inquiry and deliberation or more diffidently as the habits of careful reading, analysis, expression, discussion—we must decide about the uses of discipline in the process. It will come as no surprise that I not only believed in a required curriculum but that I also believed students should be required to do, should acquire the habit of doing, the work. But requiring something and getting someone to do what is required are two different things. The problem was to get our students to do what we thought they should do.

To begin with, for the familiar range of idealistic reasons, we denied ourselves the usual array of sticks and carrots. We decided not to have examinations or to give grades. The university had just begun to experiment with a pass/not-pass system, and we were given permission to use it, stretching its limits a bit. Everyone whose performance did not merit expulsion from the program was simply given a "pass"—a grade that would not enter into determining his subsequent grade point average. No one was ever expelled from the program for any reason other than serious performance delinquency. We put up cheerfully with intellectual inadequacy. I should say, on this score, that our students were good enough to have been admitted to Berkeley, but were not admitted to the program on the basis of any special distinction. We did not want to run an "honors" program; we wanted as typical a group as we could get and simply chose haphazardly from a large number of applicants.

There are situations in which there are examinations and grades and in which the student is told that he can do as he pleases about attendance and all that sort of thing. He will be tested and judged; how he prepares is his business. We were, I suppose, at the other extreme. There was no terminal

35

exam to prepare for, no grade to certify anything. What we insisted on instead was that the student *be there*, with work at least more or less prepared. What we could not tolerate was no exams, no grades, *and* no prepared presence. Essentially, to stay in the program meant to be there and to do one's work.

This choice of a mode of operation created many unfamiliar problems for us. The faculty had disarmed itself, put aside the usual disciplinary weapons. Nonattendance? We'll catch him on the exam. Sloppy work? Do you want a C or D? It's all so easy, so familiar. We wanted something better and discovered the challenge, the difficulty, of developing other modes of intellectual motivation and student-teacher interaction. I had a great skiing instructor whose diagnostic and instructional technique had impressed me as a paradigm of the teaching art. I tried to imagine him watching me turn my way down the slope and then saying "C+. Next time try to ski better!" But I have seen instructors hand back a paper with the notation "C. Try to write more clearly," and then argue with the student about whether the paper really deserved a B.

We wanted something else. We wanted habitual prepared presence because nothing much could happen without that. But we wanted to improve the quality of intellectual activity. We wanted to find the useful thing to say about a student paper without—instead of—giving it a grade. We wanted to get the student to work harder and more fruitfully without the prod of grading. It was not easy and, at times, we wondered why we were making life more difficult for ourselves. But we persisted in the attempt to provide something other than extrinsic motivation for the exercise of the mind.

Students sometimes missed grades. One student announced that she was going to transfer out of the program. She was a good student and, had there been grades, would have rated an A. She liked the work, she said, and she thought she was getting a lot out of the program. And she really didn't mind just getting a "pass." But she couldn't stand the fact that her friend down the hall in her dorm wasn't doing much, was always going out on dates, and was getting a "pass" too. It wasn't right. Would you like it better, would you stay, if you got an A and she got a C, she was asked. "Of course!" she said, and departed for a fairer world.

Well, the path we chose required the insistence on a timely adherence to a sustaining common routine. But, from start to finish our performance was sporadic. The faculty had its hawks and its doves. Students defied expectations, and it was difficult to do much about it. We could expel or threaten to expel, but that often seemed too drastic and was, from our point of view, an admission of failure. We hated to be reduced to nagging or disowning or, for that matter, to coaxing. Toward the end of the second run I began to entertain the heretical thought that we should reconsider the abandonment of grades. Grades don't really bother the good student; they serve as a prod to the middling; they provide retribution to the delinquent. I expressed my doubts to my second-run colleagues and was thoroughly raked over the coals. They are probably right; grades are a second-best device for a second-best world. It no doubt reveals my condition when I confess that the issue does not seem to me as important as it once did.

Meiklejohn, I believe, was more tolerant of student "independence" or "nonperformance" than I was, and I was inclined to think he might have been out of sympathy with the spirit in which I was approaching the problem—that a late paper or missed lecture was not a minor failing but a sign that one's life was fundamentally out of control. Some students thought so too. The reproach pinned to the wall "Joe, Joe, what have you done to my idea?" signed "Alec," was, no doubt, a forgery, but, I was prepared to concede, not a bad one. Meiklejohn, I believe, had had—had been required to have—grades.

But whatever the verdict about grades as a motivational and disciplinary device, I am not in retreat at all from the view that a college, a program, a *community* of learning is not a collection of individuals each pursuing his own firefly, but a company taking thought together, sharing a common life, a common discipline, a common ritual. I suppose I prefer the fellowship of the Round Table to the solitary quest for the Grail.

Towards the end of the second run a committee of the college of Letters and Science looked into what we were doing and made a recommendation that eventually resulted in the college's giving its approval to the program on its academic merits while, at the same time, expressing the cautious view that continuation would depend on the availability of fairly scarce resources. I was pleased, since all I wanted at that point was academic approval. I did not know how much was generally known about our internal storms. Our students were also involved, to different degrees, in the campus life of the time. I remember being strangely pleased when, during a general student strike they would show up for work, announcing that they were on strike against the university but not, obviously, against *us*. The student movement was leaving us in peace, practicing benign neglect. I knew some of the leaders, and while I was almost always opposed to what the movement was doing on campus, I was not terribly active in the fight. On the educational front, it was generally known that I held to the reactionary view that the faculty was to govern education (my burden was that I defended the faculty's authority even while I despised the way the faculty exercised it) and that I had scant sympathy for student participation in curricular matters. As a matter of principle this was anathema to the movement, and they could not embrace the program as a step in the right educational direction. On the other hand, the program was at least a radical innovation and an expression of the university's concern with undergraduate education. So the movement neither supported the program nor opposed it. I welcomed being left alone and would not really have known what to do with student "support," would have been embarrassed by it.

The university faculty, initially a bit apprehensive that I was launching an undisciplined educational spree, seemed reassured by rumors that I was really trying to run a sort of boot-camp. An unexpectedly candid report I wrote after the first year evoked many expressions of appreciation and good will and by the time we were well into the second run I felt that the faculty was amiably tolerant, although far from accepting the validity of fundamental conceptions underlying the program.

The administration—at least in its higher ranks—continued to be supportive (although I was aware of some hostility at the decanal level). We were receiving favorable national publicity as educational innovators, somewhat offsetting the charge that the University was involved in research to the neglect of undergraduate teaching. Even some regents, at one of whose meetings a prominent member had, before we were launched, criticized us as planning to teach (incite?) revolution and had demanded, in vain, a letter supporting free enterprise from each of the program faculty, were, informally, offering encouragement.

In short, as we neared the end of the second run the auspices for continuation were generally favorable, and I welcomed the academic approval of the college as a minor vindication and as a necessary precondition of a move from "experimental" to "regular" status. But I was undecided about what to do. The past five years had been exhausting, and I needed some leave. The program faculty needed to return to their regular positions elsewhere. Continuing meant gathering a new faculty, and while some of the second run faculty were perfectly capable of running the program and were willing to continue, they could not simply stay on without resolving ambiguities about permanence that could not, at that stage, be resolved. I realized that to have a break in continuity would be to lose some momentum, but I did not have the heart to scramble to put together a third trial run. Two experimental runs was enough, I thought, and now the university should make a decision about permanence and, if it wanted the program, settle upon the basic conditions of its existence. (A canny institution builder might have tried to prolong the trial period indefinitely.)

For the student of institutional reform the situation was not without interest. I see it now as an encounter between the enduring and the ephemeral. The enduring university is rooted in departments, themselves based on the great cognitive disciplines that, over time, may merge and split, slowly altering the geography of the mind. But the basic fact of modern university life is the department; the faculty members home is the department. That being said (and this is an oversimplification) we will have to recognize that the university will also seem to be a great collection of institutes, schools, colleges, centers, programs. Some of these may be quite enduring, but they are administrative modes that facilitate the transdepartmental activities of department members. Such activity may be quite important, exciting, fruitful, opportunistic, and the nondepartmental organization enables the university to respond to challenges and opportunities without having to endure frequent or traumatic fundamental restructuring. The key to the relation between the enduring and the ephemeral is the institution of tenure. And tenure is something you have (with a few ignorable exceptions) in *departments*.

This, then, was the context in which the question of the future of the Experimental Program presented itself. Should it, could it, how could it move across the line that separated a trial venture from a regular more or less permanent part of the university. Let me say, to begin with, that the university—the great ponderous soulless "multiversity" of popular caricature—had shown, in my case, remarkable openness and flexibility. As a professor, I had presented to the university, from the back benches, a radical educational proposal and within a year the program was in existence. During that year I was teaching a full load of courses in philosophy and serving as chairman, so that arguing for, planning, and launching the program were essentially spare time activities. It was an adventure, but the real point is that the university listened, smiled faintly, nodded, made a slight adjustment in the distribution of its resources (nothing much— perhaps a million or so) and said "go ahead." Now, four years later it said "not bad" and waited for me to make the next move.

But while the university had been flexible and hospitable, I had done nothing to get the program rooted in Berkeley's soil. The first run Berkeley faculty had returned to their departments and had no continuing connection with the program. The visiting second run group had gone home. I was left, panting, in my home department. Where was the program? Who cared? The house, unused, was, by a delicate act of university courtesy, held for my decision until I relinquished it. But I had no working colleagues on the scene and was uncertain about what to do. On the one hand, the prospect of continuing to work in—to live within, really—a program with colleagues like those in the second run was very appealing, although I liked normal academic life. On the other hand, the tangle of problems and decisions that loomed over the path to permanence—and as I said, I would not do another trial run—was daunting. Overshadowing personal considerations, although intertwined with them, was my loyalty to the idea of the program as a great educational form and the sense of guilt that overwhelmed me at the thought that the program might go out of existence because I lacked the energy or ingenuity to keep it going.

Everything was in limbo when I got a call from a newly appointed vice chancellor. He had himself been appointed by a newly appointed chancellor. (Chancellors were ephemeral in those days. This was our third or fourth in about as many years.) The message was that the new chancellor wanted me to continue the program. Would I draw up a proposal? So I drew up a modest proposal. A program to start each year with about 150 students and six professors in each group. I suggested that three of the faculty were to be permanent, tenured faculty who understood and were committed to the program and who could guide the three transient faculty members and provide stability and experience. In addition to thus keeping the program in existence and available on a modest scale for Berkeley students, I wanted, by inviting the right visiting faculty, to foster imitation by state and community colleges for whom such a lower-division program might be a boon. Finally, I proposed that we undertake to become a center for the study of higher-education teaching, the absence of which had seemed to me to be a scandal not mitigated by schools of education. I gave the three-page proposal to the vice chancellor and within a very short time he told me that the chancellor was sold on the idea and wanted me to go ahead. So, what did I want? What should we do?

I was not surprised that the chancellor wanted the program. I thought any educator in his right mind would want it. It was inexpensive, unobtrusive, daringly innovative, serious, highly regarded throughout the country and even abroad, worth its cost in public relations alone—to say nothing of the real point, that it was a great educational program. I agreed to go ahead and got down to cases with the vice chancellor. He was a very engaging young man, apparently marked for high administrative positions. But at that time he seemed to me to be quite naive about the academic facts of life, not knowing what was easy and what was difficult, not knowing the score, hardly knowing what the game was. But enthusiastic.

I went to the heart of the matter quickly. There was only one thorny problem: faculty. We would need a skilled cadre. I could not do it alone. I would need colleagues. I already had three in mind, all of whom held tenure positions at their own very respectable institutions. I had taught with them and knew they were very good. I could probably induce them to come. But I would only invite them if I could offer them tenure. So besides myself I would need three to five tenure slots. Everything else was easy. I think my request seemed reasonable to the vice chancellor. He raised no objections and said I'd be hearing from him.

But I did not hear from him for quite a while. I did not expect to. I thought he would be discovering the difficulties in the way of capturing tenure slots. Hard-nosed deans might not make a fuss about temporary programs they did not believe in, on soft money. But tenure slots were a different proposition. They were precious, and departments fought over them. Their assignment determined the fate of departments and the shape of the university's future. Toleration for an ephemeral maverick program was one thing; giving away tenure slots was quite another. So I waited, knowing the vice chancellor would be encountering static. As the personnel deadline approached I indicated that I needed a decision. Eventually the vice chancellor informed me, with some irritation, that he was not going to turn over a half dozen tenure slots for me to dispose of as I wished (not that I had put the request that way). I did not argue, and the deal was off.

But this was rather uncharacteristic of me. I had not, in the course of establishing and running the program, acquired the habit of taking no for an answer. So why did I not try to go around the vice chancellor, or over his head, to the chancellor, or even the president, as I had been prepared to do in the past when necessary. That is an interesting question, and when I try to put my finger on the crucial point at which the program lost its life it comes to rest here. Not with the denial of the tenure slots, but with my decision not to fight the denial—even though, in the end, I might have lost that fight. It was convenient for me to explain, when I was asked, as I frequently was, why the program went out of existence, that the university was unwilling to assign the necessary tenure positions. That answer, while true enough, sounds as though I am placing the blame on the university, on the vice chancellor or on the lesser satraps who were stiffening his spine. They were, no doubt, formidable adversaries, but not as formidable as my own doubts that paralyzed me at what might have been the moment of battle.

My own doubts. I could not solve the tenure question, in principle, to my own satisfaction. As I have mentioned, tenure was only granted to people in departments and on the recommendation of departments. Two of the people I had in mind held tenure positions in their own philosophy departments. Should I approach the Berkeley department with the proposition that they should take on my candidates as tenured members of the philosophy department, grant them indefinite leave to teach in the program with the option of deciding, at any time, to teach philosophy courses instead. The department had, in fact, recently gone through a bitter battle about such a case and I knew how hopeless such a request would be had I the gall to make it. I won't elaborate on the complexities of this situation, but it was clear to me that I could not hope to plant the cadre in various departments, enjoying, as absentees, the privileges of tenure.

The alternative was to consider tenure without departmental status—an almost self-contradictory notion. We now have a few "university professors" whose tenure may transcend departments and even a particular campus, but in those days they had not yet been invented, and they were not designed for our situation. So how about simply pressing for tenure in the program as a justified novelty. I thought of it, of course. But first, who knew how long the program would last? And if it terminated, tenure would not persist like the grin of the Cheshire cat, it would vanish with the program. But besides the risk that I was unwilling to invite others to assume, it was not at all likely that the highest university authorities would approve some form of nondepartmental organization supporting tenure appointments.

And if, in spite of the odds, it did—and this was the crushing difficulty, the one I never discussed but that weighed on my mind—I was not sure that I would want it or could recommend it. I knew how intimate and abrasive life in the program could be. I thought it very likely that sooner or later friends would fall out, would disagree in ways that would make working together impossible, might get fed up with each other or with the program, or with students at less than arms length, or would, in sheer exhaustion over the toil of collective life, yearn for the healing privacy of a course of one's own. A yearning we could not satisfy in the program. I was not unaffected by the falling out among friends in the first run and was even more troubled by the fact that in the second run, in spite of my caution, I had invited a friend who became so upset by his disagreement with the rest of us about how to teach that he soon withdrew in embittered rage from communication and interaction and was a dead weight for almost two years. We were stuck with him because I had invited him for two years and he had taken leave, etc. Suppose he had had tenure? This experience points up the virtue of departments. A department member does not have to get along with anyone. He can despise his colleagues to his heart's content. He need have nothing to do with them. And he can get on with his teaching and research as he pleases. Tenure in *that* made sense; but tenure in a program? I was baffled. Tenure was necessary. Tenure in departments was not in the cards. Tenure in a program alone worried me. I anguished over the problem. I considered all the things you are now about to suggest. But baffled I remained.

And I was unnerved by other doubts, not about others, about myself. Life in the program, especially during the second run, was enormously exciting, and I was really willing to do it again. But why was I so exhausted? I remember one day in the first run when, late in the afternoon, as I was settling down to some task, I saw our mathematician sauntering towards the door. I must have sent him a reproachful look because he turned back to me. "I know what you're thinking" he said, "but let me tell you something. I do all my work, all the reading, attend everything, meet my seminars, confer with my students. But I'm not going to overwork like you. I'm going to work the way a professor should work. This is an educational experiment, but if it can only work if the professors overwork, the experiment is a failure. You're working too hard. I'm not going to, and I'm right. . . . " He was right, of course. I did work too hard. I realize that the work of establishing a new program was far greater than the work involved in teaching in an established, ongoing enterprise, that life in a continuing program would get a bit easier. But at the very least, teaching in the program was a heavy, full-time job, whereas, at Berkeley, teaching was considered only part of a professor's work. He was supposed to be doing scholarship, research, writing as well, and his relatively light teaching load reflected that fact. Was I to become a full-time teacher? I didn't really want to, although I was devoted to teaching. I wanted—should I be ashamed to say?—to live the life of a normal Berkeley professor. Sometimes, during the program, I would cross the campus to see old cronies at the Faculty Club. I was like a harassed mother who had escaped her demanding brood for an adult lunch-break. I felt the seductive charm of "normal" academic life—the intellectual tension, the pervasive wit, the intellectual privacy, the leisurely autonomy, the cool arms-length, controlled, well-mannered involvement, on one's own terms, with others. I missed it, and I shrank from the thought of giving it up for the unremitting intensity of life in the program. And if I felt that way now. . . . Well, these were secret thoughts, unsharable, treasonous. Was I really prepared to wrestle endlessly with the recalcitrant for their own unrealized good or to live the life of a missionary in a corner of a gaudy rialto. The very question was enervating, demoralizing.

So, when the vice chancellor told me there would be no tenure slots I did not argue. I did not spring into battle in order to face, if I won the battle, a problem for which I had no solution. Perhaps it was simply weariness. Perhaps something was operating at a deeper level, something that I have no desire to understand. I let it go. But now, when I think about the program's failure to graduate from "ephemeral" to "enduring," in spite of its unique quality, I do not blame the university, I blame myself.

The fundamental delusion may have been to suppose that it was possible for a great organism like the university to nourish or sustain for long an enterprise at odds with its essential nature. The mode of life required by the program was not congenial to the normal Berkeley professor, violating the basic assumption that one teaches what one is expert at, as one thinks best. Experts teaching their subjects to students who want to study it is our ideal condition—the best experts and the best students. Some requirements, some structured sequences. Courses, courses, courses—the established American pattern of schooling producing, not infrequently, the tough, provocative course that lingers almost alone in the fond memories of alumni. The pattern common to Harvard, Yale, Stanford, Berkeley, Swarthmore, Oberlin, Wesleyan, Amherst, Smith, Michigan, Wisconsin, Columbia, Fresno State, Ohio State, and almost everywhere else. It is easy. We know how to do it. It may not be all that good, but it cannot be all that bad. It has, after all, made us what we are. So it is not surprising that our basic pattern persists, taking ephemeral challenges in stride. A daring young president summoned Meiklejohn to Wisconsin and gave him some running room for five years before the weight of the patient regular faculty prevailed and the Experimental College vanished. Hutchins, with great energy and flair, created his college (not really all that radical) at the University of Chicago and, as he told me ruefully, the university proceeded to dismantle it as soon as he left. Scott Buchanan and Stringfellow Barr launched St. Johns on its significant path and it is still alive after half a century. But it is not a part of a university; it stands apart, a church served by its own devoted priesthood. The University of California's Santa Cruz campus flirting initially with a college organization and, never trying anything terribly different, becomes more normal every year as the department, under a different name, increases its dominance over the college. The fact is, our prestige institutions are content to be what they are—course-givers with, perhaps, a few local variations. The key is, of course, the faculty. It is what it is, not something else. It does what it does best, and it is hard to get it to do anything else, and perhaps unreasonable to try. Meiklejohn and Hutchins tried to do different things with specially recruited faculties living as second-class citizens within the domain of the regular faculty. St. Johns does different things, but with a "different" faculty and lives beyond the main stream. Santa Cruz wanted to do different things, not really knowing what they were, but it wanted to do them, as I learned when I was asked to serve on committees, with a Berkeley-style faculty. In the program at Berkeley I wanted to avoid the second-class citizen problem by getting some Berkeley faculty to act differently, and ended up in the war of the first run. For the second run I gathered a non-Berkeley faculty that did different things brilliantly, but I could not solve the problem of turning them into Berkeley faculty.

The nature of the faculty sets limits to the possibility of reform—taking reform to mean not mending one's evil ways but rather reshaping the structure of learning and teaching (and, of course, the better the faculty the more difficult it is to expect it, or even ask it, to change its ways). Within our conventional limits we hail as innovative the establishment of the great course. It can be a course in Western civilization, or in great books, or integrated humanities or integrated social science, or American civilization, or citizenship, or world culture. . . . Each is an attempt, frequently successful, to mitigate fragmentation and excessive specialization, to provide some integration and perspective. They are usually founded by the vision and energy of a powerful faculty member and persist, even with diminishing élan, as cherished and distinctive features of the institution. Birth by committee is, I believe, rather rare, but I am not opposed, *a priori,* to miracles. Beside the special course and the addition of new courses, the educational change generally compatible with the basic structure is tinkering with requirements and sequences, sometimes sparked by genuine educational considerations, sometimes by political pressure triumphant, even, over responsible faculty qualms. To a disappointed or frustrated idealist like me these minor matters are barely worth the candle substantively but may be grimly amusing to observe as they reveal the interplay of intelligence, habit, power, of self-interest, ignorance, and irresponsibility in the conduct of affairs in a great institution.

Well, in the immortal words of Edith Piaf, I regret nothing. It was worth doing. For many of us, it was a uniquely great educational experience. I am proud of the exasperating, ephemeral, now-vanished child. The house is still there, and, as I said, when I drive past it now nothing happens. Almost nothing. The other day as I drove by, a small drama from the past popped into my mind. I had walked in at about 7:00 A.M. No one was there. I looked with distaste at the disorder, the weary furniture, the carelessly strewn objects. Then I stared in irritation at the enormous poster, the head of Dylan (Bob, not Thomas), lording confidently over the great hall. Unavoidable, dominating. It had annoyed me for weeks. On a reckless impulse I stood on a chair, unpinned the poster, rolled it up and carried it off to my office. Some hours later an indignant young man stomped in. "What happened to my picture?" I looked at him coolly. "I took it down." "Why did you take it down"? It was not really a question. I parried with "Why did you put it up?" "I put it up," he said, contemptuous in advance of an assertion of authority, "because I felt like it!" "I took it down," I said, "because I felt like it." He stood silent for a rather long moment. Finally he nodded. "Fair enough," he acknowledged, reached for his poster, and left with the head of Dylan under his arm. Whim baffles whim. The memory of that small triumph of reason warms me.

In the end, the program must be judged to have made no enduring difference to the quality of education at Berkeley. The sea of normal life has closed over the sunken hope, the surface now unbroken, the depths unvisited. I have never been tempted to launch a salvage operation or to get back into the educational wars, since, apart from other reasons, I seldom see a banner raised that seems worth repairing to—only trivial proposals, not worth fighting for, not worth opposing. I have had my chance.

When I look back at the program through the haze of present distance, ignoring the details of small triumphs and small tragedies, banking the glow of old animosities, stilling regret over misplays or false moves, several things stand out. First, the struggle to achieve something of a working intellectual community—a group of faculty and students engaged in a common enterprise, creating a structure of ritual and habit triumphant over the impulses of disintegration—an intellectual community as a way of life, sustained for a significant period of time. It was, in a world of discrete, self-contained, autonomous classrooms, a glimpse, a reminder of the quality of a pre-Babelian world. That glimpse of community is, perhaps, the most dominating of all my memories.

And second, the curricular conception—the attempt to provide for our present crises the cultural context within which they are to be understood. Something has happened when you can grasp the thread that runs from Orestes and Antigone to *West Virginia v. Barnette* and the presidential campaign of 1988. When you can see that the attempt to impose the tablets of the law upon the worshipers of the golden calf is the same struggle as is involved in our attempts to make the constitutional covenant and the law prevail over our hedonic impulses and narrow partialities. The failure to provide this great context is to send our students, robbed of their proper clothing, of their proper minds, naked into the jabbering world. It is stupidly irresponsible of the university to allow this to happen. It is a betrayal of its trust. It is, as I used to say, a consequence of the fact that the university, simply by being what it is, has killed the college.

These convictions, with which I began, survive in me unimpaired, although shadowed now by frustration and defeat.

CHAPTER 2

EXPERIMENT AT BERKELEY

PREFACE

The Experimental Program was conceived as an attempt to reincarnate the spirit and principles of the Experimental College. That college, founded by Alexander Meiklejohn at the University of Wisconsin in the 1920's, had a brilliant but brief life. It was only a memory when I was an undergraduate at Wisconsin, a legend, an educational Paradise Lost. I have always regretted that I missed it, and several decades of university teaching strengthened my belief that it offered the solution to the central problems of undergraduate education.

A concrete proposal was developed in the spring of 1964, and preliminary discussions had begun when, in the fall of 1964, the Free Speech Movement burst upon the world. This coincidence has supported the assumption that the Experimental Program is a child of the student movement; but the child does not, in any important way, resemble its putative parent. It is undoubtedly the case that the depth of student unrest and disaffection shook the complacency of the faculty and made it more receptive to drastic innovation. It is quite possible that without the prevailing sense of urgency and crisis the program would not have been authorized—at least not without considerable delay. Student unrest was, in this way, involved in the establishment of the program. The spirit of the program, however, with its completely required faculty-determined curriculum and structure, is utterly alien to the spirit of "student-initiated" programs that involve students in the creation and planning of courses in

---

This is a somewhat shortened version of the book *Experiment at Berkeley* (New York: Oxford University Press, 1969).

which they are interested, or which, in one way or another, turn them loose to educate themselves.

During the three years the program has been in operation the world has experienced the eruption of student discontent in contagious and striking form, and everywhere there is anxious concern over how to deal with it. Are there "rights" we have failed to recognize? Are there legitimate demands that must be met? Is it an irrational storm we must try to ride out? Can we anticipate and prevent? Will minor concessions do? Or do we need fundamental reform not only of the educational institution but of society as well? Is the inherited conception of the university—whatever it may be—no longer appropriate, and must we, therefore, reshape it to a new conception of the relation of thought to action, understanding to involvement, university to society?

The Experimental Program has had its own internal struggles in its attempt to establish a radically different mode of educational life. It is not easy, under the best of circumstances, to change deeply rooted habits. But the program does not, for good or ill, exist as an island in the midst of a calm sea. We had an educational idea, and we were trying to carry it out. It is so fundamental a departure from the current educational pattern that most of the current educational controversy and agitation seem altogether superficial and irrelevant. Arguments about how to improve courses sound quite unreal and remote when you have simply abolished "the course" altogether. We recognize that people are still taking and giving courses. They have our sympathy, but we cannot regard their quarrels, their politics, their participatory gestures, their ad hoc concessions and innovations, as very important. Why get excited about educational battles with insignificant educational stakes? When all the dust has settled things will look very much the same. Only some names will have been changed to confuse the innocent. The Experimental Program goes deeper and reduces current battles cries to triviality.

So, regarding its terms as beside the point, we stand outside the mainstream of current controversy. Student dissatisfaction with college education is real and justified, but the demand for student participation in educational administration is a futile and misguided remedy. The faculty is right in trying to retain its educational authority, but its exercise of that authority within the habit of the course structure amounts, at the lower-division liberal arts level, to a feeble joke. On behalf of the student we oppose faculty practice; on behalf of education, we refuse to defer to student inclination or power. In the politics of education, our alliances are precarious.

We have worked during the past three years in complete freedom. The administration has been generous in its support and has imposed no restrictions upon us. At no point have we had to accommodate our educational judgment to supposed institutional, administrative, or political necessities. No one has interfered. The student culture has been generally sympathetic and supportive, even though the scale and complexity of the program make it seem, to some, at best a token remedy and not a massive solution to a massive problem. The faculty, which with some misgivings authorized the program, has been tolerant and even sympathetic. Much of its opposition based on misunderstanding has disappeared. The opposition based on understanding is yet to be reckoned with.

December 1968

CONTENTS

Introduction

I. The Teacher

II. The Student

III. The Curriculum

IV. Draft of Report on Program, January 1968

Postscript, July 1968

INTRODUCTION

The campus may well emerge in the modern world as the successor to the marketplace, the cathedral, the factory, the financial district—as the pivotal social institution. That the campus is in turmoil is, in fact, a sign of its vitality. We are fighting about its constitutional structures, and the stakes are high.

The most significant conflict on the modern campus is not the most dramatic one. It is not between students and administration, or faculty and administration, or faculty and students; it is the subtle conflict between the university and the college. It is a peculiarly internal conflict between two tendencies within the same company of men, two purposes, two functions.

The university is the academic community organized for the pursuit of knowledge. It is arrayed under the familiar department banners and moves against the unknown on all fronts. Its victories have transformed the world.

The university is a collection of highly trained specialists who work with skill, persistence, and devotion. Its success is beyond question, but it pays the price of its success. The price *is* specialization, and it supports two unsympathetic jibes: the individual specialized scholar may find that, as with Oedipus, the pursuit of knowledge leads to impairment of vision; and, the community of scholars, speaking its special tongues, has suffered the fate of Babel.

The men who are the university are also, however, the men who are the college. But the liberal arts college is a different enterprise. It does not assault or extend the frontiers of knowledge. It has a different mission. It cultivates human understanding. The mind of the person, not the body of knowledge, is its central concern. This, I am sure, is the heart of the matter. I hope it is clear as it stands, because I despair of explaining it. Knowledge is related to understanding, but understanding is not another subject that can be taught. Wisdom can escape the expert; there are learned fools. Folklore and dark sayings, but I will rest on that for the time being. The university for multiplicity and knowledge; the college for unity and understanding.

The college is everywhere in retreat, fighting a dispirited rear-guard action against the triumphant university. The upper division, dominated by departmental cognitive interests, has become, in spirit, a preparatory run at the graduate school, increasingly professional. Only the lower division remains outside the departmental fold—invaded, neglected, exploited, misused. It is there that the college must make its stand.

The cast of characters—students, faculty, administration—is standard but sometimes misunderstood, so a few cautionary remarks are in order.

First, "students" are not "scholars." This is not a complaint. It is a fact, and not even a deplorable one. It has nothing to do with intelligence or the capacity to learn. Some students will, of course, become scholars, just as some will become dentists. But it is a mistake to think of "training scholars" as the same thing, in principle, as "training students." The American college student is simply a normal American who has behaved well in high school and who can afford to go to college. He is there because it is the natural place for him to be, not because the life of reason beckons, or because he wants to grow up to be a professor, or because curiosity is his master passion. His being there is important. His education is important. But whether he becomes a "scholar" or not is not important.

Second, speaking of the faculty, a "scholar" is not a "teacher"; a "professor" is not a "pedagogue." A scholar is a man with something on his mind and with the skill and determination to pursue it; a teacher is a cultivator of other minds. A university usually hires scholars and hopes that they will do as teachers.

Third, the administration is not the bureaucratic agent of alien claims upon the academic community. It is, on the whole, the conscientious guardian of the integrity of the institution, negotiating support while fending off distorting influence from the outside and confronting internal self-interest with the legitimate claims of the institution. It is, on the whole, probably too weak; and its "corruption," its misuse of the institution, is invariably less than that of the faculty and of the students.

The radical improvement of educational life within the university is not a narrow technical matter. It involves the reorganization and redirection of educational energies within an institution whose members and resources are already fully engaged in activity believed to be significant. No one is going to wipe the slate clean and start all over. Whether desirable or not, no quick, drastic, or massive change is likely. For to change education is to change the behavior of the faculty. Minor change, of course, is continually taking place. New courses are created, programs are renovated or reconstructed, lectures improve and deteriorate, requirements are changed; but the basic pattern is much the same.

The American college must rediscover and renew its commitment to its fundamental purpose. It has a purpose, and that purpose is, for the sake of all of us, for society and for the individual, to develop our rational powers, to heighten sensitivity to and awareness of fundamental human problems, to cultivate and strengthen the habits and dispositions that make it possible for humanity to displace the varieties of warfare with the institutions, the practices, and the spirit of reasoning together. The college is not the blind or servile tool of transient arrangements, but it is not neutral as between reason and unreason, between freedom and frenzy, between civilization and chaos. It stands with Apollo, not with Dionysus.

The college must rediscover its purpose and must assert itself. It is not the marketplace that it has come, all too often, to resemble: professors crying their separate wares in their separate stalls, student customers wandering and loitering through the maze, consulting private shopping lists. We like the marketplace; it strikes us as an ideal situation—a social institution that caters to private desire. Let us have the market if we must, but let us not confuse it with the college. Free men are not produced in stores.

Nor is the college a professional school. It may prepare for, but it does not directly train for, the great professions. It has its own mission: to fit us for the life of active membership in the democratic community; to fit us to serve, in its broadest sense, our common political vocation.

A college consists of faculty and students appropriately related by and involved in a plan or program of study. This would seem to be an irreducible trinity, but there are heresies abroad in the land which, in one way or another, are antitrinitarian.

The familiar "personalist" heresy runs something like this: it is all a matter of human relations, of communication—the teacher and student relating as persons, breaking through the artificial barriers of roles and authority and engaging in dialogue in small discussion groups, preferably unstructured. That gets rid of the program of study. If the faculty won't play, the attempt at transgenerational tolerance or understanding is abandoned and stress is placed on peer group interaction—"students educate each other." That gets rid of the faculty. In some versions the "others" disappear altogether, and we are left with the solitary individual in search of himself.

There are, no doubt, other versions and other heresies, but I shall take it as obvious that the college has a faculty and that it has students (although there are some utopian visions . . .). That there is always a program of study must be asserted with less confidence. Students always have work to do, but a miscellaneous collection of courses does not constitute a program. The deficiency, is most serious at the lower-division level, and it calls for drastic treatment.

The attempt to create a coherent first program brings to the test the entire range of educational resources and ideas. It imposes tasks upon the faculty that require it to re-examine its teaching theory and practice; it forces a reconsideration of the status and the needs of students; and it calls for a re-examination of basic curricular conceptions. That re-examination, if we undertake it, may revitalize our higher education.

I. THE TEACHER

The art of teaching, in its broadest sense, is the art of creating and maintaining an environment and a structure of activity conducive to the proper development of the mind. The teacher himself is an active feature of that environment, and he applies energy and judgment in different ways at different points to stimulate growth and development. Teaching resembles gardening, except for the propensity to lecture to the roses.

The individual teacher tends to take the institutional environment as given—by the nature of things, by tradition, or by administrative decision—tests the system for flexibility, accommodates himself with varying degrees of eccentricity to its limits, and settles for jurisdiction over his own courses as providing the arena within which he practices his art: his course, his subject, his students. Left largely to his own devices, the teacher comes to identify good teaching with "giving good courses." He masters a subject and develops a way of dealing with it. He lays out a course of study and sets out to be helpful—to sustain interest, to analyze and explain, to encourage and correct. He develops and comes to terms with his powers as a lecturer, works out a mode of individual consultation, and learns to accept with remarkable patience the shortcomings, the gratuitous indifference, and the occasional cruelty of students.

Undergraduate liberal arts teaching accommodates itself to the structure of the course and develops some distinctively course-related characteristics. It is necessary to mention the obvious because the course is so pervasive that we have come to regard the conditions of course teaching as the conditions of teaching in general.

The course forces teaching into small, relatively self-contained units. Horizontally, courses are generally unrelated and competitive. That is, the student is taking three or four or even five courses simultaneously. They are normally in different subjects, given by different professors, and, with rare exceptions, there is no attempt at horizontal integration. Thus, each professor knows that he has a valid claim to only a small fraction of a student's time and attention. The effect is that no teacher is in a position to be responsible for, or effectively concerned with, the student's total educational situation. The student presents himself to the teacher in fragments, and not even the advising system can put him together again.

What is worse is that the professor knows that even his fragment of the student's time must be competitively protected. If he does not make tangible, time-consuming demands the student diverts time to courses that do make such demands. It becomes almost impossible to set a reflective, contemplative, deliberate pace in a single course. The tendency is to over-assign work, with the expectation that it will probably not all be done. The cumulative effect on the student is brutal. To survive he must learn how to not do his work; he is forced into the adoption of the strategies of studentship; he learns to read too fast, to write and speak with mere plausibility. His educational life, through no fault of his own, becomes a series of artificial crises.

Horizontal competitiveness and fragmentation of student attention are limiting conditions of which every sensitive teacher is bitterly aware. But there is nothing he can do about it. He can develop a coherent course, but a collection of coherent courses may be simply an incoherent collection. For the student, to pursue one thread is to drop another. He seldom experiences the delight of sustained concentration. He lives the life of a distracted intellectual juggler.

The vertical aspect of the course structure mitigates, in principle, the separateness or independence of the individual course by providing sequences and treating some courses as prerequisite to others. The student, in this dimension, moves from the introductory through the intermediate to the advanced. While some sequences are obvious—as, for example, foreign language study—it is not always the case that the sequence is technically developmental. It may be a movement from a preliminary survey, historical or systematic, to courses with a narrower focus; and in such cases the preliminary course is not indispensable. The student may wish to go directly to the more specialized course, and the professor may be glad to admit someone who is interested in his subject and may waive the general introductory prerequisite.

Thus, while vertical sequence, integration, and development are features of the course structure, they are not as significant or pervasive as might appear. With some exceptions, courses come in clusters rather than in chains. The bearing of this on the planning function (or burden) of the faculty is significant. A chain takes more planning than a cluster. The internal structure of a particular course is more affected by its position in a chain or sequence of courses than by its location in a cluster. The former requires some faculty cooperation; the latter permits greater teaching autonomy. The faculty, like any group, finds cooperation difficult and prefers autonomy. Thus, in the absence of strong countervailing forces, a natural law of the universe finds expression in the curricular law, "chains give way to clusters."

The point is that such sequential organization as exists tends to be fairly loose, takes the course as its building block, and does not dominate its internal structure. The course is identified and located by name or subject and number. There are some college rules about courses and some departmental policies, but within those limiting conditions, the professor can shape his course as he thinks best. He practices the art of teaching within a quarter course that constitutes about 1/45th of the student's undergraduate education.

The teacher is thus stationed at a particular time and place in the educational process. Students come and go; he tends his station. It is inevitable that the rhetoric of discontent should seize upon the "cafeteria" and the "factory" as telling metaphors. It is also obvious that the criticism or defense of the quality of the courses offered is really beside the point. The difficulty is not with the quality of the particular course but with the course structure itself.

Even within these limitations there is a lot of good teaching going on. Professors normally put a great deal of thought and effort into their courses. Their devotion and diligence keep an essentially absurd system afloat. Their efforts may be appreciated, but they are seldom celebrated.

What usually comes to attention and acclaim as "great teaching" is a more spectacular sort of performance. "Performance" is the right word. The "great teacher" is, all too often, a great performer on stage. Articulate, witty, rhetorically versatile, he captures and holds his audience. He has ideas, and he makes the most of them. His course is a good show, and he usually plays to a full house. He is not necessarily eccentric, although there is a familiar type who is academically unconventional—the "professor as rebel." He attacks his colleagues, his guild, his discipline, his institution, his society. He is original about grades, examinations, schedules. His course is a charmingly defiant exercise in self-expression and self-indulgence. He has not been conquered by the system. But he confuses "students" with "audience."

It is a commonplace that the university does not sufficiently recognize and reward good undergraduate teaching. The university feels quite guilty about it and is always trying to make up for its neglect. But the instinct that keeps it from freely bestowing tenure and promotion for "good teaching" alone is, I think, quite canny. On the one hand, there is the generally invisible but adequate—even good—course teaching; on the other hand, there is the star performer. The former is not worth rewarding because course teaching itself is, as I have suggested, a generally fruitless form of teaching; the latter we are reluctant to reward—although we do reward it anyway—because something tells us, although we are afraid it may be jealousy, that there is something suspicious about it. It is as if we had some awards to bestow for excellence in swimming and found ourselves confronting candidates who on the one hand were managing to keep afloat in a well or who, on the other hand, seemed to be walking on water. Treading water and walking on it are peculiar kinds of swimming. Tending the courses that mark the stations of the student's cross and giving brilliant lectures are peculiar kinds of teaching. They are, I suspect, adequately rewarded.

We have gotten about as far as the course can take us. Energy spent in improving them produces only marginal gains and is energy misdirected. We have reached the point at which, if we are to improve college education significantly, we must create a real alternative to the course system itself and reduce the course to a peripheral feature of the educational structure. The only effective unit for educational planning is the program. And the Experimental Program has shown that it can be done even where it is most difficult—at the lower-division level.

A program of sufficient scope drastically alters the teaching situation, eliminates some problems entirely, and presents us with interesting new challenges.

First, the competitive horizontal pressures are removed. A single outside course can be accommodated without distraction (although more than a single course would probably destroy everything). Attention can be focused or concentrated, and decisions about simultaneous lines of activity can be made within the program on purely educational grounds. We can make possible exclusive attention to a single work for a sustained period. We can integrate or coordinate virtually the entire range of the student's academic activity—reading and writing, lecture and discussion. We can set our own pace and establish our own rhythm.

Vertically, continuity for a two-year period seems about right. While a single year is better than nothing, the second year brings to fruition and reinforces what the first year only begins. Two years is far more than merely twice as good as a single year. Such continuity provides ample opportunity to develop curricular themes and variations and to ensure variety and balance. It also makes possible a relaxed, confident, long-range approach to the development of particular skills and powers. We can, for example, think in terms of a sustained two-year program of writing. Development is discernible and can be fostered.

The program, unlike the course, is a workable educational unit. It presents us with the whole student for a significant period of time. It restores to the teacher a rather frightening share of responsibility for the student's education—a responsibility that seems to evaporate from the interstices of the course system. Educational decisions become necessary; more importantly, they become possible. The program recaptures for the teacher the possibility of giving a reasonable structure to the life of learning.

The shift from the course to the program has, however, a revolutionary effect on the teaching situation. A single professor can teach a course; he cannot teach a program. "What should I do with my students?" gives way to "What should we do with ours?" Unless structural reform entails the substitution of the latter question for the former, it will have only minor effects on the quality of education. We must move from individualistic to collegial teaching. That is a drastic move, indeed; "revolutionary" is not an exaggeration.

We sometimes speak of a faculty as a "community of scholars," and the expression is, as often as not, used with irony. "Community" applied to scholars is like "pride" applied to lions or "school" applied to fish. But we do not even say "community of teachers." Scholars may collaborate and cooperate. But teaching, even after we make the necessary exceptions and qualifications, is normally regarded as a solo performance. The program necessitates the collaborative teaching that the individual course prevents or discourages. It involves professors in a genuinely common teaching enterprise. It gives the teacher real working colleagues.

Anyone familiar with the facts of academic life is more likely to shudder at this prospect than to welcome it. One's colleague is one's cross. The faculty meeting—college, departmental, or committee—is a familiar butt of academic literature. It is the abrasive ordeal from which one flees to the delicious, healing privacy of one's own course. There, the teacher cultivates his own field in peace. Publication subjects scholarship or research to the judgment of one's peers; the privacy of the classroom shields teaching from the critical scrutiny of colleagues.

Even academic freedom seems to be involved. Academic freedom, properly understood, is a doctrine that assures to the academic institution the power necessary for the performance of its function and freedom from improper external interference. It is a grant of autonomy to the institution not in order that it may do as it pleases, but in order that it may best do what it is supposed to do. The institution is empowered to exercise its own best judgment in fulfilling its responsibilities.

The academic institution has its own system of internal government. Some decisions are made collectively—by the school, or college, or department. And some matters, by a delegation of institutional authority, are left to the judgment and decision of the individual faculty member. He is, in some areas and to some degree, self-governing or autonomous. That autonomy is highly valued and gives to academic life much of its distinctive character. The professor in full cry is pretty much his own master.

But the claim to autonomy as a teacher does not stand on quite the same ground as the claim to autonomy as a scholar. A collection of scholarly experts is not a collection of expert teachers. The college professor is a professional scholar but only an amateur teacher. Autonomy in the classroom is not strongly buttressed by claims to expertness in "teaching." I am not proposing that we invade the classroom. I do suggest, however, that the claim to teaching autonomy is less firmly based than the claim to scholarly autonomy.

The course taught by a single professor is not sanctified by the law of nature; it is not a mandate of the charter of academic freedom; it is not triumphantly vindicated by its fruits. It is simply a customary, archaic mode of academic organization. It is supported by our habits, and it confirms us in our vices. It puts the professor, wrapt (rapt!) in his subject on the center of the stage, converts him into a verbose performer, and pawns this off as a paradigm of the life of reason.

The program gives us the teaching colleagues we so badly need and imposes collective responsibility at the working level. Faculty egos check each other, with the inevitable result that the student, not the performer, moves into the center of the picture. The teacher finds himself worrying less about what to say next than about what the students should be doing next. Genuine teaching problems move onto the faculty agenda, and teaching practice, under the stimulus of example, discussion, and criticism, improves steadily. The experience is both exhausting and exhilarating. It can shake the teacher rather strongly, but it can only improve him.

A program must be based on and dominated by a single, fairly simple, curricular conception. That conception must have, so to speak, constitutional status, and it must remain beyond challenge for the duration of a cycle. Fundamental questions must be faced in the process of conception and the answers, however tentative, must be embodied in the constitution of the program. Fundamental changes may be warranted by experience, but they cannot be made in mid-stream except—if there is an exception at all—by the unanimous and genuinely uncoerced consent of the staff.

The constitutional conception must be the basis upon which the faculty is gathered or recruited. Whether it is framed by one person or by a group, no one should be invited or allowed to teach in the program unless he commits himself to its basic terms.

The point is not to make disagreement impossible; it is rather to make disagreement possible and fruitful. We can only disagree within the program if we agree about it. Constitutional disagreement while a program is in process threatens to destroy it; "legislative" disagreement (if we may use that contrast) can enrich it. While many decisions can be left open to be made by the faculty as it proceeds, the constitutional structure must be decided from the start.

The importance of constitutional clarity and commitment cannot, I think, be too strongly insisted upon. The faculty member is an individualist. He not only has ideas, he is used to being able to act on them. In a common program he cannot do everything his own way, but his tendency will be to attempt to recreate the conditions within which he is habitually successful and at ease. Differences in teaching style and practice are deep-seated, and they are usually supported, if questioned, by a theory of education. In a teacher of any experience—especially a successful teacher—to challenge them is to challenge him. Many views of teaching are incompatible with each other. In a system of individual courses that does not matter; but some differences make teaching together impossible. Constitutional clarity can prevent some disasters.

Even so, we can count on misunderstandings that will raise fundamental questions and will pose some threats to the program. One danger is that the faculty will split into factions on the nature of the program. And that kind of disagreement, on top of the normal range of problems, is almost too much to live with. If decision is forced "politically," then the losers can become disaffected and withdraw spiritually from the common effort. If, to avoid that, we try to compromise, the result is, like any educational compromise, a mess that pleases no one, and that makes one long for his private course where at least someone's conception of what is best can be controlling. Factionalism and compromise are the banes of the common program, and prior constitutional clarity and agreement are the necessary inoculation.

The "constitution," overbearing as it may seem in this a count, really contains little except what is necessary to preserve the common enterprise and encourage fruitful interaction: (1) central curricular conception, about which I shall say more later and, as a corollary, the understanding that all students are to study the same thing at the same time. That is, no special reading list for "one's own" students. If in the judgment of a faculty member something should be added (or omitted) he must raise the matter for common consideration and decision; (2) a single common lecture program in which all participate and which all attend. This is an especially valuable unifying force. (3) A single common schedule of seminars, conferences, and writing.

These principles protect the common program against the tendency to become fragmented internally, force the faculty to develop and apply collective judgment to common educational problems, and provide sufficient stability to encourage fresh- ness and flexibility.

Each faculty group will, of course, develop its own institutions of discussion, deliberation, and decision. It was not until the third year of the Experimental Program that we developed a really successful pattern. Its elements include:

(1) Prior summer support so that the faculty can prepare itself for the program. This permits some intensive planning of the curricular and pedagogic pattern and time for preparatory reading and study.

(2) During the teaching year, provision for regular faculty meetings. A meeting over coffee for a half-hour prior to the lecture twice a week is sufficient to take care of most minor matters. But the significant institution

is the faculty "seminar." Once each week, through the entire academic year, the faculty met for dinner and discussion. Mostly, we discussed the program reading, argued about the ideas involved, and considered their educational significance. In spite of the heat that was sometimes generated, these meetings—which normally lasted about four hours—were delightful and exciting. The seminar shaped and supported the lecture program, brought out the issues, and made individual experience and insight the common property of the program. It is not too much to say that, in fact, the seminar made the program. In retrospect, much of the internal difficulty during the first two years seems due to the fact that we had not yet developed the regular evening faculty seminar.

If a program faculty develops the proper *esprit de corps* it will, I believe, seldom find itself voting about anything. It is a small group and attitudes quickly become known. It is genuinely collegial and, given the constitutional commitment, questions of formal democracy or equality seem quite irrelevant. Consensus usually emerges from full and free discussion, and when it does not and some decision is necessary it is probably better to let someone express the decision of the group than to count heads. If that becomes an important question itself, the faculty is in trouble, and counting heads—although it can be done—won't help much. Voting, in an educational program, is only for matters that are not worth discussion.

The rewards of involvement in a successfully functioning group are very great. It is an unforgettable experience. It is also an experience of unusual intellectual and psychological intimacy that can, if things do not go well, be very trying. Personal sensitivity, pride, vanity, insecurity are always with us, and friendship is an indispensable balm. Friendship is, in fact, an important recruiting principle and should be recognized as a legitimate one.

This sketch of the internal situation may suggest some of the reasons for difficulty in recruiting faculty members to teach in programs. It sounds a little like trying to convert the prosperous small businessman to socialism. Moreover, the Experimental Program, in tackling the problem where college education is at its worst, in the lower division, faces special difficulties.

Let me refer again to what I have called the "three program" structure of the university. This consists of the graduate program, the upper-division major program, and the largely nonexistent lower division or first program.

To some extent the graduate or third program already embodies principles upon which the Experimental Program is based. It is not generally course dominated, and it involves vertical continuity over a sustained period of time with only minimal horizontal distraction. It is subject to and even requires cooperative staff planning and direction.

The major, or second program, places at the disposal of the department roughly half of the student's academic time over a two-year period. The educational potentialities of this situation are in most cases unrealized because departments usually define the major program in terms of sequences or clusters of individual courses. But there is very little standing in the way of a department's deciding to organize its major program differently—to assign a tutorial staff to an appropriate number of students for a two-year period and to commission that staff to work out a two-year program of common reading, writing, and discussion. This is well within departmental discretion and would raise very few, if any, legislative, staffing, or budgetary problems.

The second and third programs have two very significant advantages over the first program from the point of view of program development. First, each is based upon or rooted in an established academic subject, field, or discipline, centered in an academic department. This simplifies the curricular problem considerably. And second, the department provides us with a continuing corps of disciplinary experts who expect to, are prepared to, and are even eager to teach their "subjects."

The special problems of the first program are revealed by contrast. Its curriculum does not coincide with an academic subject or fall within a department's discipline. And, since the college faculty is departmentally organized and recruited, there is no easily available or continuing first-program staff.

To involve a member of a department in a first program requires that he be able, for a time, to free himself from his normal departmental responsibilities and also that he be willing, for a time, to work outside the area of his specialization. These are formidable obstacles.

But the lower division is an educational wasteland. We cannot abandon there whatever is left of the possibility of liberal education. The first-program conception can save it, and we cannot accept present obstacles as permanent barriers. There are, I believe, two complementary possibilities which, if pursued, might make at least a dent in the problem.

First, we must devote more attention to, and learn to deliberately reap the benefits of, the distinctive phases of the normal academic career. That a professor moves through intellectual phases is a fact not a disgrace. But it is sometimes supposed that he should race continuously and triumphantly on the straight and narrow path on which he starts and that to waver or to leave that path is to begin to decay and die. That is not quite the correct description of the civilization of a barbarian or of the development of a mind. The mind, too, has its seasons, and the periodic breaking in of wisdom redirects and alters the mode in which we pursue knowledge. An analytic, technical mood gives way, for a time, to a reflective or synthesizing mood. There are times of assessment and reorientation as well as times of confident exploration.

The professor is not, therefore, at all times or at all stages fit for the same kind of teaching activity. There is a time for graduate students and there is a time for freshmen—graduate students when he is developing knowledge, freshmen when he is seeking wisdom.

The task of educational administration is to provide opportunities for teaching that correspond with the phases of the teacher's career and to facilitate and encourage flexible and timely involvement with first, second, and third-program teaching.

Fortunately, the phase of the academic career during which the institutional and personal pressures operate most strongly against first-program involvement is also the phase during which the professor is least fit for first-program teaching. There is a good deal of misplaced regret over the fact that junior members of the faculty, the assistant professoriate, are under heavy pressures of research and publication. "Publish or perish" is not entirely a myth, but we often overlook the fact that it does not express merely an external institutional demand. The decisive pressures are internal. The candidate for academic life is a professional intellectual in his novitiate. He is interested in knowledge, attracted by ideas, anxious to solve problems. He wants to make a significant contribution in his chosen field. He is eager, driving, ambitious, enthusiastic. It is likely to be a decade before he emerges from his first great "technical" phase. During that initial phase he is best suited for graduate or upper-division teaching. He is likely to be more specialized than he will be later and should probably be encouraged to mine his particular vein to its limit before he is diverted by teaching demands that require a different frame of mind. Junior teaching energy tends to be most professional and, in character, furthest removed from first-program teaching. It is fresh and enthusiastic; but it is also likely to be subject-centered, self-centered, and missionary.

So we should not waste too much time and energy bemoaning, or fighting, the difficulties of freeing the junior faculty for first-program teaching. We should look to the tenure ranks in terms of both suitability and availability. Readiness for ventures into first-program teaching should be seen as marking the end of academic adolescence.

It must be acknowledged, however, that there are many members of faculties who are really never fit for first-program teaching. They are merely scholars, specialists, technicians without mitigating philosophic or reflective resources. They have an honored place in the university. They may be quite productive in the current mode of their discipline, and they play a large part in the training of graduate students. But they have one-track minds, and if derailed they simply come to a stop. Whether he is still a rampant young lion or is subsiding into "old Blank who is still doing research in X," he is not much interested in teaching callow freshmen who aren't "motivated." He believes in scholarship and in his discipline (as he knows it, or knew it), scorns the dilettante, and wouldn't be caught dead outside his special field. He is useful where he is, and is best left undisturbed. He does not understand the first program and is opposed to it by instinct. The university is full of such citizens who will never be suitable or "ready" for the first program.

And second, we must, to take advantage of such faculty readiness as there may be, provide a first-program structure-in-being with which a willing faculty member can easily associate himself.

The only feasible solution is, I believe, to establish, in one way or another, a regular first-program core staff. To develop a separate lower-division or first-program faculty would, apart from other objections, defeat the purpose of encouraging the regular faculty to move through the whole range of teaching situations. But to have no permanent staff at all to provide experience, continuity, and stability would mean that we would have few, if any, first programs at all.

This conclusion has been reached with great reluctance. But faith in the continuous spontaneous generation of programs is now dead. The obstacle course is too difficult.

A permanent core staff would have responsibility for developing and modifying program constitutions, for recruiting faculty to join in the program for a period of one or two years, and for providing leadership for the teaching staff. If we consider a normal program as involving six faculty and 150 students, we should plan on a core staff of two or three for each faculty group of six. Two is certainly a minimum.

It should be said that this account of the staffing difficulties reflects the special bias and condition of a university with a dominant graduate school and upper-division concern. The regular four-year college has easier solutions at hand, and the lower-division junior or community college can shift to a program basis quite easily, if it can free itself from the tyranny of transfer requirements.

It is clear, I think, that the problem of establishing the first program is quite extrinsic to its educational merit. If the program were only as good as, or slightly better than, the present pattern of lower-division education, it would not be worth bothering with. It is not just a little better. It is infinitely better.

The difficulty is due entirely to the established teaching habits of the contemporary professoriate and to the institutional structure that reflects and reinforces those habits. Those habits—as teaching habits—are appalling; they need reformation. But the case is one in which the physician must heal himself. No one else can really do it. The gradual replacement of the individual course by the common program is probably the only real therapeutic device on the scene.

But all this sounds unnecessarily and misleadingly grim. The life of the faculty in the program is deeply exciting, satisfying, and refreshing. What, after all, does he do? It is a full-time commitment, so, for a year or two, he puts other things aside. He reads and studies, with other faculty members and with students, a coherent and varied sequence of great, readable books dealing with the great human questions. He joins in a lively faculty seminar. He discusses what we read with students. He reads and confers with students about their papers. He gives occasional informal lectures. He is an active member of a genuine working community, involved with people and with ideas. He is still a teacher, but he sees, in a different context, what the art of teaching really is. Life in the program is, without question, a great and unique experience.

II. THE STUDENT

Students en masse are apparently a disturbing spectacle. Beards and mini-skirts, mysterious potions and simple musical instruments, evoke ancestral memories of nymphs and satyrs. In our puritan nightmare they have emerged from the wooded fringes and swarm unheeding and shameless in the public streets, the parks, and the campus—dazed or frenzied litterers. Or, in the other nightmare, the sullen cast of *Lear*—Gonerils, Edmunds,

Regans—monsters of ingratitude, are turning heedless and destructive energy against the aging nurturer.

The college, when it is not blamed for causing all this, is at least expected to cure it. And the danger to the college, as it comes in crisis to the center of public attention, is that its own internal efforts to understand and to improve itself will be impeded by the overwhelming emphasis on visible disorder. Of course disorder is a serious problem. But it may be the symptom of deeper problems and stirrings, and we must aim at more than a premature subsiding of symptoms.

The college is the point at which three parties meet and make demands of each other. These parties are, in fact, deeply interdependent, and the college is, in principle, a point of cooperative integration. If it has come to resemble a battlefield it is because each party comes with two sets of banners—one set authentic, the other a subtle caricature which, when raised, seems authentic enough, but by insensible degree breeds chaos.

First, society is a party to the college, and to meet society's legitimate demands is not a betrayal. It asks the college to prepare successive generations to carry on and develop the life of the culture, to provide for both continuity and change, for appreciation and criticism, for transmission and creation. That is the authentic banner, and who cannot rally to it? But the caricature is different. It says "accept," "conform," and "who pays the piper?" and it gets the response it merits.

The second party is the faculty, the keeper of the college. Its task is complicated, and its corruptions are subtle. I shall not linger here but will put the matter crudely. Its authentic banner says "cultivate wisdom"; its seductive caricature says "pursue knowledge." (Or perhaps "be reasonable," and "be inquisitive.") And the difference in emphasis eventually converts a college of intelligent teachers into a collection of mere scholars.

Finally, the student. He is a party to the college. He is there, and importantly there, although transitory. He is there because we care about him, because he needs special treatment, and because the life he may live is not altogether his own.

When all is right with the world, the student, who is, after all, a student, sees the college as a school and respects its character as a place of tutelage. When times are out of joint, he may see it simply as his place, his scene, his city and, in a premature rejection of tutelage, raise the counterfeit banner of self-determination, autonomy, democracy, play generational house, or sally forth to claim and change the corrupt old world. Moses, descending from the heights, faces the crisis of the golden calf—the schism between those who think that the journey toward freedom still lies ahead and those who think they have arrived. School, he declares, is not over.

It is not necessary to imagine what it would be like if everything went wrong and the hosts were marshaled under the counterfeit banners. It has happened, and the tumult is all too familiar and, by now, boring. Outraged society pounds the table and growls for order and discipline; the faculty is busy doing research; and the students are beating their chests and chasing their tails. The American college of the '60s.

Serious discussion of education in this situation is almost impossible. The noise level is too high, and we are soon shouting at each other. How can we discuss and maintain the delicate relations between the society and the college in an atmosphere marked by fear and suspicion on one side and defiant dependence on the other? How can the faculty clarify its responsibilities to society and to its students when, enthralled by the pursuit of knowledge as an end in itself, it sees their claims as secondary and distracting importunities? How can we expect students, in this atmosphere of competitive self-assertion, to lend themselves to purposes other than their own, to not see themselves as a neglected interest group whose hopes depend on the assertion of student power? Initiation into what? Tutelage for what?

Reasoning together is displaced by negotiation, and the campus of the future, we are told, will rediscover community only by accepting a pressure group view of itself and by admitting, in the name of freedom and democracy, the once silent and oppressed majority to the corridors and seats of governance. But the view of the college as a political democracy is nonsense. It may be, at this time, unconquerable nonsense, but it is nonsense nonetheless. Of course, a college is really not "undemocratic" either. The concept is simply inapplicable, and anyone who knows what a college is understands the point. "Democracy" applied to a college makes about as much sense as "democracy" applied to a rainbow or to a baseball game.

The effect of the prevalence of this nonsense is that education in the college is now under the pressure of misguided student demands which, even when educationally motivated, are so imbued with a consumer-oriented pressure group quasi-democratic ideology as to place only another set of obstacles in the path of real educational reform.

These demands are, in large measure, going to be granted. Administrations, accustomed to dealing with pressures, are prepared, or soon will be, to deal with one pressure group more. They have, quite properly, considerable concern about students, and they know better than the faculties that the students have valid complaints about education. Long experience has taught them that the organized faculty is too strong to be moved educationally by administrative effort. Student-faculty "encounter" may at least bring some countervailing power to the table and produce more change than can be produced by the usual application of administrative energy to faculty inertia.

The faculty member, on the other hand, is quite prepared to make concessions that do not require him to change his way of life, that do not restrict his authority over his own course or class. There is a whole set of currently fashionable student demands that have that virtue: more student control over "student affairs," more freedom from formal requirements, credit for student-initiated courses; and supporting those demands has some attractions.

> After all, it is only simple justice. Here am I, doing what I want. Why shouldn't the student do what he wants? Who am I to impose my values on him? He has watched television all his life, and he's an adult now. What he does on his own time is his own business. Why ask him to study what he's not interested in? Who likes a captive audience in a required course? Why not let him initiate courses if he can find some faculty member who feels like taking it on? Why not give him credit for going to Mississippi? He might learn something. If we grant all this, maybe things will calm down. And if I vote "Yes," I can be a liberal educational reformer.

Seldom in the history of education has reform required so little of so many.

The argument is almost irresistible, and the student, I am afraid, is doomed to get what he wants. Or thinks he wants. Instead of curing the disease, it will simply move us into its final stages.

I am reluctant to waste much time trying to meet the argument for the further extension of the principle of *laissez faire* in the college. The principle itself is disastrously inappropriate for education and its further extension is merely a depressing exercise in futility. To dress it in the rhetoric of freedom, democracy, and community is to indulge in sick parody approaching blasphemy.

The college is still a place of schooling. To affirm this is not necessarily to deny the adulthood of the student but rather to assert its irrelevance. Students come to us in various stages of development—physical, emotional, intellectual. In some respects they are quite mature, although American culture does not notably value or encourage the dubious blessing of early maturation. Very little follows educationally from the explicit assertion of adulthood, although, since adolescents are so touchy about it, it is tactless to deny it. Facing the facts about time, with equanimity, is hard even for adults who have had more time to get used to them.

Perhaps the only significant point about maturity is its bearing upon educational motivation. With infants and children we exploit "interest"; with adults "purpose" becomes dominant, and we hear less of "but I'm not interested in" as a reason for lack of educational engagement. The adult has learned that interest develops with and sustains fruitful activity; it does not necessarily initiate or guide it. The "not interested" whine is the dirge of the undeveloped mind, and the elective system panders without nourishing. As a solution to educational hunger it is candy for children. To treat students as adults is to not worry so much about their views about what they are interested in.

If we consider, beyond this, the wisdom of placing upon the student, adult or not, the burden of constructing the mosaic of his own education out of the mass of discrete courses in the catalogue, the answer is obvious. It is not lack of intelligence or lack of maturity, but lack of experience and knowledge that is decisive. The college has no right to evade its responsibility for educational planning by the specious device of treating the student as an adult who should plan his own education.

As for student-initiated courses, they are just courses, probably all right as courses go, probably inferior to faculty-initiated courses. Not much harm, not much gain; a pointless diversionary move that allows some youthful energy to spend itself in premature educational entrepreneurship. It only strengthens the course system and does not improve education. It is not worth fighting for, or against.

So much for shadow boxing with folly under the counterfeit banners.

The crux is freedom. Liberal education aims at the free mind. Every aspect and device of the Experimental Program is intended to serve that end. If we could force men to be free, we would; as it is, we can only try to help them. Once we understand what freedom of the mind is, the paradoxical quality of that statement disappears. Minds are not made free by being left alone. Nor are students.

We are told that there are two concepts of freedom; one good and one bad, one simple, one complex, one safe, one dangerous. The nice freedom is, of course, the absence of coercion or external constraint. Chains and bars limit our freedom; laws, threats, and sanctions also constrain us. They limit our freedom by preventing us from doing as we wish. The fewer the barriers the greater the freedom. This is the simple and safe view. Even assuming that it is clear, it presents us with several small flaws. First, the mere removal of external barriers does not touch the disparity between the weak and the strong. How valuable is the absence of external restraint in the absence, as well, of positive power or capacity? And second, suppose one acts, in the absence of external restraint, in a way that is harmful to oneself. In that case, freedom turns out to be bad for us.

Defenders of this conception of freedom may wish to meet the first point by embracing "equality" as a supplementary good or perhaps "equality of opportunity and the devil take the hindmost." As for the second point, you can't have everything! Freedom is good, but it includes the possibility of doing the wrong thing. Better to suffer and learn caution than to limit freedom; or if not, limit it a bit.

It turns out, apparently, that, on this view, freedom is not a "good" for the weak and foolish; he cannot do much, and he is likely to do the wrong thing. It is a "good" for the strong and wise, for the "able."

It should not surprise us, therefore, that a second concept of freedom arises—one that seeks to define freedom so as to preserve its character as an unmitigated "good thing." It seizes on precisely these qualities that make the absence of external restraint a good thing—strength and wisdom—and defines the free man as one who has the power to achieve what is indeed good. This, of course, is the "positive" or dangerous view of freedom.

It is dangerous because, if government is to promote freedom, it may no longer be the case that that government is best that does the least; it must do something to develop the powers and the wisdom of its citizens; it must see to it that minds are cultivated; it must, in the almost unimaginable extreme case, create and maintain a system of public schools. It is a license to meddle.

Moreover, the "freedom" that once seemed so easy—*laissez faire, laissez aller*—now becomes something difficult, an achievement. It is not the sort of thing which someone can simply be given "now" by an act of Congress. To turn children loose is not to make them free. One is free to swim only if he knows how.

It is, of course, only freedom in this positive sense that is relevant to education. And that is not because educators are professional meddlers who cannot bear to leave people alone and who, therefore, prefer the "positive," the "welfare," or the "authoritarian" state to its less intrusive alternative. It is rather because the mind is not the sort of thing, or entity, or process, to which the notions of physical constraint (or barriers) apply. The mind is not something that can be held or pushed, except in a metaphoric sense. And the metaphor can easily mislead us. We can think of a body as moving freely when unobstructed and, in a materialist tradition, can describe a man as free when, unhindered, he can do what he wants or go where he wants to. We sometimes try to apply this notion to the mind and speak of the "freedom to believe." But it does not parse. Can we believe as we please? Only if we are insane. A healthy mind, a functioning mind, a free mind, is not a mind that believes as it pleases.

Thus, in thinking about the mind, or of the person, we can easily fall into a confusion of categories and systematically misuse the language of objects. About "freedom" the sin is habitual. For the mind to be free is for it to be able, to have the power, to do what it should do. That is the freedom with which education is concerned. For the student who seeks freedom, the implications are drastic. He must submit himself to the imperatives of the quest for genuine power. He must incorporate in himself the power of the culture of which he is the creature.

Satan's great flaw, in *Paradise Lost*, is his inability to enjoy the given. "Better to reign in Hell than serve in Heaven" is not the cry of a lover of freedom but of one who would reign at all costs and who does not understand what "serving in heaven" means. He is mixed up about freedom, power, and goodness, and the pandemonium he creates is a dark parody of the order he rejects. He is enamored only of his own creation and cannot accept the good when it comes as a gift. He is surly about gifts. His missing virtue is docility.

Docility, acquiescence, deference—these appear to our present mood as weakness if not vices, as predemocratic attitudes, close kin to humility and respectfulness, conservative tools of exploitation and suppression. But they are in some circumstances really virtues, and their current disrepute is part of our problem.

Let me say at once that I consider docility to be a necessary element in the character of the healthy student. Docility is not merely a matter of obedience, although intelligent obedience is also necessary. It is a complex set of attitudes toward the world and the immediate context that is a condition of growth toward freedom. This has been expressed canonically

74

in the promise that only the docile shall inherit the earth, that unruliness is self-defeating.

Docility is destroyed by fear or anxiety. It is a kind of spiritual relaxedness, a looseness, which comes from faith, hope, love, trust, confidence—from the sense that something good is going on and that one wants to, and can, join in. To join in what is going on, to be led in, inducted, initiated; not to destroy by breaking in and breaking up. Anyone who has watched an instructor teach skiing or tennis or swimming will find this very familiar. "Relax, relax. Don't fight it, use it. Try it this way and you'll see. Don't be afraid to . . . don't worry about . . . don't tighten up." What the pupil learns, if he learns at all, is that the world does most of the work, and that his job is to learn how to cooperate with it and to accommodate himself to its requirements if he wishes it to support his purposes. This piety of the body is the germ or paradigm of the more complex piety of the mind or spirit. "Docility" is, perhaps, a nondenominational or secular term for "piety."

Not fear, then, but a positive set of attitudes. Affirmation and enjoyment of what is good; acceptance, with shameless gratitude, of gifts, of goods we have not created but that are there for us; appreciation of the continuity and fellowship of human achievement; respect for the craft and its masters; the faith and trust of apprenticeship. These are the facets of docility.

Without docility we learn, if we learn at all, the hard way. If we do not let the world teach us, it teaches us a lesson. So it is, in tragedy, that the indocile—Creon, Oedipus, Lear—learn only through bitter suffering. Socrates suggested a better way.

Student indocility is a serious problem, but it is a sickness not a crime, and it cannot be cured by a lecture. If we wish to blame someone let us, at least, not blame the victims, but look to the social institutions and their trustees who have nourished disillusion, rejection, and distrust, and who generate alienation in absurdity instead of membership in community. The immediate question is whether the college can cope with indocility and even cure it, or whether its own structure and operation make it worse. The short answer, I believe, is that the standard lower-division structure makes it worse, but that the pattern established by the Experimental Program, while it cannot cope with everyone and everything, is fundamentally helpful.

The student who enters the program does so by his own decision. It is very much a decision taken in the dark, since he has no experience either of the program or its alternatives. But it is his own decision about his education and, if he remains in the program, it is the last administrative decision about education he is called upon to make for several years. Whether he realizes it or not he has, through an accidental combination of circumstances, committed himself to something by an act of faith.

The student finds himself in a program that is overwhelming in its givenness. Its curriculum is set and completely required, and he is not consulted about it. When he is curious or anxious about its general structure, he is given a correct general answer and told, also correctly, that he won't really understand the answer until he has been through the program. We advise him to relax, to take things as they come, to try to enjoy the present, and that he will soon be catching the drift.

The structure of work, although it leaves much to the student, is also fixed and given and presents the student with a reasonable but inexorable schedule of writing, conference, discussion, and lecture. It is, for him, a novel pattern, and he is expected to adjust to it. It may take some time, but we do not waive the demands.

Early responses are, of course, quite varied, but we are now familiar with some significant symptoms and can even risk generalization. The "healthy" response seems to have two elements: first, the student is moved by what we are reading and is enjoying it, and second, he is discouraged by his inability to work as hard as he thinks he should be working and by the realization that his work, chiefly his writing, isn't very good. Both responses are encouraging signs. They reveal that he is accepting the task, not fighting it, and that he is open, perceptive, and even objective. We encourage the enjoyment, try to cheer him up about his performance, and settle down to constructive work.

The first symptom of trouble, on the other hand, is lack of enjoyment. It is not simply a matter of taste. If we are all reading and talking about Homer, for example, not to be enjoying it means that something is wrong. It may mean—and usually does—that the student is not reading or is not trying to read. Why not? At this point we begin to sense, in one form or another, the drive for autonomy, the existence or emergence of private plans, and even a strategy of self-defense. Why are we reading this instead of something else, why this kind of paper assignment, why so slow or so fast, can I do something else instead? General dissatisfaction with what is given. It should be stressed that this mood is more likely than not to be the accompaniment of not doing the work or at least not doing it very well, and also that the student may have a higher opinion of his written work than is warranted. That is, he is not happy with, engaged with, or enjoying the program, and he appears to be fairly satisfied with and defensive about the work he does. He is like a student who for some reason signs up for a tennis class, doesn't seem to enjoy the game, doesn't practice much, always thinks the teacher is doing the wrong thing, and is impervious to the teacher's criticism and judgment of his strokes.

This is the indocility problem, and it is not easy to deal with. We resist as long as possible the temptation to say simply, "If you don't like it here why don't you go somewhere else?" In any case, the answer is likely to be, "I don't like it there, either." The student is encased in armor that hinders his movement and growth, and our task is to free him if we can, and if he stands still long enough. But he is not always ready to get rid of his armor. It is home-made, fairly comfortable, and still useful for combat. His reasons for acquiring it are still operative, and he distrusts the invitation to take it off. The world that lies before him seems rotten and hostile, the establishment is powerful and corrupt, and the college is its tool. He cannot relax.

The stultifying self-protective capacity of the indocile student is formidable. We try to create an environment in which trust is reasonable, and we practice patience. But in some cases nothing seems to work, and the student never really gets involved, although this is not always marked by formal separation from the program. He may, as a rebel, move into the shrill culture of "activism" and learn its thin lessons. He may go completely, if temporarily, out of reach in the faubourgs of contemporary Bohemia and learn the lessons of its illusions. Or he may find less dramatic ways of getting lost. We regret the foolish choices we cannot prevent.

The program is a better school, but it can be fought, resisted, or rejected by those who do not understand, or who lack the power to fulfill, the commitment of enrollment. "Commitment" is worth lingering over. There is a moral dimension to the problem. The program is a voluntary undertaking and there are reciprocal obligations. There are "oughts" for the faculty and "oughts" for the student that go far beyond mere academic criminal law. What is required is a good-faith effort. And there can be failure at three levels: misconception or failure to understand what an undertaking is, or that this is one; bad faith; and failure of effort. The last is merely a matter of weakness. We expect it and attend to it. The others pose deeper problems of morality.

I do not intend to pursue here the discussion of student academic morality, although it is underdiscussed. The theme is freedom and the free mind. To be free, I have argued, is to be able to do what one should. Lack of understanding, ill-will, and bad habits (or incapacity to work)—this is the simple profile of the unfree man. Freed from external restraint only his incapacity postpones disaster. In the incubator of the program we cherish docility. It is not all of virtue, nor its final form, but it is the embryonic precursor of freedom.

I turn now to an explanation of how the process of involvement in the program supports the student's growth in power or freedom.

Interest

The first problem is that of liberating the student from thralldom to his so-called interests. He may arrive under the impression that he knows what he is interested in and also that he knows that he is not interested in certain things. He may believe that he does well only in doing what he is interested in and he is inclined to want, naturally, to pursue his interests further. The student who "doesn't know what he is interested in" tends to be worried about his condition, is discouraged about his apathy, and is anxious to get interested in something, to "find himself."

Perhaps the worst thing that can happen to the student at the start of college life is that his interest-condition should be allowed to determine the shape of his education. The student arrives at college a creature of circumstance struggling to take charge of himself—of this time and that place, of home, town, school, friends, games, trials, triumphs, and errors. Interested in law, or medicine, or science, or literature? Why? A parent, a relative, a local hero, a television program? Did a high school teacher praise his verse? Was math easy? Did he fall in love with his motorcycle or have an underprivileged friend? Did girls like him? Was he too fat to run? Did he work for his allowance? Was his mother nervous? We should help spring him, if we can, from the trap of accident.

An interest, unlike a headache, is not an item of immediate indubitable awareness; it is not revealed by a simple act of introspection. Interests come in layers, they change and develop, they even come disguised. Knowledge of ourselves is a difficult achievement, and the deeper pattern of our interests may escape our scrutiny.

At what point and to what degree a student's conception of what he is interested in should be allowed to shape and direct his education is a difficult question. But it is, I am sure, a disastrous mistake to let it dominate or seriously influence the lower-division years. It will, at that stage confine and limit him. The alternative, of course, is not to hurl our own discrete and varied interests at him, but rather to construct a required program that involves what he should be interested in. That is not as difficult or as ludicrous as it may sound. It is another way of saying that the curriculum should be about what is centrally important and that it should be deep and difficult. "Important" for the liberal arts lower division in America today means "moral," "social," "political"; it means freedom and authority, the individual and society, conscience and law, acceptance and rebellion. That is what the student ought to be interested in and that is what he will find that he is interested in, although it may surprise him. "Deep" means that the curriculum must push beyond the current cliche and surface of the problem to its fundamental terms. "Difficult" means that it should be intelligible but inexhaustible.

In such a program the "interest" question gradually subsides or is displaced by the discovery that enjoyment is more crucial and is more likely to evoke interest than to be produced by it. The student grows less temperamental about his work, less finicky, more confidently omnivorous. His latent self gets some nourishment. Involvement in the program, given and required as it is, helps in removing the "interest" barrier from the path of development.

Habit, Power, Self-Discipline

With rare exception the intellectual habits of the student who arrives at college are those of a defensive scrambler. His experience is primarily of crisis response to varied, fragmentary, unrelated demands. He has risen to these demands and crises or he wouldn't be where he is, but the experience has left its mark on him. He can marshal facades to meet tests. But his reading and writing habits show the effects. The crisis must be abated, and the habits it generates must be displaced by others. Examination is a disciplinary device, but it is not the only one and is not in the long run a good one.

Unfortunately, the usual course pattern in the lower division continues the crisis pattern of the high school and even increases its pressure. Successful adjustment by the student only confirms him in bad habits. He may learn quite a lot, but he does not significantly gain in effective mastery of his intellectual energies. The senior, all too often, is simply a tired freshman who has been through the mill.

The Experimental Program breaks away from the usual pattern and provides a different environment for a sufficiently long time—two years—so that the student can gain, or regain, some effective autonomy on the basis of reasonable habit. We try, as far as possible, to avoid crisis, haste, and pressure. We have eliminated all examinations and tests; assignments are quantitatively light; grades are effectively out of the picture. The stage is set for a long, unharried pull.

The program is a set of clear and unavoidable demands presented at a steady pace—a regular schedule of reading, of discussion, of writing, which must be done on time. Constant timeliness, however, is our aim, not the mere meeting of deadline, although the deadline has its place. We really have no make-up devices. Our interdependence in a common program requires that we discipline ourselves to the common pace, that we keep current.

Old habits persist, however, and some students will inevitably recreate for themselves the crisis conditions to which they are accustomed. Postponed reading, consequently unprepared discussion; hasty, last-minute, gimmicky and superficial papers. Indolent distraction followed by unproductive frenzy. Since there are no grades to encourage self-deception, the student will usually recognize the unproductiveness of the pattern and will be troubled by it. As he tries to break out—if he tries—he is likely to discover how little he is master of himself. It is a lesson in the difficulty of freedom. He wants to; he resolves to; he tries to; but nothing happens. He cannot sit down or sit still; he cannot resist an invitation; a change in the weather and he is undone. Master of his fate and captain of his soul! A routine that makes the old habits pointless and that encourages and supports new and better ones is what the student needs. The external discipline makes sense only when it promotes self-discipline. It is a bridge between the old and the new—a necessary bridge.

The program has such a routine, but it is not foolproof. A student who lets it take over finds himself gradually working with more effectiveness and self-reliance and with a greater sense of power and freedom. We are not policemen, however, and a student who wants to play more familiar games can do so for a while until he either decides to try, or to leave, or until we decide he should be dropped. Resistance is utterly pointless and profitless, but it occurs anyway.

Individuality

All this talk of docility and discipline might suggest to the unwary that the program is a sort of boot camp designed to stamp out such vestiges of individuality as have survived the flattening effects of mass culture. This is not how it looks from the inside.

We cherish individuality and strengthen it. The common program, and the community of students and teachers it makes possible, is precisely the context in which individuality is revealed, encouraged, and developed. We are not a series of transient and sporadic classrooms. We are a working group of students and faculty who are closely related for a long time. We know each other. Our freshmen receive more faculty attention, on an individual basis, than do virtually all but the most fortunate graduate students. It is not a situation that demands or promotes uniformity.

The common program of reading, discussion, and writing serves as the background that heightens awareness of individual difference. It is only when we read and discuss the same thing, tackle the same task, that we discover how individual and different we are.

It is the same old story and one wearies of telling it. Polar notions involve each other; they do not destroy each other. "Change" is not a denial of "permanence"; "only the permanent changes." Sameness and difference, unity and multiplicity, public and private, individual and social—variations on the same theme. A collection of solipsistic eccentrics is not a collection of individuals. If you want individuals and individuality, create a community. Our students are unmistakably individuals.

We do, occasionally, get the echoes of a current generational slogan: "Don't let them get at your mind" (a polite version), and it has an ironic ring in an educational institution. But it is quite understandable. It is held that we are a sick society, that our good human nature has been corrupted and warped by bad social institutions and ideologies guarded by the established powers and propagated by the mass media and the servile school system; that most people, especially adults, have been tricked into taking absurd games seriously and behave with systematic insanity, moving through their destructive and joyless paces like zombies. A student who holds a version of this widespread and interesting view of things is also likely to think that he has, through accident, some "outside" help perhaps, and his own efforts, escaped or thrown over control. "They" (we) want to recapture him and will, if he does not guard it, invade his mind.

So he guards his mind and his hard-won and precarious individuality. Beleaguered and suspicious, he won't play. Sometimes he really won't, and there is nothing we can do except stand by patiently while he wanders through the faddish anti-establishment world looking for a home, starving the individuality he is trying to protect.

There are some games we refuse to play. "Solitaire" is one; "participatory democracy" is another. Each, in its own way, destroys the learning community that is the essence of the Experimental Program.

Relevance

What makes everything go, of course, is the curriculum, the ideas with which the program is involved. It dominates everything, and sustains us when we falter. I will discuss the curriculum more fully later, but here I wish to consider some general features of its relation to the life of the student.

The demand for "relevance" is hurled at the university in so many foolish ways that a self-respecting scholar may be tempted to dismiss it as an expression of self-centered impertinence, as misguided narrow-mindedness and short-sightedness. It is sometimes just that.

Many things are studied in the university that are not relevant to the war in Vietnam or the war in the ghetto or the war on poverty. The university is the kind of institution in which that sort of thing goes on and should go on. Whether the justification is that knowledge is an end in itself or that the strangest things turn out to be useful, we will, I am sure, resist any attempt to make immediate relevance to today's crises the test of whether something should be studied or taught, whether the attempt comes from economy-minded legislators or from crusading students.

More immediately annoying is the student who finds that the course he has enrolled in is "not relevant to him" and who seems to think that it should be made so at once. The professor is likely to think that the student should accommodate himself to the demands of the subject—not the other way around. "Irrelevant" sounds, sometimes, like "I'm bored," and only politeness keeps the professor from making the obvious replies.

But these unfortunate misuses only tend to discredit a concept whose legitimacy, at the lower-division level, must be recognized and honored. The graduate student who chooses to work for a degree in a particular field should expect to be required to show signs of becoming relevant to it. He, not the field, is on trial. To a lesser degree this holds also for the student pursuing the upper-division "major" of his choice. But the lower-division situation is quite different, and the problem of relevance cannot be put aside.

We should consider what a freshman is. He is a person who has arrived at a crucial stage and is confronted with an array of incredibly difficult decisions that may set the pattern of his entire life. He has acquired or developed a set of ideas about the way the world is and about himself. These are of vital importance to him and to us, and they must be taken seriously.

I have already suggested that the entering student is, to a considerable degree, a creature of circumstance, and his ideas reflect the circumstance of intellectual and moral fashion. I have, elsewhere, given a caricature of the freshman philosophy of life and treated it as a bill presented to us as the belated price for the sins of the fathers. They are eating the grapes, and our teeth are set on edge.

They arrive with ideas, swinging between dogmatism and despairing uncertainty. We can systematically ignore the ideas or, if we know what we are doing, we can, in a special way, build the curriculum on them. That is what we must do, and that, in its proper sense, is what the demand for relevance is about.

To do this is not to pander to superficial interests but to respond appropriately to real needs. And we must do it our way, a way appropriate for a college, digging below the shrill level of fad and fashion to the bed-rock resources of our culture. If we try to do this, we discover that the great problems of today are, for the most part, the perennial problems in modern dress; and we discover also that the resources of the culture are far from depleted, archaic, or irrelevant. They are real resources, and if we use them properly we subject our own ideas to the kind of ordeal that constitutes education.

When I say that such a curriculum responds to real needs, I do not refer to the student's alone. They are the needs of the society as well. To the student, the question is, "What should I do with my life?" Before society answers, "Do this," or "Do that," or "Above all do as you're told" it had better take the occasion to ask aloud, "What are we up to?"

The lower division is the ground upon which these two questions meet and interact. Other things may intrude, but they are irrelevant. Scholars who are unwilling or unable to address themselves to these questions should, at least, stay out of the lower division. They are usurpers there, and if they have their way they displace the real curriculum and exile the big questions to the television talk show and the street-corner microphone.

One of the implications of this curricular conception is that the dominant perspective of the lower division is moral rather than scientific, normative rather than descriptive. The student is seen as an agent or a potential agent, and the organization of knowledge is shaped by relevance to action. "What should we do?" is the typical question in this perspective. It is a stage at which knowledge is instrumental to purpose. I have discussed elsewhere (*Obligation and the Body Politic*, Oxford Press 1960) the contrast between the normative-practical and the descriptive-predictive perspectives and the relevance of that distinction to the education of the political agent, the ruler, the citizen of a democratic polity—to "liberal education"—and I shall not retrace that argument here. It accounts, however, for the displacement of science, social as well as natural, from a central role in the lower-division curriculum. "What is to be done" takes precedence over "What is the case." This is a point of considerable controversy, and the argument is an easy one to lose in the university where the priorities seem quite different, and where the pursuit of knowledge, scientific or scholarly, organizes itself in its own terms and claims autonomy. It accounts, also, for the anomalous status of the lower division in the university structure. For it does not really share the primarily cognitive bent of the upper and graduate divisions. It is captive to them, however, and in its institutional weakness it suffers from the inroads and demands of the heedless and hard headed.

The moral perspective is, of course, the perspective of induction or initiation. It enters the quandary of the young student faced with the decisions of adjustment to, rejection of, or participation in the life of the society. It is the perspective that entertains his problems; it is also the perspective in which society solicits his full membership, explains its commitments, and invites his participation in its troubled but rewarding life.

It is a scene of wonderful confusion and misunderstanding, of mistaken and challenged identities. We think we are offering a generous invitation; he has heard of Greeks bearing gifts and looks the horse in the mouth. We take him to the mountain top and offer him power to turn deserts into gardens or offer wisdom in human affairs; we think he may have a divine nature; he thinks he hears a forked tongue and sees a cloven hoof—that we mean to turn gardens into deserts and take power over human beings. The commitment of membership in community is mistaken for bondage; slavery to desire and whim is mistaken for freedom.

We need to straighten it all out if we can. It is, no doubt, deplorable that the problem should arise. Where is the family? Where is the church? What has happened in the nursery school? What has become of the Boy Scouts? Alas! It is up to the college.

III. THE CURRICULUM

Within the course system the problems of the curriculum are quite familiar—what collection of courses, what subjects, what order, what degree of concentration and diffusion, what required, what elective. The substitution of the program for the course does not eliminate all these considerations, but it drastically alters the context and form in which they appear. It brings the problem back to the teacher, to the teaching staff, as an integral part of his teaching activity. When the teacher gives a course he is responsible for its internal organization, but he can largely ignore the problem of intercourse or foreign relations. He may consider those problems as a member of his department or college, but he does not need to, except as they affect his own course. In the program the problems are internal and inescapable and go far beyond what is involved in the planning of a traditional course or course sequence.

The curriculum of the Experimental Program is, I believe, a meaningful and powerful one. It is a joy to the initiated and a stumbling block to the unsaved. Its principle of organization is difficult to express with clarity in familiar terms and appears subject to a host of academic questions and objections; and it seems, in addition to and also because of its organization, to pose insuperable teaching difficulties. I wish to explain its principles more clearly, and to explain away the difficulties if I can.

The principle that underlies everything and which creates most of the trouble is that the normal categories in which the university organizes knowledge and administers its pursuit are irrelevant to our purposes—to the purposes of first-program education—and should be ignored. We do not think in terms of "humanities" or "social science"; we do not even think in terms of "history" or "literature" or "political science" or "philosophy." It is not that we want to replace these categories with others. We do not quarrel with them; we simply do not use them, and, if they prescribe limits, we do not observe them. We read Homer, Thucydides, and Plato; but we do not say or think, "Now we are on literature," "Now we turn to history," "At last we come to philosophy."

These categories are quite legitimately the organizing categories of the university, of its schools, divisions, departments, and the faculty thinks of knowledge quite naturally in these terms. This makes communication somewhat baffling, and when we shrug off the politely proffered "interdisciplinary?" "integrated?" and mutter "No! Subdisciplinary," "A-disciplinary," incomprehension dawns. This is a university. Where does that fit in? The first difficulty, then, is that we do not use the normal categories.

A second and related difficulty is that we do not accept as a governing mission direct introduction to or preparation for the academic fields or disciplines that dominate the upper-division and graduate programs. The first program comes before the second program, and our students, we know, will continue into the upper division and should be able to handle it. But there is an important sense in which we are not "introductory." Not in disciplinary terms.

This separates us from a whole tradition of lower-division curricular devices—the elements of X, an introduction to Y, sampler survey of Z. And also from an interdisciplinary introduction to XY or an integrated introduction to division H. Who else is there? Nothing, really, if we accept the conception of the lower division as essentially introductory, finding its *raison d'être* in the major and the graduate school. But we think the lower division has its own integrity, and we resist the facile demand for "continuity" that only serves to facilitate and perpetuate the domination of the college by the graduate school. Not disciplinary, not introductory, unless it abdicates its real function and allows itself to become the neglected captive of the professionals.

I suppose this rejection of the academic discipline needs more explanation. A discipline is a way of studying something. What it studies is a particular aspect of a complex situation. The choice of aspect is definitive of the field, and the tools of the discipline are the techniques, skills, and practices appropriate for dealing with that aspect of things.

A man pauses in a public square to listen to someone speak. This is a crude macroscopic description of a fragment of what is going on at a moment of time in a particular place. A body is in motion, it has a chemical composition, glands are secreting, digestion, respiration, blood-pressure rises, languages, emotion, a political allegiance at stake, a moral crisis, an official mistake, lives take a different course, institutions tremble, a dozen histories take a sharp turn. How many aspects of this fragment of event can we describe or study? Physics, chemistry, biology, psychology, sociology, history, rhetoric, linguistics, political science, logic, ethics. Grist for all our mills.

Each discipline abstracts what concerns it and places it in its own context of classification, law, and explanation. Each has its own story to tell. There are many stories and most of them are probably true. An academic discipline is a sustained attempt to tell a particular kind of story—about poems or organizations, about very small things, very large things, short-lived or enduring, about warring, sheltering, growing, healing, trading, about people, animals, societies, rocks.

The ways we study and know the world reflect the structure of the university. The ways are varied, intensive, skillful, and, of course, specialized. No one has invented a better way, although we all have our particular complaints.

I do not quarrel with the conception that the upper-division experience for the student should be primarily that of catching a glimpse of the way things look from the perspective of one of the academic disciplines. Not only for what it shows him about the world but for what he learns about how seeing really goes on and about the significance of "seeing" for "doing." Nor, of course, do I quarrel generally with what the graduate school is up to. But what has all this got to do with the lower division?

The freshman is there to learn but not yet to learn to be a professional scholar. Some may become professionals, but that is only accidental. We can even encourage the choice later by those who show special fitness. But that is no more the aim of the lower division than it is the aim of hospitals to turn its patients into doctors. Putting it crudely, freshman courses—if we must have them—in literature, history, or philosophy should be conducted on the assumption that the student is going to be a dentist, stockbroker, or a civil servant, rather than a professor of literature, history, or philosophy.

What the freshman is going to become vocationally is really beside the point. He is already something that he will continue to be—a member of a society, a social individual, a center of values and awareness, a person required to act on our common stage. He needs to get his bearings there so that, if he doesn't wander off, he can understand the part he is to play.

So we come again to the perspective of the agent and its problems as shaping the lower-division curriculum, not the perspective of the academic discipline and its problems. That is why the first program is neither disciplinary nor introductory.

There are two aspects of the first-program curriculum which need consideration. First, the problem of shaping, forming, or constructing a particular curriculum without the familiar disciplinary guidelines; second, the problem of competence to teach such a curriculum when the teacher himself is where he is because of his own training and expertise in a discipline.

If our general thesis is accepted, the purpose of the first program is to lead the student into a broad and sustained examination of the "moral" dimensions of the situation in which he and we find ourselves. The curriculum is a concrete plan for doing that. Let me present some preliminary assumptions underlying the Experimental Program's curriculum or, perhaps, its search for a curriculum.

First, it must be related to the deep controversial issues of our time . This is not to say that it is about current events or that we even necessarily deal with the problems in the language and temper of current controversy. This particular war is concrete and unique. But it is also an exemplification or instance of war, and the problems it poses are not unique. Conscience confronts law in a particular circumstance today, but the terms of that confrontation are ancient and familiar. To understand our situation requires not only that we be acquainted with it in its concrete particularity but that we see it also as an instance of a kind of situation. We must study our problems; but not always or necessarily in current terms.

Second, the program is primarily reflective rather than experiential. Our concern is with gaining understanding rather than with gaining experience. It is temptingly easy to misunderstand this point. We recognize the complex interdependence of understanding and experience, the need to have real examples to think about, the need to attach understanding to what we are living through. But it is a matter of emphasis and timing. The student comes to us already overwhelmed by experience he is struggling to understand. He is soon involved in the exciting and broadening life of the modern university community. He will graduate to half a century of active life in the world of events and actions. We believe that his time in the program is best spent in the program, not in the world. Our curriculum is, without apology, bookish, not activist.

It is difficult to discuss the "construction" of a curriculum. There is no recipe for putting one together. I think the reason is that "construct" and "put together" convey the wrong impression. A curriculum is a work of art. It is based on an inspiration, and its history is the working out of that inspiration in appropriate forms. As with other works of art, a curriculum can be subjected to the process of analysis and criticism; we can discern its structure and come, perhaps, to understand the basis of its power; we can learn to develop effective variations and modifications. But the process of analysis and dissection, of appreciation and justification, is not to be confused with the process of creation. Making up a game, and describing and appreciating it, are two quite different things.

We are not swamped with first-program curricular inspirations. The standard lower division is a distinctly uninspired habit, and apart from it there are few candidates. St. John's rests on an inspiration. There is a cluster of institutions living on the student-interest-centered unstructured "happening" inspiration. Perhaps something more, but the field is thin. The Experimental Program lives on the inspiration of Alexander Meiklejohn's Athens-America curriculum, established for a brief time at Wisconsin in the 1920s. We have our own variation—we are captivated, not enslaved—but the Meiklejohn conception was there from the very beginning. Without it, in fact, the Experimental Program would not have been created.

I am now convinced that a dominating idea must come first. Without it nothing happens. This has some implications for first-program curricular planning and educational reform. It means, I think, that we should expect nothing, or very little, from academic committees, commissions, or task forces, in the way of real innovation or reform. They are, at best, midwives; they may encourage fertility and even help with delivery, but they neither conceive nor bear. Nor can we simply bring together a small group of faculty members and ask them to work out and teach a first program. Unless they are already all dominated by a common conception the faculty will either fall apart or will work out a compromise or *modus vivendi*. They may put something together, but it will not have much life.

The first-program curriculum, in short, cannot be simply put together. It must grow out of a simple idea and be developed by a group committed to the idea. The heart of the program "constitution," of which I spoke earlier, is the commitment of the faculty to its governing inspiration.

But if there are not very many distinctive first-program curricular ideas around, we do not, on the other hand, need very many, and there is no need to be discouraged by the relative infrequency of radical curricular inspiration. A few basic conceptions given institutional form can serve as models to be adopted, imitated, or modified. Creation is difficult; intelligent imitation and modification will serve the ends of education.

What is required, therefore, is not a handbook on how to invent programs, but an analysis of a program in being. We think that our curriculum is successful, that it is not dependent upon any of the peculiarities of our university (in fact the distinctive character of the university at Berkeley creates only added difficulties and obstacles), and that it is easily adaptable and adoptable.

The starting point was Meiklejohn's Athens-American conception—a two-year integrated program focusing, the first year, on the Greeks, the second year, on America. We did not try it quite in that form. A whole year on Greece seemed a little too much, and seventeenth-century England—the Puritan revolution—had some special attraction, so we divided the first year between Greece and England. For the second year, we planned to begin with the period of the constitutional convention in America and end with the contemporary scene.

The program as it was presented for approval thus seemed to have four segments. Each segment was full of crisis and turmoil, and we succumbed to the temptation to describe the program as a study of culture in crisis—four different crises, four different periods, apparently a peculiar "historical" approach. We bore with cheerful indifference the criticisms that since we settled on crises we were "teaching revolution" and that for a "historical" program we had some strange gaps.

Our preliminary description was far from satisfactory, and by degrees we shifted emphasis from periods to problems or issues or themes. But if we said "war and peace" or "freedom and authority" we had not yet accounted for our doing it in this way. It is not a bad formulation and perhaps it will do as well as any as long we are restrained by modesty or by fear of uproarious and inextinguishable laughter from stating what is closer to the real case—that we have hit upon, in manageable form and extent, a rich version of the basic moral curriculum of our culture.

The Greeks constitute for us a great exemplary episode. Its dramatic center is the Peloponnesian War seen through the eyes of Thucydides. But everything we read illuminates that tragedy. Homer is in the background, Aeschylus, Sophocles, Euripides are brooding commentators, Plato reaps its lesson. It is an unparalleled chorus for the basic human plot. We echo it in everything we do. It is the great introduction to ourselves.

We do not really care about the seventeenth century after all, exciting and crucial as it is. It happens to be where we pick up the other great cultural strand of our lives. It gives us the King James Bible, Shakespeare, Hobbes, and Milton—the Judeo-Christian tradition in a strain especially constitutive of the American tradition and character.

As for America, we take the covenant, the Constitution, the law, and the court, the living complex institution, as the thread that guides us in the attempt to understand what we are up to. We have followed this thread haltingly but we will persist with growing confidence. We are the people of the law if we are anything.

This is the structure of our curriculum—an episode, a strand, an institution. It is deep and varied, fundamental, relevant, and even cumulative.

It is possible, I suppose, to substitute another episode for the Greek one. I doubt if anyone who knows it will be tempted to do so. It is possible to pick up the Judeo-Christian tradition in another way, but the cost in loss of fringe benefits would be high. It is possible to reject law as the center of the American year, but also at a sacrifice. Tinkering is allowed, and we may even do some ourselves. But it is great as it stands; and within it, as it stands, there is a good deal of flexibility.

To the charge that this is all Western provincial and that a citizen of the modern world needs to know a "foreign" culture, we have a standard two-part answer. Our real culture is a foreign culture to most of us; and, you cannot understand a foreign culture if you do not understand your own.

To the charge that it leaves out too much of importance even in our own cultural tradition, the reply must be that, of course, it leaves out much. There is no alternative. We cannot include everything. If we try we end up scurrying frantically and hopelessly through masses of material, without enjoyment and without understanding. We must select carefully and be ruthless in rejecting great things.

I turn now from the problem of the construction of the curriculum to the questions of its teachability. However attractive a curriculum might appear, if it cannot be "taught" or if professors cannot be found to teach it, or are unqualified to meet its challenge, it isn't of much use. Let me first marshal the standard objections:

> The program violates the first principle of university teaching: an expert should teach what he is expert in. The good faculty member of a good university is a man who has taken a particular branch of knowledge as his province, who has become a specialist capable of contributing to the advancement of knowledge. He knows more than anyone else around about his part of his field. When he teaches he should teach what he knows, communicate his special insights. Thus, his teaching goes hand in hand with his other work and is not entirely a distraction. At the same time, the

student can be assured that he is getting his information or his particular training from a certified source. Teaching by experts; learning from experts. That is the rock upon which university teaching and learning rests.

But the curriculum of the program neglects the use of our assets, it ignores expertise. It ranges from epic through tragedy and history and philosophy, from ancient to modern, from the poet to the judge. The same staff teaches everything and most of the time the teacher is out of his field. Even if he is willing, he will need to prepare himself, and that means a decision to put aside "his own work" as a scholar. It is a full-time involvement, so he drops out of the race for several years. Scholarship suffers, his career suffers, and the student gets some amateur teaching. It makes no sense.

Of course, there may be some people around who would like to teach in such a program. Scholars who have tired of scholarship or become bored with their fields and want to "teach." They are usually gambles the university has lost. They might be happy as "generalists" teaching in the lower division. But the true scholar belongs in his classroom or seminar teaching what he really knows. And even if he would want to, he cannot really know what the program curriculum requires him to know well enough to teach it. And anyway, a proper selection of courses will give the student everything he could get in the program—and expertly taught.

This is the standard barrage. It sounds formidable, and it is. "Barrage" is perhaps the wrong word. It is the siren song and who, in the university, does not hear it without longing? Knowledge, certainty, security, an unchallengeable status, a tight little island, a chosen few, a mine of one's own, digging, finding, eureka! I confess I hear it too and am sorely tempted. . . . Well, warm the wax to stop the ears, get tied to the mast, issue strict orders; row on.

The question of expertise is intrinsically related both to the kind of materials or books that make up the curriculum and to the kind of use we make of them. A discussion of these matters will, I think, put the problem of expertness in a different light.

We read great books, classics, masterpieces, and very little else. If we deny that we are a "Great Books Program" it is because we do not use the selective and organizing principles, and perhaps do not share the educational and metaphysical assumptions that have come to be associated with the Great Books Program. But we prefer great books to lesser books.

This is not simply an innocent preference for high quality. The classic (as I shall loosely call it) that we read has some important features beyond the fact that it is a great achievement of mind and art. Quite simply, a classic escapes from or transcends its generative context. It retains its intelligibility and significance when it is taken out of context. It is self-contained, a world of its own. Like a pearl, it can gain from its setting, but its best setting is not its oyster, and it really cannot even be said to belong there.

I am not saying that a classic is not evoked by the situation, that it does not use the materials at hand, that it is not, in its time, timely. But its response to what evokes it is a response at a level deeper than the current surface of things. If it stays on the surface it is gone with the surface and to read it later requires that we reconstruct what is gone. But if it is deeper, it takes us, when we read it, below our own surface to the common bedrock level. The historical context may explain some things about it, but the classic is fundamentally intelligible and significant without it. It is not a period piece.

You do not have to know anything about Greece or about Plato in order to read and understand and enjoy the *Republic*. It does not need background. You can read and enjoy King Lear without knowing anything about Shakespeare or his England. A reading of the work may produce an interest in its genesis, and what we discover if we pursue that interest may contribute to our understanding. It may also distract us, and if we shift our attention to the context we may well impair our experience and appreciation of the work itself. If we must commit the genetic fallacy at least let us not commit it prematurely.

This is a controversial point, but I shall not push it. I have said enough to indicate that the program's use of the classic is not "historical." We are more concerned with the truth or validity of an idea than with its history. Whether Plato is right in what he says about show business is more important than why he happened to say it, more important to us, at this stage of the game.

But besides being detachable from its historical context, the classic is not dependent upon the various disciplinary contexts in which the university is prone to place it. Plato's *Republic*, let us say, belongs to the philosophy department, and there it takes its place in the field of philosophy, preceded by the pre-Socratics, followed by Aristotle, related this way to Hegel, that way to Plotinus, the fountainhead of this movement, the whipping boy of that. For "philosophy" the *Republic* may shrink to the "divided line" and "the form of the good" with much of the rest passed over as of no special philosophical interest. What is left over, other departments can have. Or consider the *Iliad*. It is in Greek so it belongs to the Greek department. It is an epic so it probably belongs also to comparative literature or to whoever takes all epics as his province. To study it is to take it in that context, subject to the categories of that discipline. Every professor belongs to a department, every department has its field, and everything we read "belongs" in one or more fields. For us to "teach" a book is to seem to invade a field without a license, to commit academic trespass.

But the classic escapes simple "belonging" in a disciplinary context. It can be put there, but it need not be. Its author was not a member of the union or discipline that studies his work. He did not write his book for professors, however confidently they appropriate it. I do not really quarrel with the appropriation for purposes of disciplinary scholarship and study. No doubt it must be done. I quarrel with the arrogance of the appropriator who thinks that because he is interested in tusks the elephant belongs entirely to him. I doubt if the tusk collector appreciates elephants the way we do.

A glance at our reading list will quickly reveal that whatever we read is independent of both the historical and the disciplinary context. It can be confronted directly. It is readable, "nontechnical," and without gratuitous complexity. It does not require the mediation of the historian or the disciplinary expert.

Of course we do not read a series of discrete and unrelated classics. We develop a sustaining context of our own. We begin cold, with the Iliad, but everything after that is read in a steadily thickening context of insights, questions, ideas. One of the delights of the program is the growing sense of relation and interconnection as we progress. Each book seems to strike a note that reveals a new pattern or develops a familiar one. What we once read is always with us, and everything seems to get related to everything else. The unity of the program is the real context of each work, as the melody is the context of the note.

The point of this discussion of the relation of what we read in the program to the historical and disciplinary contexts is that the usual forms of university expertise are irrelevant to teaching in the program. It does not require expertness in the particular books we study. It requires of the teacher intelligence, the ability to read, and some understanding of the teaching process.

There is really no mystery about it. Let me illustrate what is involved.

We come to Hobbes's *Leviathan*. We have already read the Greeks, including Thucydides' *History* (which Hobbes admired and translated into

English). Leviathan appeared in 1651. Hobbes was a refugee from revolution and civil war. He is responding to the turmoil and destruction England was experiencing. There is no doubt about that. But he analyzes, diagnoses, and prescribes in general terms. What shall we make of *Leviathan*? Do we need to know about the civil war? About James and Charles? About Parliament and Pym and Wentworth and Cromwell? It is interesting, and it does no harm if we know something. But it does not help very much, and it is, above all, not necessary. The general statements Hobbes makes about the causes of conflict and about what is necessary for peace constitute a coherent argument. If we want to "apply" it to a concrete situation, to test it against examples, we do not need to use his situation or his examples. We do not need to try to acquire information about the seventeenth century—although we can if we wish and someday we may wish to in order to test Hobbes's theses. We can place his theory in the context of our day, our conflicts, our attempts at remedies. This will not only test his theory more effectively than it would be tested by our feeble, second-hand knowledge of the seventeenth century, it will also help us understand our own situation better—whether we agree with Hobbes or not. We can, in short, free the *Leviathan* from its seventeenth-century context and dip it into ours. Its relevance is then inescapable.

Again, *Leviathan* is the third attempt Hobbes made to write on this subject. For a student of Hobbes the successive shifts in formulation are exciting and illuminating. Should we not read *De Cive* as well? Trace the development? Look at his other works? The answer, I am sure, is "no!" We are not that interested in Hobbes. (Some of us are, it so happens, "professional" students of Hobbes, and we are interested; but the program is not, and we need to restrain our private passion.) *Leviathan* is more than enough for us, and it stands on its own feet. We do not need to read something else first.

And again, Hobbes is a figure in the history of political theory. Do we need to know how he fits into that story? How he is related to Locke and Rousseau, to Bodin and Grotius, to Aristotle and St. Thomas? No, we do not; not now.

There is really no escape. We must simply read *Leviathan*. Why the struggle? It is better than anything written about it. It is clear, powerful, imaginative, beautifully written. To read it, as Hobbes would say, is to "read oneself." Are we like that? Is that what we must do? Can't we get out of it?

The book itself, the context of the program, the context of our own day—that is what is essential. What does he say? Is he right? These are the questions.

Let us consider another example, a different kind of book, the *Iliad*. What are we to do with it? As usual, there are a number of fascinating things we do not do. The poetry? Not really, in translation, although we are grateful to Lattimore. The Homeric question? She remains a mystery to us. The structure of the epic? The oral question—can a Yugoslavian bard really do it? Was there a Troy where someone said he found it? Was Odysseus a bear, or a Jew? When did it happen? Who monkeyed with the catalogue of ships? What can we infer from the description of the cap worn on the raid and the judgment scene on the shield of Achilles, the lump of iron given for a prize, the human slaughter on the pyre? We do not pursue such questions. We are not that lucky.

We try to read the *Iliad*. What do we find? First, a human city: walls, shrines, homes, fathers, mothers, children, husbands, wives, an inner order, a way of life. Opposed to it a line of beached ships: an expedition, men on a mission, leaders, followers, comrades, rivals, mixed motives in a common cause. Between the city and the ships, a field of war, a scene of courage, fear, strength, weakness, weariness, endurance, and poignant, brutal death.

Why are they there? For Helen? To recapture and hold elusive beauty? To restore one shattered home by destroying another? To honor treaties? To satisfy ambition, to win glory and loot? Why does Troy fight? Must it defend its errant son? Does it harbor injustice? Is it the innocent victim of aggression?

They are caught up in war. They are tired of it. They want to stop, but cannot. So the destruction goes on, and in its course we see it touch almost every possible human relation, evoke every emotion, test every character. In camp, city, and field we see humanity at war, helplessly destroying and weeping. Homer may nod, but he misses very little.

We live with the *Iliad* for a few weeks. The strangeness wears off. A terrible question creeps up on us. Has anything changed? Are we still on the plain before Troy? That is how we begin.

What discipline? What expertise? The only problem is to learn how to read, to let Homer in. That is difficult enough. Not reading words, but reading a mind. The fact is that reading is, today, a highly undeveloped art. There is a good deal of justified complaint about student writing, but student reading is probably worse, and the deficiency is more serious. It is almost enough if the faculty can teach students how to read.

This discussion of the classic nature of our curricular material and of the way we read it is an oblique response to the charge that the program violates the university principle: "experts teach what they are expert in." The charge is only partially admitted. The program does not follow that rule in its ordinary sense. But we do not violate that principle in the sense of using nonexperts to do what experts should be doing. Ordinary university disciplinary expertise is simply not called for. It is not relevant to what we should be doing The program is not a place where experts can teach what they are expert in.

The question, then, is not whether the university should tolerate a program that violates its formal teaching principle, but whether it should tolerate and even support a program to which the principle does not apply. Or, to put it another way, the question is whether the lower division belongs in the university at all.

If my general argument is sound, there is real curricular discontinuity between the first program and the other two programs. The discontinuity is great enough to enable us to face the question of administrative and even physical separation with equanimity. The association is a peculiar one. The first program, the lower division, does not need the university and is not intellectually dependent on it—although it is subservient. The university gets all the benefits. If it lets it do its job it gets better educated students. And when it does not let it do its real work it uses it as a recruiting ground and preparatory school for its own professional concerns. It is grudging, predatory, and ungrateful. The lower division would be better off on its own. But the university community would be poorer without it. In spite of everything the lower division is the only civilizing influence it has left. Without it the university is only a glorified trade school.

But the concrete problem, as long as the first program retains its position as part of the university, is that of getting the university faculty to undertake the teaching of the first-program curriculum. My only concrete suggestion is the combination of a permanent core staff and greater attention to the professors' first-program readiness. This may not be enough. But the curriculum, at any rate, is teachable.

The program, its curriculum, is suitable for anyone and everyone faced with the necessity of living his life in today's world. It will, of course, not be available to everyone, and we enjoy the principle of toleration that allows us to exist as one of the many options that should be available to entering students. Since it is unlikely that we will be able, immediately, to solve the staffing problem in a way that would support more than very limited expansion, I will not push the argument that every freshman should enter, or be required to enter, a program like ours. The practical limitations make it unnecessary to grapple with some bad arguments.

The program would be good for everyone and probably especially good for those who are least likely to choose it. If the lower division is terminal for many students they would be infinitely better off in the program than if they wander through the standard collection of introductory courses, and many of them might discover that they are not terminal after all. Students "who know what they want to be," and who are required to devote their lower-division years largely to technical preparation for the major deserve sympathy. They cannot fit the program in, although they need it. Some of the sciences are the worst offenders in this respect, but it is unlikely that they will do anything about it. They are too strong to move, and they are full of reasons why it is necessary for the entering freshman who wants to be an X to immediately take this and that and the other. They are sorry about it and wish someone would whip up a nice compact liberal education that their students could swallow in their spare time. They are, I think, in more of a hurry than they need to be; but they probably think not.

The curriculum, incidently, is not only good for students. It is an educational experience for the faculty, and if we all took a hand in teaching it we might rediscover what "academic community" means.

To sum up, the first-program curriculum is easier to teach than to construct. It is not the introductory stage of training in the academic disciplines; its orientation and perspective is "moral." The material is "classic," and its proper use does not involve the ordinary academic expertise. It is, in principle, good for everybody. It is about, and it cultivates, freedom. It should probably be required for everyone, but we are neither institutionally nor intellectually ready for that.

CONCLUSION

A sustained attempt to improve the quality of education reveals, as perhaps nothing else does, how deeply we, as a society, are imbued with the ideas and attitudes of competitive individualism. We do not really think of man as a political animal or even understand what that means. We think of him as essentially a private person created, by God or by himself, complete with mind, self, goals, rights—autonomous and naturally sovereign over himself. All relations are foreign relations, entered into for private reasons, justified in private terms. Even when these ideas get shaken the attitudes persist, and we prefer patching up the worn spots with a sentimentality in which we do not really believe to giving up the old familiar ideas. We are attached to the weapons with which we have fought and won some earlier battles. Even our misconceptions, we think, have served us well, and it seems safer to cling to them than to risk "philosophy."

So we remain individualists. Children of the polis, we deny our generative source and then enjoy our crisis of identity. We search for ourselves in all the wrong places.

We are, characteristically, uneasy and ambivalent about the exercise of the teaching power. On the one hand, we have created a system of public education on an unprecedented scale; on the other hand, we are extremely reluctant to face the implications of this massive "governmental" involvement in the shaping of individual mind and character. We believe, apparently, that if we don't think about what we are doing we are safe; to even describe what we do seems "totalitarian." Government (the school?) is to leave the mind of the individual alone, although, of course, it should eradicate racism and all that sort of thing. Salvation is another empire to be acquired in a fit of absent-mindedness.

The relation of society and government to the mind of the citizen is the most crucial and neglected of problems. This is not the place to pursue the subject, but we can stand a passing reminder about democracy and freedom.

Democracy is not anarchy; it is an organized and complex way of life, and it requires the cultivation of its appropriate state of mind. That state of mind, which alone can sustain the institutions of democracy, does not develop naturally or by neglect. The democratic nature is also a "second nature," and it needs deliberate nurturing. To be committed to democracy is to give a special mandate and a special character to the school and college.

Freedom is the fruit of the successful operation of the teaching power. Freedom is power and it, too, must be deliberately cultivated. It rests on discipline, not whim; on habit, not impulse; on understanding, not desire. It is a difficult achievement.

The American college today betrays its function if it does not take its democratic tutelary and initiatory tasks seriously. In cultivating freedom, the college can neither abandon the student's mind to its own devices nor abdicate to him the responsibility for creating or administering the conditions conducive to his own growth. At these points, as at others, we see the doctrines of individualism playing havoc with the spirit and operation of constructive institutions of growth and liberation, dooming us to a life of change through weakness and conflict rather than through strength and understanding.

The university, enterprising in the pursuit of knowledge, is a stronghold of individualism. But its own distinctive problems have not been my concern here. I have touched on the university only as it distorts and destroys the college. It has been a Procrustean host, and the college sleeps uneasily in its embrace.

The college itself, especially the lower division, needs fundamental reconstruction. But it is firmly set in its joyless ways and, under current pressures, is likely to drift in the wrong direction. The faculty, which alone can save it, is, regrettably, the vested interest most difficult to move. It acts out of conviction and habit, but what it has created and what it maintains is in educational, social, and human terms a disastrous failure.

The Experimental Program has attacked the problem root and branch. It has shown that there is another and a better way. The only question is whether it can survive and grow against the inertia of prevailing institutions.

The prospect is not hopeless. The task is not, at this point, to effect a total conversion of any particular college to the first-program pattern. It is, rather, to gain an exemplary foothold wherever possible. There is really no reason why every community college or junior college, every four-year college or university—public or private—could not, within a short time, have a first-program unit in operation. Every institution has at least the necessary handful of faculty who could do it, and that is all it would take. It is not expensive or elaborate or cranky.

If the program can gain a foothold for fair trial it will prove itself in many ways. It may even turn out that sanity and joy are contagious.

IV. DRAFT OF REPORT ON PROGRAM, JANUARY 1968

The American college is the setting for a crucial rite of passage. Parents see it as the place where they lose their children. The son or daughter who leaves, uncertainly, in September reappears briefly in December moving to the music of some strange pied piper, lost forever. To the student, it is a world of peers without parents, the threshold to the broader stage of fools.

100

To the society, which creates and sustains it, the college is a mysterious institution into which turbulent generations of adolescents are fed and from which are to issue, each year, intelligent, appreciative adults ready to take their places among the guardians of civilization.

The teacher knows that the college is the most crucial of battlefields. It is not simply that it is a place of confrontations—youth and age, feeling and habit, impulse and discipline, innocence and experience. It is the place where the essential vitality of the society is tested, its capacity to claim and harness the energy and commitment of its youthful self. The society brings itself, in the college, to public trial. There, before a skeptical, and even hostile, jury it must state its case. It must recollect and clarify its purposes, aims, and values; it must justify, if it can, its current interpretations of these purposes; it must acknowledge its shortcomings, explain its difficulties, justify its procedures, and reveal opportunities for creative and constructive action. The college is the point at which society comes to self-consciousness.

It is forced to do so by its very nature. It is the great social initiatory institution. It must make sense of the enterprise to which society expects the younger generation to commit itself. Habit goes a long way, and sheer momentum can carry us over some rough spots. But, in the end, we need more. In a "free" society the commitments of membership must be rooted in understanding.

The capacity of the college to make sense of the society that sustains it is the ultimate test of social vitality. If we cannot pass that test, we are doomed more certainly than by mere physical devastation. We cannot survive the breaking of the generational succession. Society, in the college, is not simply battling for the souls of men, it is fighting for its life.

The American college has been described in many ways, not always, or even usually, in these terms. The society that sustains it expects some return, but usually in the form of heightened competence for the professions and the more complex careers. The student sees it as serving his private needs. The faculty tends to think of itself as pursuing and transmitting knowledge. All these purposes find some measure of expression in the college. But they obscure the most significant fact. The college has come, more than any other institution in our secular "pluralistic" society, to fill the gap left by the separation of church and state; it performs some of the functions of an established church. It is the institution of initiation and confirmation. It is our failure to see this that is responsible for so much of the futility of current college reform. It is a failure of perception, and it is also a failure of nerve.

The society that imposes this task upon the college does not make the task an easy one. It sends to it sons and daughters already deeply disaffected and disillusioned. They take for granted a fairly high level of material affluence, but they are not grateful nor are they impressed by the quality of life it has brought to their parents. They are deeply troubled by the war and the race question and tend to see these as the characteristic expressions of a society that has betrayed its ideals. With youthful ruthlessness they see the gap between professed ideals and practice as evidence of hypocrisy and condemn impatiently all tempts to "explain the complexities" as mere establishment rationalization, as a defense of the "status quo."

The teacher, in this situation, rediscovers, if he has forgotten, the tale of the two cities—the enduring and the temporary, the invisible and the visible. He must fall back upon a conception of the community as enduring through time, an organization of intentions that, at any particular moment in its history, are imperfectly or inadequately expressed in the shape of its external and visible institutions. The mystery of initiation is that it is the joining of the invisible city, the commitment to ideals and institutions, not the mere acceptance of current practice. In short, the student has seen through some myths; he must now be initiated into the mystery. This initiation is not only the basis for appreciation, loyalty, and commitment, it is also the precondition of genuine dissent. It provides the understanding without which "dissent" cannot rise above mere opposition.

The visible gap between our ideals and our practice makes the initiatory task extremely difficult. At the same time, the disarray of the visible world forces the college, to its profit, to develop its philosophical resources. In meeting the challenge the college, out of educational necessity, may reforge a coherent and intelligible theory of the state.

Nothing is more badly needed. We have been drifting thoughtlessly on the wreckage of a shallow commercial individualism. But what has seemed to serve the father can no longer serve the son. Every bad theory exacts its price, and we are paying now.

It is deeply fitting and ironic that the students whose behavior most disturbs the adult world come to the college equipped with a "philosophy" that is only to a slight degree a parody of that of their elders. It is not the newness of the ideas that shocks; it is their haunting familiarity. Ivan is being confronted with Smerdyakov. Shall we review the standard items?

"The only language they understand is power." Authority? Legitimacy? Nothing but power clothing its nakedness in rhetoric. Principles? Rights? Rhetoric, unless there are battalions of bodies. International law and morality? It comes down to power. Therefore, student power. Very perceptive; very orthodox.

"Trust feeling; distrust reason and the word." If you buy and sell the mind, your children will become misologists. If you turn radio and television over to commerce, don't complain about the suspension of belief. A healthy organism tries to protect itself; the assaulted mind will turn against the word.

"Anyone over 30 is either dead or can't be trusted." Who do they know over 30? And how, in any case, can you expect the young to resist the impact of the vast cosmetic industry that has sold the cult of youth to rueful parents.

Drugs? The obvious and traditional response of a consumer civilization to the news, "The Kingdom of Heaven is within you."

"It's my life." An outrageously silly application of a primitive notion of property to something the claimant has neither created nor nurtured.

"Everyone should do what seems right to him." Apparently the ultimate moral principle, casually relegating law, politics, experience, authority, knowledge, humility, and all that, to the dustbin of history. Moral solipsism and self-righteous idiocy. We do not see, apparently, that this is the classic characterization of the state of war.

This is a short way with a short list. But it suggests the problem. Students do not learn these things in college; it is part of their baggage when they arrive. They did not make it up. It is their going-away present from the middle class.

The college must transform this state of mind—which at most can barely support a shallow and parasitic private life—into something capable of sustaining and developing the life of a democratic society. It is not an easy task. And it is not clear that the college has either the will or the capacity to succeed. But it is the last hope, and the battle must be joined there.

The college faculty, if it had a voice, would raise it in indignant and horrified protest at this description of its function. It would say:

We are not a church; we are not an institution for moral reclamation; we are not the spiritual arm of the political state. We are a secular institution of higher learning in a pluralistic society. We are not the priests of your invisible city. Moreover, this is a democracy, and democracy is based on individualism not on your kind of thought control and—yes— totalitarianism. And furthermore, who are you, or we, to judge, to presume to teach virtue, to impose values on others. No, thanks! We are independent scholars, not grand inquisitors; humble truth seekers, not soul savers.

Objection for objection, the guilty uneasiness of society and the desperation of the disillusioned student are as nothing compared with the adamant self-assurance of the faculty.

If there is a reply it must begin, I think, with an insistence on the distinction between the idea of the university and the idea of the college.

The university is an organization of scientists and scholars engaged in research. Its concern is with knowledge. Its teaching is professional and technical, centered in the graduate school. So great is its attractive power that it has warped the college into its own orbit. The college of letters and science has become simply a part of the university, a holding company for a large number of university departments with administrative responsibility for undergraduate education. But it has lost the sense of any independent mission. It measures success in terms of students sent on to graduate school; it is content to be a preparatory school for the professions, academic and other.

The college has drifted into this condition because it has never understood, or taken seriously, the implications of democracy. First, that democracy imposes on everyone, in the name of dignity and freedom, a political vocation. And second, that this vocation demands a special education. But the American college turned its back on this opportunity; and its institutional structure and the character and bent of its faculty make it highly unlikely that it will seize it now.

One of the consequences is that the college is ludicrously unprepared for the crisis in which it now finds itself. Its intellectual guns are trained in the wrong direction. It expects the administration to cope with major student unrest as if it were chiefly a question of bad manners. It meets the charge of educational irrelevance with bland incomprehension. Faced with a major moral and intellectual crisis, it presents its kaleidoscopic array of courses in subjects leading, ultimately, to the Ph.D. It does not see that this form of salvation is, for the college, only another way of dropping out.

The renewal of the college can and must begin with its first two years—the so-called lower division. The student is relatively free from immediate vocational pressure, although his search for a significant role is intense. His expectations are high; he is ready to turn over a new leaf; and he has not yet been discouraged into academic apathy by the discovery that his "important" problems are extracurricular. He is ready for education.

Moreover, the college is less confident about its handling of the lower division than about the rest of its life. The major program is still generally confined to the upper-division years, and it is recognized that the student's college education should consist of more than a major. But what that "more" should be is not so clear, and the college is open to suggestion. I suggest that we consider this question under the rubric, The First-Program Problem.

The program is the significant educational unit. Programs may be, and usually are, constructed out of courses. The course is a familiar unit for teaching purposes, but it would generally be recognized—and the quarter system has brought this point home—that a single course is a fragment, and that much of its significance depends on the context of courses and other modes of organized intellectual effort in which it is placed.

Graduate work—the third program—is a program of sustained study designed by the faculty as adequate preparation for teaching and research in a particular field or area. A Ph.D. program may involve courses, but it is defined in terms of the mastery of knowledge and techniques, tested in various ways, and is thought of as a more or less coherent program.

The upper-division major—the second program—while it may often be defined in terms of courses is, in principle, a more or less coherent plan of study designed to give the student some immersion in the basic concepts, the problems, the lore, the methods and techniques that characterize one of the great academic disciplines. It is supposed to be more than just a collection of courses in a department. It is, in intention, a coherent program.

The difficulty is with the largely nonexistent first program. (We seem to cover the range from programs without courses through programs with courses to courses without programs.) Can we construct and maintain, largely within the framework of our existing resources, a suitable variety of coherent and appropriate first programs?

What we have now, instead, is a loose system of "requirements." These have a long history and reflect genuine educational considerations. But, I believe, there is general dissatisfaction with what they add up to or fail to add up to. They are conceived as guarding against premature specialization by insisting on "breadth, a minimal sampling of courses in various areas; as providing for the tools or skills a college graduate should have, e.g., the ability to write and knowledge of a foreign language. To these general requirements are added those that departments impose as prerequisites for the upper-division major, amounting, in some cases, to as much as half of the student's lower-division course work.

The result is that, for most students, undergraduate education involves a single program (the major), supplemented by a variety of fragmentary courses. The suggestion here is that we think of undergraduate education as involving two programs and attempt to reclaim the lower-division years for appropriate first programs. "Appropriate" means, at least (1) some measure of coherence and integration, and (2) an organizing principle different from that upon which the second program, the departmental major, is based. It is also suggested that, for the sake of the integrity of the first program, departments be encouraged to claim a larger share of the student's time during the upper-division years, and, in exchange, minimize the lower-division prerequisites for majors.

We must expect, realistically, that for the immediate future, at least, the course will continue to be the unit out of which most programs will be constructed. Two encouraging tendencies are discernible, however: the student course load appears to be moving from five to four or even three, so that his attention is less fragmented and distracted; and we are beginning to think of double and even triple courses as providing greater opportunity for real curricular planning.

We need now, as we try to clear the ground for significant first programs, to consider whether the time has not come to loosen further or even drop the general system of requirements that give us the illusion but not the substance of educational planning. What would happen if we dropped them? Students would still, in large numbers, pursue the study of languages, although many who now go through the motions would not. Students would still seek courses that offered them an opportunity to improve the clarity and coherence of their writing. Our general requirements are a substitute for a serious educational advising system. If we do not feel that we can safely drop the requirements and rely on advice, we should at least be prepared to waive the requirements where they interfere with an acceptable first program. We should also avoid adding to the requirements on an *ad hoc* basis.

But to clear the ground for the first program does not tell us what it should be. We need to apply creative educational energy to this problem to develop a number of reasonable programs. The essential point is that each should be powerful enough to give character to and to dominate the student's lower-division years and should be distinct from but complementary to the upper-division major. There are some traditional precedents: Western civilization, world civilization, integrated humanities and integrated social studies, American studies. Such "core courses" might well be expanded in scope and treated as "double courses" and extended over as much as a two-year period. Foreign culture or area studies, heavily language-based, could be developed. Or urban studies. The first-program problem is not unsolvable. It simply needs to be recognized as the problem, and the ground needs to be cleared so as to encourage a variety of solutions.

The Experimental Program

The Experimental Program, now in its third year, is a first program. Technically, it can be regarded as a triple "course" extending over two years. Except for a single outside course each quarter, it constitutes the student's total program for his lower-division years. It is regarded as satisfying the reading and composition, social science and humanities, and American history and institutions requirements. The outside course permits the student to satisfy the language requirement and either the science requirement or some prerequisites for the upper-division major. The program is limited to 150 entering freshmen selected randomly from among applicants and is staffed by six full-time faculty members. Almost all of the students avail themselves of the pass-not pass option.

While the program has been conceived from the beginning as an integral whole, it is possible to distinguish two aspects: its curriculum or "subject," and its pedagogic structure. Each is an important part of the experiment, but it has always been considered possible that the general structure might commend itself to some who would not approve of the particular curriculum and who might wish to experiment with something like the same form and a quite different curriculum. I therefore shall discuss separately the curricular and structural aspects of the program.

The curriculum—"what we study"—always has been the most difficult aspect of the program to explain. Not only difficult, but really, when explained, so controversial and subject to misunderstanding that there has been a tendency on our part to settle for accurate but superficial descriptions rather than to face the serious task of explanation. Thus, we have pointed to our list of reading—a list so powerful as to seem self-justifying or to support a number of justifications.

Or, falling back on the original source of inspiration—Alexander Meiklejohn's experimental college—we have described the program as a variation of the Athens-America curriculum, focusing on Greece, seventeenth-century England, and America. True enough, but the program is really not "historical" in its conception or orientation.

It is more revealing to say that the curriculum is "problem-oriented," using materials that are, to some extent, historically clustered. The problems, however, are fundamental and perennial—that is, as contemporary as they are historical. Against the background of war and conflict we see men struggling to achieve peace and freedom, attempting to supplant power by legitimate authority, to embody moral values in a legal order, to reconcile submission to authority and the claims of conscience and individual judgment, to curb passion with reason, to tame destructive pride, to make wisdom operative in human affairs.

That we begin with the Greeks and end with America only serves to give force to the conception of a human culture persisting as it develops different forms, enduring in various modes of expression. The underlying assumption is, therefore, that there is indeed a common set of fundamental problems and that liberal education is the process by which we become more perceptively and sensitively involved in them. That these problems are supremely urgent and relevant today is obvious, especially to anyone who is at all aware of the freshman state of mind crudely sketched earlier in this paper. I argued then that the function of the college, as distinct from the university, is to deal with that state of mind as part of the process of initiation into the life and work of society. The suggestion that the lower-division first program address itself to this task finds expression in the curriculum of the Experimental Program.

In Homer and Hesiod, Herodotus and Thucydides, Aeschylus and Sophocles, and in Plato we have a constellation of fresh and powerful minds grappling with central issues. To continue the argument in seventeenth-century England—with (yes!) the King James Bible, Shakespeare, Hobbes, and Milton—is to tap the other great stream in our living tradition and to set the stage for the American venture. The study of America presents great curricular challenges and difficulties, and we are planning revisions in the second year of the program. But we certainly will retain, as a central thread, the concern with the Constitution, politics, and law.

So much, then, for the "subject." I turn now to some of the curricular principles involved.

1. Everyone is to study the same materials. This is a practical necessity, if there is to be a useful set of common lectures and seminars. But it is more than merely a practical necessity. It is a necessary condition for the development of a learning community with all of its sustaining qualities. A student who chooses to enter the program finds himself subject to a completely required curriculum for two years. It is, moreover, a curriculum determined entirely by the judgment of the faculty. We consider curriculum construction to be one of our central responsibilities, and we are not apologetic about the assertion of our authority at this point. It is almost the main service we perform for our students.

This means that we are not impressed with current tendencies to allow or encourage each student to pursue his own "interests" or to encourage students collectively to participate in curriculum determination. Students will have the rest of their lives to plan their own learning programs; in college, such planning is still the responsibility of the faculty. As for motivation, students are interested in fundamental problems, and a program that deals with such problems intelligently will elicit and sustain interest and effort. Moreover, the chief problem for the student is not interest but habit. Finally, a healthy student will be interested in what he should be interested in, whether he knows it or not. Our problem is to shape programs that embody what the student should be interested in. If we do that there will be no real problems of motivation.

2. The common reading list should be short. Serious reading is almost a lost art. Rapid reading under pressure is killing it. It is essential to restore the activities of reflection, of questioning, of appreciation to the reading process. This takes time. Students must be given the chance to read at a more leisurely pace. This means staying with a relatively short list of readings, allowing sufficient time for each, and reading one thing at a time. For example, we spend three or four weeks on Plato's *Republic*. Since it is the only thing we read during that period, the time available is at least the equivalent of a major quarter course. Lectures, seminars, and papers during this period also are focused on the *Republic*. This adds up to an educationally unique experience, and the program is designed to provide an integrated sequence of such experiences—intense, but unhurried and undistracted.

The pace of the reading is always a difficult matter of judgment, but our situation is kept flexible so that the tentatively scheduled time for a particular work can be shortened or extended as we think desirable.

We are, of course, confronted with some difficult decisions and temptations. There are too many good things not on the list. We have Plato, but why not Aristotle? Why not more Euripides? *Paradise Lost*, but why not Dante? The temptation is always to add good things, but we are convinced that that is the shortest path to disaster. No doubt it is possible to draw up a sequence of readings quite different from ours—perhaps equally good, perhaps better—although I doubt it. But it is not possible to draw up a list that would include every reasonable suggestion and still be an intelligible or manageable educational program. Choice is necessary, and it must be guided by considerations of thematic development, by concern for significance and variety, by a broad range of considerations that, for a teacher, are often intuitive; and experience will suggest modifications.

Our curriculum, then, takes as its "subject" a cluster of perennial moral and political problems and takes as its materials a relatively short and varied list of great works drawn from the Western tradition, to some extent historically clustered, and culminating in the study of these problems in the American context.

This particular curriculum is not an inherent or necessary part of the idea of a first program, and we can imagine a range of variations from those that keep the same central concerns but substitute other books for ours, to those that substitute major historical "clusters" including "non-Western" materials, to those that would depart radically from the central moral and political themes.

But a common, required, faculty-determined curriculum is an essential part of this conception of a first program.

The structure of the program makes a radical break with the course-classroom-examination pattern of educational life. But the problem is not simply to free the student from the traditional routine and turn him loose. It is, rather, to establish a ritual that will support and encourage the development of a set of intellectual habits consistent with a reasonable, effective, and continuous use of the mind. The association between "taking courses" and "getting an education" needs to be broken. But something must be put in the place of the old destructive routine. Just as we regard the development of the curriculum as a faculty responsibility, so also we regard the establishment and maintenance of a structure of educational occasions, activities, and demands as a faculty responsibility. The teaching art at this point is the art of maintaining an environment and ritual conducive to the development of intellectual powers and habit. The chief resource available, apart from the curriculum itself, is teaching judgment and energy, and the problem is to determine the structure of its most fruitful application.

The program makes use, in its own way, of the traditional techniques and forms: lectures, discussion, writing, conference.

Lectures

While we do not regard lecturing as the chief mode of teaching, it does have a significant place in the program. The dangers are familiar and obvious. The lecture can shift the work from the student to the teacher and encourage passivity; it can explain what the student should be trying to figure out himself; it encourages the confusion of "telling" with "teaching"; it presents the teacher with temptations. Nevertheless, meetings with a large number of students during which the faculty is being heard can, if properly conceived, be very useful. We have two such regularly scheduled meetings (each about 1.5 hours long) a week, and all students and all faculty members are expected to attend.

The lecture program is coordinated with the readings, and its main function is to stimulate and deepen the reading process. We operate with a few simple rules. We do not lecture about what has not been read; and we do not generally present background or supplementary information. We try, instead, to raise questions, to offer suggestive interpretations, and to sharpen and deepen the issues or problems latent in the reading.

We have tried a variety of forms: occasionally a single speaker lecturing for almost the standard hour; sometimes two speakers for shorter periods; sometimes even three. We have had a few panel discussions. There is almost always a question or discussion period, with the faculty, on this occasion, given priority. Students have a chance to hear the views of the entire faculty, and while we do not strive artificially for controversy, it takes place quite naturally.

The common lecture program is quite indispensable. It is the only occasion on which we are all assembled. It ensures that common themes are developed, and it reinforces the unity of the program. It keeps the faculty working closely together and gives the student a sense of involvement with more than members of his own seminar group. As the function of the lectures has become clearer the pressure on the faculty has virtually disappeared. We are not, except accidentally, academic experts on the material studied, and any attempt to give conventional academic lectures

111

would be misguided. But we are not using the materials in the usual academic way in any case, and the faculty quite easily can develop, with the aid of a good deal of free internal criticism, the capacity to respond fruitfully to the materials. There is scope for a wide variety of approaches and styles. In short, the lecture program has become an interesting challenge to the faculty and a stimulating and unifying feature of the program.

Seminars

The seminar is the occasion for discussion, in a small group, of the curricular materials and ideas. We began with a single two-hour meeting each week with 15 students. This was found to be unsatisfactory because 15 seemed to be too large a group, and because one meeting a week did not seem to be enough. We then tried groups of about eight, each group meeting twice a week—once with the faculty member present and once without. This was much better, although it quickly became apparent that the second meeting, unattended by the faculty member, needed more attention. We are now going to try groups of 10 or 11, with increasing concern for the second meeting. The complexity of the seminar situation is so great that, for example, the faculty spent hours considering the advisability of the shift from eight to 10.

The question of appropriate size is, of course, related to the conception of the function of the seminar—more particularly to the role of the faculty member. If he is, in effect, to lecture there is not much point to smallness. If he is to dominate and direct the discussion to themes or ideas he believes to be most significant he may well be able to work with a larger group. If students are to be encouraged to discuss with each other, a small group is desirable and the discussion may move in directions the faculty member may not think most fruitful; and, in any case, his participation takes on a different character. A dominant role for the faculty, member means that the two seminar meetings are radically different in character. Should the objective be to foster the art of discussion so that the faculty member's presence becomes increasingly unimportant and the two meetings come to resemble each other in character? These are fascinating pedagogic questions, and the staff is not fully in agreement about them. There is general agreement, however, that the seminars are to focus on the current reading.

The regularly scheduled seminar without a faculty member present seems to us to be a promising institution adaptable to situations other than

112

ours. It puts burdens and responsibilities squarely upon the students, and they are often surprised by the discovery of the extent to which they are, disappointingly, faculty-dependent.

Writing

The program makes it possible to think of student writing as a central educational discipline sustained over a two-year period. While there is some difference of opinion on this point, we do not, on the whole, think of turning students into "writers." We are more concerned with the practice of writing as an activity that reveals the mind at work and aids in the development of clarity, coherence, and understanding. Whatever else it may be, writing is, for us, a powerful pedagogic instrument.

We expect, or hope, that the student will spend at least an hour a day writing—every day for two years. We assign a formal paper about once every two weeks. And we ask the student to write every day in his journal. This is not a personal diary. The student is to develop some idea growing out of the reading, discussion, or lecture, and the journal is to be available for faculty scrutiny.

We are moving, with increasing conviction toward formal papers on clearly assigned topics and in a prescribed form. And we are discovering that we have much to learn about how to formulate paper assignments so as to increase the possibility that the writing will be educationally productive.

In the past, we have returned the papers with written comments and corrections (keeping a copy for the student's file) and on occasion have discussed the paper with the student in individual conference. But we are not too pleased with this method. Paper reading is a lot of work, and written comments are not always helpful or effective. We are now going to try regular tutorial conferences. We plan to see each student once every two weeks for a half hour, during which we will read and discuss the paper with the student. We hope this will provide for an effective level of attention, analysis, and criticism. The provision for this regular individual conference is related to our decision to increase the size of the seminar to 10 students.

The writing program heightens our awareness of the problems of habit. Our students, for example, have coped effectively with high school demands. The standard habit is deadline-oriented: reading delayed until late, a writing strategy adopted, a last-minute sustained writing session, a marginal revision while typing. It is difficult and necessary to break this

113

pattern and to develop another. The crucial experience is probably that of the student's own ruthless criticism of his first draft and the rethinking involved in writing the second draft. But this requires early reading and thinking and an early writing of the first draft. Everyone knows this should be done, but it is easier said than done. Similarly, everyone agrees that the daily journal writing is a good idea. But apparently it is very difficult to find an hour each day, to sit down and try to write. It takes character and discipline.

Individual Conferences

We have always assumed that our faculty-student ratio precluded regular tutorial sessions with each student. Our policy has been to consult individually with students whenever "needed." This has worked fairly well, although it is possible and inevitable that a student who needs a conference may go unnoticed. Our decision to handle the formal papers on a conference basis will alter this situation. We will see every student once every two weeks. If this proves to be an adequate way to criticize the writing, we will have gained tutorial advantages as well.

Informal Associations

From the beginning we have regarded a physical "center" as essential to the program. We have relatively few formal "classes" or meetings, and we count on informal association and contact to strengthen the sense of the common enterprise and community. A reconverted fraternity house on the edge of the campus has been assigned to our exclusive use and has been adequate for our needs. It is near the auditorium that we use for the lecture program and, except for the lectures, all our academic activities take place in the house. Keys are given to students on request and the house is available for use evenings and weekends.

It is hard for us to think of the program without the house. But it must be admitted that the house has been and continues to be a source of disappointment and anxiety as well as of enlightenment.

Two Passing Observations

1. This description has stressed the fact that both the curriculum and the structure are faculty determined, and that the program is, internally,

"required." This obviously raises questions about "freedom" and "authority" in education at the college level, and the program may seem reactionary and authoritarian in spirit. That is, it may seem so to those who understand neither freedom nor education. I mention this point only to indicate that I am perfectly aware of this misconception. Freedom is the essence of the program.

2. In this account of the Experimental Program as a "first program," I have distinguished the "curriculum" from the "structure" and have suggested that the conception of our curriculum is not necessarily built into the broader idea of the first program. And in an obvious sense, this is the case. A different curriculum could be adopted. But I would be less than candid if I did not express my intolerant conviction that our curriculum comes close to being essential to the conception of a significant first program. I do not mean that this or that particular book is essential; or even that different historical clusters might not be used. But rather that the curriculum must be concerned with central moral, political, or social problems, that it must be concerned with initiation into the great political vocation.

I have little expectation that this view will be widely accepted. However, I believe that the first program, even apart from the curricular question, is a neutral and useful conception. It sharpens and clarifies some aspects of the question of how to handle the lower division.

The Problem of Institutionalization

The institutional fate of the Experimental Program is still to be determined. There are two questions. First, does the program, as a mode of educational life, commend itself to the university as a reasonable and acceptable form of lower-division education? And second, can the university provide for its continuity and continuing vitality?

Evaluation is difficult. The traditional lower-division "programs," if they can be called that, are not really evaluated. Individual courses generally are sponsored by departments and approved by faculty committees, but beyond that there is little "evaluation." We rest on tradition and *ad hoc* judgment. The Experimental Program, as a drastic departure from standard practice, will seem to need special justification, but it is difficult to see what that would be.

Of the 150 students who entered the first class, 90 completed the program. Roughly, 20 students left the program at the end of each semester. Most transferred into the regular program, some left school for a variety of personal reasons. Of the 90 who completed the program, about 15 are taking a junior year abroad or elsewhere, a few have dropped out for a while, and the rest are continuing at Berkeley. It will be some time before we even know how they fare in their upper-division programs, and it is not clear what that will prove.

We are skeptical about evaluation procedures and reluctant to get heavily involved in them. We recognize, however, that if the program is to continue it must receive faculty sanction beyond the authorization sufficient for its experimental phase. A case for the program will have to be made, but apart from giving its rationale and reporting the experience, we do not really know what to do or what will be required.

Moreover, the problems of continuity or institutionalization are so complex that, unless we can see the way to their solution, there is not much point in worrying about evaluation.

The chief problem is staffing. The difficulty of first-program staffing in an institution like the University of California at Berkeley, especially a first program like the Experimental Program, is so great that it is tempting to abandon the task as more fitting for institutions with a primary commitment to undergraduate education. But Berkeley does have a lower division, and what it does with it can have a significant effect on the freedom of other institutions to experiment with first programs. It should and must exercise some leadership in this field. Unless it loosens up, other institutions, confronted with the transfer problem, are unable to do so.

The heart of the matter is that a university faculty does not take naturally to college first-program teaching that is not "disciplinary." It can provide excellent lower-division courses that are introductory to majors, but it has great difficulty in doing anything else. All of the pressures, personal as well as institutional, drive the faculty into research and the research-related teaching that is the primary function of the university. The kind of lower-division teaching we tend to have is the kind that can be done without drastic or sustained diversion from research. The alternatives seem to be either to recruit a separate or special "college faculty" or to take more advantage than we now do of the different phases in the career of the faculty member. He is not always in a "technical" phase, and there are times when a different kind of teaching would be refreshing rather than distracting.

116

The separate college faculty problem is an old one, and no one is very eager to follow that path; certainly, not on a large scale. But it does not seem unreasonable to consider a small number of permanent appointments of men of high intellectual quality and training who are good at and committed to undergraduate teaching, and who would provide leadership and energy.

The Experimental Program has found six faculty members and our initial group of 150 students a satisfactory arrangement. A single faculty member permanently assigned to the program probably could handle the recruiting and orienting of the temporary staff (one or two years) and provide direction for the program, although a core staff of two would be much better. A half-dozen permanent appointments would keep the program going at its present scale with a class beginning every year. The nonpermanent staff would be recruited from the regular Berkeley faculty or from other institutions.

But "permanent" needs some qualification. A tenure appointment would be necessary. But we do not know how long one could take the strains of this form of teaching; or how long one would stay fresh. So we are back to joint appointments with alternative academic status and function where necessary or desirable.

The difficulties stressed here are those related to establishing and maintaining a nondisciplinary first program in a university setting. Many of the difficulties are diminished in colleges that do not think of themselves as universities. And, in universities, they become less formidable to the degree that first programs are conceived that draw more directly on the normal disciplinary competence of the faculty. But the danger to the university-dependent first programs is precisely at that point. The application of the disciplinary competence to the first program can easily mean an earlier professionalism barely mitigated by familiar pieties and clichés.

For lovers of knowledge, worshiping the sun, real lower-division first-program teaching is the descent into the cave.

POSTSCRIPT, JULY 1968

I. Tutorials

Our initial view was that our student-faculty ratio precluded regular individual tutorials, that we were to be available for conferences "as needed." This meant a fairly heavy, though irregular, conference schedule, usually focused on student papers; but no attempt was made to see everyone routinely. In the winter quarter of 1968 we shifted to regular individual tutorial sessions and, after two quarters experience, regard them as an economical and essential feature of the program.

We introduced the system when attrition had reduced the student-faculty ratio to 20-1. We proposed to meet each student once in every two-week period—10 tutorial conferences each week. We planned on 30-45 minutes for each conference, although in practice it often ran longer.

The tutorial was devoted, for the most part, to analysis of the student's written work. We had found—what I suppose everyone finds—that taking a batch of student papers home, reading them, correcting mistakes, and writing comments intended to be diagnostic and helpful is among the more depressing and futile of academic exercises. A conscientious paper reader may spend an hour reading and marking up a five-page student paper, and the student may spend five minutes looking at the comments with very little profit.

It is an altogether different situation when the student and professor, each with a copy of the student's last written effort, settle down to consider it. The professor is reading it for the first time, questioning and commenting as he does so; the student is responding and explaining and often is giving his own paper its first objective reading. A characteristic mode of expression or error can be discussed until the point is grasped. And the discussion can cover a range of related questions.

The importance of such a conference needs no laboring. What is very worth noting, however, is our discovery that it adds up to a saving in faculty time. The instructor does no paper reading outside the conference session. And the regularly scheduled conference serves in lieu of a schedule of general office hours and obviates most of the need for special conferences. Faculty time is valuable, and eight hours a week is about the limit of time available for individual tutorials. This requires a rather severe limit to about 30 minutes when the ratio is around 25-1. An extra 15 minutes makes a significant difference, and as students, inevitably, drop out, it becomes possible to extend the time of each conference. Even a relatively short conference, however, is extremely valuable, and we are very happy about the way the tutorial has worked out.

II. Teaching Assistants

In view of the practice of making heavy use of graduate students as teaching assistants in lower-division courses, something should be said about our unwillingness to employ them in the program.

In our first year the staff consisted of five regular faculty members and five teaching assistants. We then discontinued the use of teaching assistants. We are convinced of the wisdom of that decision.

Graduate students are, of course, interesting and able young men and women. Many will soon be regular members of faculties and already at this stage of their careers display qualities that mark them as gifted teachers. But their situation, and their stage of development, precludes their general employment in lower-division "nondisciplinary" programs.

Graduate school is essentially a professional school, and a graduate student is preparing himself technically for entry into a profession. He can without too serious diversion from his primary task acquire some teaching experience as an assistant on a part-time basis. But this requires a carefully structured situation in which his developing technical competence can be used. To ask him to teach materials that lie outside his field makes very little sense. He should, at this stage, be immersed in his field; he is a young technician. If he is not, he will not be a graduate student very long.

The general use, and misuse, of teaching assistants in lower-division education is a major problem bordering on scandal. Limited technical use can be justified. But beyond that his use in free wheeling, lower-division programs is a disservice to student and teaching assistant alike. It is a temptation that must be strongly resisted.

III. The American Year

Two classes have gone through the first year of the program, and we have great confidence in its structure and value. The second, the "American" year, presents more complicated problems. It is not simply that the great books are not as obviously there. It is rather that we are more directly involved in and concerned with the *context* than we are during the first year. That is, our concern with America is different from our concern with Greece or England, which provided the setting for our study of general ideas. But America is the living society we now try to understand in the light of fundamental ideas that it embodies and issues that it faces. It is an oversimplification to say that we move from the general to the particular or from the abstract to the concrete or from the timeless to the temporal. But these contrasts suggest something of what is involved.

The curricular problem is a challenging one. There is, of course, American literature, American philosophy, American history to draw upon, but it would be a mistake to construct a second year that is simply a lesser and parochial version of the first year. Nor are we tempted, in our concern for the concrete and immediate, to fall into a "current events" curriculum.

We turn for salvation to the law and the court as the curricular basis of the second year—a solution that is itself characteristically American.

The Constitution has a place of special significance in American life. Seen as a "new covenant" it is an attempt to embody the moral and political experience of the old world in a framework appropriate for the new. The Supreme Court has produced a body of materials—interpretation, reflection, deliberation, argument, decision—of unusual educational fertility. This aspect of "law" has been badly neglected as a resource for general education, and it presents some difficulties. But to study the Supreme Court is to study the mind at work, attempting to deal with concrete and urgent problems in a context that demands justification in the light of laws, rules, principles, and purposes. Its failure and its triumphs, its confusions and its insights, its complexities and its simplicities are alike instructive. The Court is forced, by its unique position, to treat the particular in the light of the general, to square theory and practice—in short, to think about what we do.

We attempted, with some uncertainty and with mixed results, to make use of law as a teaching instrument in our first attempt at the second-year program. We will try again with greater confidence, determination, and experience.

We will not, of course, use constitutional and legal materials to the exclusion of everything else. But it will be the organizing focus of our work.

IV. The Physical Setting

Academic architecture presents us with the multipurpose office-classroom building on the one hand and the residence hall or dormitory on the other, and very little in between. The former is appropriate for the usual course-classroom mode of instruction and inadequate for anything beyond that. The residential center has its own peculiar shortcomings, but its possible use as a center of educational significance is a standing challenge.

Since some physical center is, we believe, essential to the development of educational programs, the conversion, and use, of the residence hall is worth consideration. If the Experimental Program is to be made permanent, and, perhaps, to expand, the question of its location in a dormitory cluster adjacent to the campus will have to be explored.

In the meantime we have had, in an abandoned fraternity house on the edge of the campus, an almost ideal home. It provides us with faculty offices, seminar rooms, study hall, and commons room. No one lives there, but it is available at all times for faculty and students in the program. Our reports in process have hinted that the house, in addition to its constructive significance, has been a more or less constant source of anxiety. It has been the island on which we have lived our own variations of the *Lord of the Flies*. It has provided a stage for the display of the roles of the guardian, the passive, the heedless, the predator. It has been the scene of both constructive and destructive energy.

Earlier hopes of Eden have been laid aside, and we now accept and value the house for what it is: a center of identification and of work, the sustainer of a common enterprise, and a laboratory that reveals to us all, faculty and students alike, the problems involved in the attempt to develop a community.

V. Grades, Discipline, Drop-Outs

Choice of the pass-not pass option by students in the program is almost universal. Most requests for grades for a particular quarter are the result of a student's being placed on "probation" when, in his single outside course, he falls below a C. Of course, grades in the lower division are not as important as they are later in their bearing on admission to graduate or professional school, and we can provide special letters of recommendation for a variety of purposes. But the choice of the option, without serious faculty pressure, is a healthy sign. The faculty is very pleased with this solution to the grade problem and with the quality of analysis, discussion, and criticism it makes possible.

Its chief value lies in its being not simply *another* grading system but in its not being a grading system at all. Thus, if we were to slide into a pass-not pass-distinction system, the whole point would be lost. There is a need for "not passed," but that comes close—as we have used it, and as we think it should be used—to "not performed."

The removal of grades affects us in two ways—and these effects must be recognized, and the needs, where legitimate, must be met somehow. First, grades are a traditional part of the incentive or motivation system; and second, they are the usual means by which students are, for various purposes, classified.

In our situation, the student and his work is well known to the faculty, and we can quite easily provide meaningful recommendations for scholarships, employment, transfer, and other purposes. We are not aware of any serious handicaps to our students on this score. But the elimination of grades does pose some marginal motivational, disciplinary, or "morale" problems. The problems are of a negative sort. That is, there is really no problem about most students, including the especially gifted ones. In spite of the fact that their experience has usually identified "doing good work" with "getting good grades" they adjust quickly to the new situation and thrive. They come to find satisfaction where it should be found—in a book enjoyed and understood, in a clarifying discussion, in a piece of writing that makes sense, in an awareness of growing understanding and power. It is only when we are confronted with the inevitable forms of student delinquency that, reaching for the familiar instrument to evoke greater effort or to punish indolence or indifference, we find the holster empty. We can require attendance, we can require papers, we can try persuasion, but our only sanction is "not pass," which amounts to ex-communication. And it is not easy to tell when this drastic action is called for.

We do not really consider the power to drop students from the program with a "not pass" for the quarter as a significant motivational influence. Work done simply to avoid that fate is not likely to be very useful. But we consider the "not pass" exclusion as necessary for the protection of the integrity of the program. The program consists of carefully scheduled prescribed work. Even in a "volunteer" student population there are some students who discover that they prefer to attend as they please, read what and as they please, and write what they please, if at all. *That* is not our program, and we do not intend to have it converted into that by students who opt for educational autonomy. When all else fails—and we do not wish to spoil the positive spirit of the program by constantly reacting to marginal delinquency—exclusion is necessary. It should be noted, however, that "not pass" exclusion has been resorted to rather rarely. Most students who, for one reason or another, become disaffected make their intention to leave the program known complete the current quarter with somewhat diminishing performance, and depart in peace with a terminal "pass."

Our most irritating problem, however, is what to do about some fairly bright students who tend to have a high opinion of their own intellectual powers, who have learned to protect themselves against education, whose work is shoddy and disappointing, but who go through the motions sufficiently to retain their standing in the program. We are strongly tempted to exclude them, but so far we have not done so, although they are doing themselves little good, tend to demoralize their fellow students, and do not entertain the faculty.

CHAPTER 3

WHY SHOULD WE STUDY
THE GREEKS?

Sometimes we are called upon to defend, and therefore to think about, what we have long taken for granted. This, for me, is such an occasion. As long as I can remember, I have loved the Greeks, have read them over and over, have taught them upon the slightest excuse to students who have seldom complained. Students are, no doubt, too polite to complain, but it is possible that they actually enjoy the experience. They may be relieved to discover that the Greek classics, as classics generally, are not spiritual or noble works to whose level they must struggle to elevate themselves for a time before sinking back into the more congenial mud baths of real life. They find themselves regaled by stories of sex—heterosexual and homosexual—of greed, ambition, war, murder, treachery, heroism, love— discovering an ultimate source of that universal art form, the soap-opera. All the familiar plots and the broad array of human types—golden playboys, strong ruthless women, clever plotters, stolid warriors, garrulous oldsters, young lovers, cowards, heroes, creators, thieves—they are all there—all the great roles and all the great stories. It is entertaining enough, and even, if we are inclined to think, thought-provoking. When one is reading the Greeks the need to justify the activity does not seem to arise. But if we ask, today, why we should read the Greeks, why they should play a central part, or at least serve as a starting point, in our college education, mere habit and mere pleasure cannot be a sufficient answer.

In our world, full of rapid change and novelty, struggling with a flood of innovations in science and technology, shaken by changes in attitudes about gender and the family, troubled by once-unnoticed forms of oppres-

---

This is more or less the lecture I gave at the inauguration of the Malespina College program at the end of September 1991.

sion, newly aware of our insensitivity to the dignity of ethnic minorities, frightened by our irresponsible power over biological destiny and precarious environment, bewildered by instantaneous awareness of what is going on everywhere, dazed by an enormous knowledge-explosion, threatening ourselves with disaster amidst the ruins of grandiose ideologies—in such a world it may seem oddly unreal to suggest to a responsible generation of intelligent college students that they actually turn from these urgencies to study the Greeks. There is much hand-wringing about our lack of computer literacy and the deficiency in mathematics and science that may doom us to subservience to foreigners toiling with grim energy to undermine the once-envied standard of living seen as the proper consolation for our fading spiritual supremacy. But among all the complaints about our educational failings few tears are shed over our dust-covered neglect of Homer or Plato or Thucydides. Why, under our circumstances, should we bother to study the Greeks? That is not an easy question to answer.

First, let me put aside or dismiss some perfectly good answers as not really good enough. The Greeks are interesting, but the fact that you find something interesting is not always a sufficient reason for doing it, especially when there may be something more important that needs doing. There are many great books, but that a book is great may not be a good enough reason for reading it at a particular moment in one's life. So I put aside the facts of interest or high quality as true enough but as not a sufficient reason to give them an important place in modern education.

I also put aside, with some hesitation, the rather odd fact that the ruling class of the small island that presided over an empire upon which the sun never set—that ruling class was raised on, fed its mind on, the Greek classics. Rulers, as we know, are not fitted for their tasks by the study of science, or even social science. They are seldom masters of the cognitive arts, of research or scholarship. A ruler, a governor, a college president is always surrounded by people who know more than he or she about almost anything. If we knew that someone was destined to be president or prime minister or king, it would be a waste of time to try to teach her physics or chemistry or even sociology or psychology. She should be raised on great literature—stories, histories, tragedies, epics, beginning especially with the Greeks. But this odd point—the special bearing of the classics and the Greeks upon the ruling function—is a point I will not linger over here—even though in a democratic age, when everyone is supposed to be educated for the ruling role, it is a point with special force. It raises the question of the difference between discovering general principles and uncovering particular plots and the proper place of each, of science and the humanities, in our education—a question I will not pursue here.

I also put aside, as not to be taken seriously, a related point having to do with "cultural literacy" or with the certification of upper-class status evidenced by the nod of recognition upon hearing the names of classical authors—the familiar nodding acquaintance with the classics.

So why?

College education is, for most of us, the last formal or official chance to deal with the two great questions that will plague us all our lives. Those questions are: (first) *What am I supposed to do?* and (second) *What is going on?* (What is it all about?)

What am I supposed to do? is, of course, the great vocational question. What am I to do with my life, what is to be my task, to what am I to devote myself, what is to be my job? This is, I think, the dominant question for all of us. Have I a vocation, a task that will absorb my energies, develop my talents, provide me with a lifetime of satisfying and useful work so that in the end I earn the great accolade "Well done thou good and faithful servant!" Are we to devote our lives to the great struggle for justice? Are we to try to master the arts of healing, to prolong life and banish pain? Are we to learn to turn stones into bread, transform swamps and deserts into gardens, preserve forests and animals and fresh air? Are we to entertain or teach and enlighten? Or are we to learn to make money so that we can do whatever we should do that money makes possible, while we make up our mind. I need not labor the urgency of the vocational question. It is only when we fail in this quest for vocation, when we remain or become physically or spiritually unemployed, that we must reconcile ourselves to the bitter life of the mere consumer, and one of the aims of education is to help us avoid that fate. Each of us must endure some version of the vocational crisis, presented biblically as a young man's temptations in the desert. What am I to do with my life? A good question!

But the other question is equally urgent and basic. If it is important to find the part you are to play, to find a part to play, to discover your vocation, it is essential to know what the game is. Finding a role, playing a part, is playing a part in an ongoing story, and not to grasp that is to go through motions without understanding what you are doing, to live without a sense of significance, to go through life as a sleepwalker. The anguished quest for a glimpse of the great scenario—a quest with which religion is concerned—is a central part of the experience of everyone who is not content to remain a mere uncomprehending cog in a machine or a pathetic pleasure seeker. "What is it all about?," "What have I been born into?" is an unavoidable question, and it cannot or ought not be altogether evaded by the institutions of education—although, it must be said, they try with considerable success to evade it.

So we are looking for an answer to "What is it all about?" That, I think, is really the same question as "What is going on?" But "What is going on?" is a more helpful way of putting it. It is as if each of us has been dropped by the stork on a large playing field and, as we become aware of things, we find balls flying in all directions and people running and clashing and shouting—all very confusing to an infant. (When we are born, says Lear, "We cry that we have come to this great stage of fools." Delivered by the stork to the wrong place!) The problem is to discover the point, to come to understand what is going on and even, after a while, to take part. Things are going on all around us, something we are born in the midst of, something taking place *now*, something that may be part of a fairly long-running game. So the great orienting question is, "What is going on?" And the problem, of course, is how to find out.

To begin with, we need to remember a simple fact about time, about the past and the present, as it relates to "What is going on." The present is sometimes thought of as a thin razor's edge, separating a no longer existing past from a not yet existing future. This thin conception of the present is seriously misleading. It is a "present" in which nothing can go on. So, as we all come to realize, the present in which we are living and in which things really do go on is not at all like a thin razors edge but is in fact remarkably thick or fat. The real present is not a discrete instant but a duration—a duration long enough to make sense of something going on, long enough, even, for a long story.

Consider a simple melody. It is, I suppose, made up of single notes, each of which sounds singly and for an instant. But if we hear only a single note, if only a single note is "present" what happens to the melody? Unless we hear, are aware of, the whole series we do not hear a melody at all. But we do hear the melody, it is the melody that is present, and the "present" thickens to the duration necessary to contain the melody. We are listening to and enjoying the melody present to us in the present. How thick is the musical present? It must vary. Some can carry or be aware of or hold in mind a fairly simple tune. Some, not I alas, can have a movement of a

128

concerto in mind, and listen not to notes or brief snatches but to a long movement as I can listen to or hear a simple melody. When a musician listens, I suppose the whole symphony may be "present" to him. There is no melody, no music, without a thick enduring present.

Or take another example. For someone who doesn't understand what he is seeing, who does not grasp what is going on, a tennis game may shrink to what his untrained mind merely "sees"—someone hits or serves a ball—an event that, taken by itself, is quite uninteresting. He may learn to follow the ball back and forth across the net for a whole point. The complex exchanges are seen as a unit. He may learn to see the point as a point in a game. If he understands more, he can have the set or the match or the tournament before him. It is the tournament that is now going on, that is present. And it is that that makes sense out of the tactics and strategy that are invisible to one who sees only the single shot in a thin present that has no time for these things. Many of us recently watched the Connors match at the U.S. Open. Consider what you had to understand, to have in mind, in order to make it more than the dull sight of two men running around, hitting the ball back and forth. You had to be aware of the saga of an aging ill-mannered millionaire redeeming himself by driving himself into competition with gifted athletes half his age, winning forgiveness for two decades of boorishness by a display of amazing persistence and courage. Unless you were aware of something like that going on—unless that whole long story was present to you—you did not see or know what was going on.

Or consider "reading." You do not merely read a word or a page or a chapter. A word does not have a plot. A book does. You read a book. That is the unit that has the plot or the story. In a real sense, that is what is present, what you are going through, what you are living through. The "present" to a reader is not like a spotlight going from word to word. If someone asks what it is all about, what you are reading, you do not glance at the next word and say I am reading "dog." To read is to endure through the present story and you cannot do that if what is present shrinks to the single word.

These examples are to say that the present—what we are living in and through—a melody, a game, a story—is an enduring span. What we are presently living through is a long story, (what Adam, in *Paradise Lost*, called a "long day's dying") part of an even longer story, an enduring now. And just as the musical present is thicker for one who grasps and understands music, as the game is richer for the fan who understands or grasps the series or even the wonderful present season or the story of the great series of seasons, as the book is richer for the one who grasps and is aware of more than the present page or even the present chapter—so a life is a different matter for someone who does not suffer a mere moment to moment existence but begins to grasp what is going on.

A life is, in a sense, a long present span of existence. For each of us there is a story—a childhood, youth, maturity, old age, a history. For each there is a biography. But this biography—and here I suppose I approach the point—is a chapter in a longer story, in the story of a family or a community or a polity or even a culture. When we ask "What is it all about?" or "What is going on?" we are like chapters looking for our books, and it is only as we begin to see that that we begin to see the significance of what we are and what we do. We are moments or episodes in a continuing series, in an enduring present, chapters in a longer book, moments looking for their explanatory and encompassing contexts. How to discover that? How to find the answer to "What is it all about" in the discovery of "What is going on" is one of the great tasks of education.

We, assembled here, are living through an episode in the present long running story of Western civilization—an episode in the history of this Island, of Canada, to be sure, but that is merely part of the story of Europe, and the earlier bits that go back, to the Mediterranean and, for our purposes, to the image of humans at war on the plains of Troy.

I suppose you may be objecting to all this and suspicious of where it comes out and are thinking of how to defend the view that everything is simply a collection of points and instants and all the rest is illusion, that the past is already gone, nonexistent, unreal. But as long as you have allowed me to go this far, let me stress that our lives are to be seen as episodes in a longer story and that that story—not itself the whole story—is the story of western civilization and that the story line runs thru Greece and Rome to Europe and England to North America. It is a complex story with plots and subplots, themes and subthemes, recurring motifs, cyclical movements, and even evolutionary tendencies. We are part of that story not because we have chosen to be but by the fact of our birth and nurture in which everything, every part of the furniture of mind and character is at least second hand, inherited. To think we have made it up is simply a parochial prejudice. We are, above all, inheritors and most of our creativity is marginally trivial. To think otherwise is the sin of pride. The play we are enacting did not begin when we opened our eyes. We are not the authors, we have not invented ourselves. At most we are part of the cast of characters challenged to play a role. If we reject this view and try to pretend we start with a clean slate, it is no wonder that we will soon complain of the meaninglessness of life and have problems of identity—just as one who thinks only the present note "exists," who insists on hearing only that, may wonder where the melody, where all the music, has gone.

And now I ask you to tolerate another stretch of imagination. Imagine that there is a creature, a person, called Western Humanity enduring all this time, to whom all this history is biography, is happening, a sort of not-quite-immortal being, and that each generation is really only a sort of regeneration, like the growing of a new skin. A single complex enduring great person whose life is the enormous "present." And now let us imagine that about every 50 years or so this person is stricken with amnesia, all memory wiped out. So we always seem to have on our hands, as part of the culture's regenerative process, generation after generation of total amnesiacs. The problem for the survivors who have not yet been shed, the dying, the teaching, generation, (Yeats' "Those dying generations—at their song . . . "), the task of those who still linger, is, before they go, to restore awareness of identity. Every new generation mutters "Where am I, who am I, what am I doing here?" as it groggily rubs its eyes and stirs into awakening. Education is the art of restoring these amnesiacs to their senses. They have to learn the language all over again, how to read and write, how to behave, and what is going on, what the game is into which they have been born with minds somehow mislaid. How would you do it?

It is really not so far fetched. Every generation, every person born into this continuing cultural life knows nothing of it, and the process of growing and learning, acquiring awareness of what is going on, may perhaps be more crudely described as initiation than as being brought to remember. In either case it involves being brought to grasp the story, being clued in to what is going on. It can take a short, shallow form or a longer, deeper form. The instruments of that initiation or recollection are the great moments, the great landmarks, the great clues, the high points of achievement. The minds that have given the culture—us—its great special shape are the Homers, the Platos, the Virgils, the Dantes, the Shakespeares, the Miltons. . . . It all begins for us, at least, for the West, with Athens, that small town in Greece, and flows in an unbroken line from then to now, from them to us in a great living present. In this great present story, it is Socrates who dies rather than give up the freedom to question and examine. It is Athena who invents law courts to settle great moral conflicts that otherwise lead to never-ending war, teaching us to subordinate moral indignation to judicial verdict. It is Antigone who, in the face of that, asserts that you are to follow your moral judgment when it is in conflict with the law. It is the story of Oedipus, that great victim of child- abuse, who ends up killing his father and marrying his mother, suggesting that if the home is dangerous to the infant, then infant may grow into a menace to a normal home, etc. . . .

It is hardly an exaggeration to say that we are still working out, moving within the framework of the great dilemmas posed for us by the Greeks, we are still singing the song they struck up, acting out the roles in the story we are still enacting. If we do not know that, we hardly know what we are up to, what it is all about. We remain children who have not yet been let in on the whole story, our cultural memory has not yet been restored, our initiation into the game has not yet been fully completed. And those responsible for the cure of amnesia, for the generational regeneration will have failed in their primary responsibility. The Greek classics are like great clues left for us to decipher. They reveal us to ourselves.

And that, ultimately, is why we should study the Greeks. Not merely because they are great works of the human mind, not because, once we get the taste for them, they give us great pleasure. But because if you are interested in your identity that is where you get a good part of the answer. You are the present note in the prolonged existence of Western civilization. You may not like that answer and may try to reject it. That is, you may have an identity crisis. But it is simply an inescapable fact. You can close your mind to it, but that will not change the fact; it will merely warp your mind.

We begin with the Greeks so you will know who you are, will begin to catch on to the game into which you have been born, will recover from the amnesiac ordeal and find your part to play in that enduring ongoing story. I stress that this is really not a matter of choice. We are a living part of a living enduring Western culture. That is a fact about us. You did not chose it any more than you chose your mother tongue, To hate it is a form of self-hatred. It is better to try to get to know it, to learn its movements and currents, to become familiar with its themes, and in the end to try to make the best of it. If you are going to look for your roots, you have to go back to the Greeks, or more broadly speaking, to the Mediterranean that adds Jerusalem and Rome to Athens.

It is from some such considerations as I have been trying to convey that the real answer to why study the Greeks gets its force. If you learn the Greek themes, nothing after that will really surprise you. I remember a rather striking time in the '60s in Berkeley—flower children, street people, drugs, strange wild music, disorder, rebellion, anti-establishment energy. It seemed to be, claimed to be, something new under the sun. But to Berkeley students in a program not unlike yours it was simply a familiar reenactment of the Bacchae of Euripides, in which, under the inspiration of Dionysus, those outside the Olympian establishment hurled themselves against the cold rational world that seemed to have no room for the passions. Just as other campus scenes were recognized by our students as a Halloween reenactment of *Paradise Lost*. What we are living in and through is a great Theme and Variations. And the theme is presented in Athens.

I suppose I should acknowledge that I am aware of the powerful challenges to this conception of education as helping us to discover what is going on and guiding us into taking part. First, perhaps, is the indignant rejection of the idea that a new generation does not start with a clean slate, free to make of the brave new world what it wills, but is born with debts and commitments, with hand-me-downs, that the note is "continuation" and not beginning from scratch, that it is encumbered by the expectation of gratitude towards its generator. I am always amused when I read *Paradise Lost* by a great passage in which Satan, launching a rebellion against his creator, is reminded by another angel of his great debt to the creator who, after all, made him what he is. "Where did you get that ridiculous idea?" replies Satan. "Who says we were created? As long as I can remember, I was there. I made myself. My generation was ungenerated. . . ." This satanic repudiation of the debt to the creator happens every year, and there are even educators who pander to it. I'm sure you recognize this mood of rejection of what exists, of the soiled, spoiled, sin-pervaded parental world and the determination to start all over, afresh, on a new game. (Or at least, as Electra swears, to be better than her mother. . . .) But, alas, the world does not present you with a clean slate.

Or, discovering that our culture is a story full of oppression, unfairness, injustice, a determination to turn ones back on it and find or make another that is not oppressive of class or race or gender and that, therefore, education should steer clear of the landmarks of the oppressive culture that, if we attend to them, will warp our minds and souls. But the path of reform or regeneration leads through, not around, the mastery of the powers of our culture—through the incarnation, not the avoidance or rejection, of those powers.

Or the objection that emphasis on a particular cultural life is an explicit or implicit repudiation of the value of other strains. There are, of course, other great cultures into which members are awakened. It would be stupidly provincial to deny that fact. But a deep initiation into one's own, whatever it happens to be, is a precondition of everything. Just as a mastery of one's mother tongue is generally a precondition of a mastery of language, and not an assertion that one's mother tongue is superior to other languages.

There are, I am sure, a host of other objections, but, on this occasion, I will not stop to pay my respects to them. . . .

Significance is not a cosmic but a human notion. It is not to be found by turning away from the human drama we are born into. We are born into a world of games, of styles, of ways of life, and it may be futile to yearn for another game, as if in that game everything will be better. I once character-ized this yearning as based on the hope that if only we had a different mother tongue all the mistakes in our language would not be made if we spoke French or Chinese instead of English.

The conception of the human person as basically a creature of his culture, not someone standing outside of it free to take it or leave it is strikingly expressed in one of the great parables in Plato's *Republic*. In what is usually called the Myth of the Metals that I take in fact to be the real heart of the *Republic*, Plato develops what I think of as the conception of the marsupial birth of the human being. We are born in two stages. When we emerge from the womb we are, of course, incomplete. We are then placed in the second womb, the community, or polis, the marsupial or kangaroo pouch, in which the crucial stage of development takes place. We are equipped with our language, habits, values—everything distinctively human—living a sort of limbo-like existence as minors—until we complete our growth and emerge or are born as adults. The community is, in this birth process, parental—and our fellow sharers of that womb are siblings or fellow citizens who are to carry on the life of the community. Note, it is not a mere handing on or transmission of a culture as if one is delivering a message. It is a carrying on of a community's life, in which each is to discover and play a proper part. Thus the art of education is the art of bringing a human being to full birth, it is an obstetric art. In that spirit, I have suggested that reading the Greeks is part of the process of bringing to birth a person fully aware of his identity. The myth of the metals is one of the great creation parables at the heart of Western culture and a clue to what education is all about.

I would like to supplement this Greek parable with our other great Mediterranean parable of the creation or growth of a human adult. Adam and Eve are seen as a young couple living not so much in a wild garden as in a model kingdom. There is a ruler. There is law. They are subjects living in a situation they did not create, with tasks or functions. They are told to perform their caretaking tasks and to use their best judgment. But there is one thing they are not to do. They are not to presume to know about good and evil, to presume to act on their own judgment against the law. The story as developed by Milton has Eve considering that the law makes no sense. Why not know about good and evil, to better serve the good and to avoid evil? The command, to avoid the fruit of the tree of knowledge of good and evil, she thought, made no sense. What made no sense did not deserve respect, an unreasonable law need not be obeyed, and, in a fateful moment she, with Adam following her lead, disobeyed the law, put their own judgment of good and evil above the law. As we all know, that moment of disobedience to the command of the parental creator when that commands seemed to make no sense, that constantly repeated moment, is one of the great crises in human development. It is the moment in which having learned to use one's reason the children turn their reason to the evaluation of the law and demand that the law make sense to them if they are to obey it. That is, having been taught to think, the pupils, the children, think about the system within which they have been raised, which has shaped their character, subject it to criticism, and, wisely or not, decide to make up their own minds about good and evil, to follow their own moral judgment. And at that crucial point they cease being children living in the parental garden and must go out into the world beyond, a world in which they will experience pain, suffering, and carry on life as they think best in a world they did not make, with what they have learned in the garden of their childhood, and must try, after the discovery, in due course, that their children are capable of murder, to recreate a rule of law all over again.

These two great creation myths lie at the beginning of the story of which we are the present chapter. The reminder that when we are born as adults we emerge from the second womb, the community, that has restored us to our senses by giving us our culture—our minds, our characters—and that it is only by virtue of this action by the community that we are really born at all, and that we owe a filial debt of gratitude to our real parental creators. The popular denial of these facts of life expressed in some forms of individualism is an act both of amnesia and ingratitude.

And the reminder that, nevertheless, we must, if we are to reach childhood's end, turn our minds, thus shaped, to a critical examination of the received law, to subject it to the ordeal of reason.

These two notes, appreciation and criticism, go hand in hand and need each other. Appreciation without criticism perpetuates the docility of the childlike inheritor. Criticism without appreciation will doom us to the futility of pandemonium—as Satan's rejection of the established order resulted only in the recreation of a feeble parody of that order. So initiation into the life of our culture requires that we do both, incarnate the powers of the culture and cultivate the habits of criticism that are themselves the habits of that culture. Both of these begin, for us, with the Greeks, and that is why an education that does not begin with the Greeks is a bit like listening to Bach's Goldberg variations without listening to the great opening statement of the theme of which the variations are variations.

So among all the possible answers to "Why the Greeks" I would rest on the fact that the Greek episode—the theme of a community developing the arts of inquiry and government and self-government moving tragically, almost irresistibly, to its own self destruction, struggling to understand freedom and authority, law and conscience, selfishness, ambition, and selfless devotion to the common good—that this episode states with clarity and depth the great theme upon which our current life is merely a variation in the song or story of the culture within which we play out our transient turn.

Implicit in all this is perhaps a rejection of the view of progress or at least of progress in everything. There are, as we know, at least two realms. There is the realm in which we seek knowledge, the world of science and of technology, in which there is clearly improvement, so that the ancients may have little or nothing to teach us about physics or biology or geology. But that fact of progress in the world of knowledge does not extend to something that may be quite beyond knowledge. Knowledge is not wisdom, and it may very well be the case that the pursuit of knowledge is not the path to wisdom—that we are not in fact wiser about life, about parents and children, about individual and community, than the ancients, than the Greek and Mediterranean generators. Technology and other trivial things change, but it may be that on fundamental matters there is no progress, merely the playing out of variations on a theme—that on fundamental human concerns, time does not really matter. The world of the *Iliad* is a world at war. There are spears and chariots. Our modern technology provides us with different weapons. But no one can read the *Iliad* without recognizing that the human beings on the plains of ancient Troy are the same as those recently deployed nearby around the Persian Gulf. In the moral domain, the domain of wisdom, as contrasted with the domain of science and knowledge, there may indeed be no progress but simply the perpetual movement between the demands of the political and the demands of the domestic, between public and private, between, as in the case of the Trojan War, the expedition and the city, the quest and the home. To say that in the moral domain there may be no progress is not necessarily a judgment of despair; it may merely be the recognition that on fundamental matters there is not much change in the human situation—that the vices and virtues are permanent features of the human scene, that there may be a deep human nature appearing from time to time in a new wardrobe, but fundamentally unchanged. This may even suggest that a common human nature expresses itself in all cultures, Western and other, and that as we come to understand our own, we can begin to understand others, but that we will never understand others if we do not understand our own. So that if we begin with the Greeks we may not only cure our own cultural amnesia but may even begin to grasp the common human basis underlying all human culture. That is why, I suggest, that we begin with our great opening act, in the midst of things, on the plains of Troy where people are displaying all of human nature while dying in the odd quixotic quest to recapture an elusive and faithless beauty.

CHAPTER 4

REMEMBERING ALEXANDER MEIKLEJOHN

I was not one of the Experimental College boys. It had shut down before I arrived at the University of Wisconsin, but I had been present, an envious intruder, at the 25th reunion. I was there as one of the later generation of Meiklejohn students, crashing the party to be in on the tribute. And now, another 25 years later, there was to be a reunion without him, a gathering of remnants, a few surviving faculty and perhaps a hundred Ex College students, all well aged, assembled now not in the presence but in the memory of Alexander Meiklejohn. Veterans of an educational war, the thinning ranks of those who remember Alec. Beyond them, scattered, the even thinner ranks of those who were there, who could remember when, as president, Meiklejohn had stirred, scandalized, divided Amherst.

I did not meet Meiklejohn until all that was over, until he had turned from the struggle to reshape institutions, had retired in some sort of defeat from administrative responsibility, had become famous for his unbowed gallantry in that great lost cause—educational reform. I met him first when he returned to the university to teach for a few years as a member of the philosophy department before retiring from academic life.

The students' lack of institutional memory always seems to surprise the old faculty hand, but to the new student what happened the year before he arrived is merely a little known part of ancient history. So, although the Experimental College had run from 1927 to 1932 and I arrived in 1933, I had never heard of it. I had not heard of Meiklejohn either. "Meiklejohn is back!" I remember the word spreading among the older students on the fringes of whose circle I drifted. There was respect, almost awe, in voices usually stridently iconoclastic. So I signed up for an introductory philoso-

---

This chapter was originally published in *Liberal Education*, 1984.

phy course he was to teach, sensing that he was a hero, but knowing very little about it. I am struck by how little was conveyed by what gossip there was about the Ex College. It was different, some sort of educational Eden, briefly flourishing before being done in for reasons or villainies I was too innocent to grasp.

He stepped briskly, smiling, into the classroom—lean, eager, complete. That is, he looked then very much as he looked to me for the next quarter of a century. He seemed old then, and he never seemed to age much after that; old but not feeble, evoking all the comments we make when the old don't act their age. He was lively, cheerful, witty, concentrated, crisp. He was also, although open and friendly, very polite and, I thought, very formal. He brought with him an air of anticipation and excitement.

We were to see Meiklejohn in the classroom, in the conventional academic setting, teaching a course offered by a department. I was not aware of the ironies of the situation. He had been, as we know, an educator—dean of Brown, president of Amherst, director of the Experimental College—concerned to create an environment in which teaching and learning would flourish. It is not too much to say that the discrete course, the self-contained class in a subject, the educational institution seen as a loose collection of courses, was the triumphant enemy against which he had always fought. And here he was, at the end of his academic career, enjoying, or condemned to, the transient hospitality of the enemy camp. He had, on equal terms, the freedom of that city. There was a truce. He was not to disturb the university's peace; he was to teach some courses in philosophy—whatever he chose, no doubt—and then, in a few years, he was to retire. I do not think he could have believed very strongly in the significance of what he was doing. But if this is true—as I am now sure that it must have been—we students had no inkling of it. He did not reminisce about the good old days. I do not remember him criticizing the educational system; he did not continue the controversy. He simply taught his courses with zest.

It was a lively class. The mode was discussion of what we were asked to read. He did not explain anything. He smiled a lot, nodded encouragement, listened intently, enjoying it all, welcoming independence, challenging, seldom if ever allowing himself to stand before us as having an idea he was anxious to give us. His enjoyment was contagious, and I remember coming into class sullen about the current shape of the universe, warming reluctantly to the discussion, almost cheerful as, at the end of the hour, we streamed down the hill in his lively wake, unwilling to let the argument end.

What was it all about? Why did it mean so much to me? Why, especially since I did not really believe what I thought he meant to say, do I think of it as the turning point of my life?

Wisconsin in the thirties was a progressive politically alert state proud of its LaFollette tradition. The university was swarming with students from the East who, fleeing or exiled from the seaboard, seemed to land either at Chicago or Madison. Madison in the thirties was, with due allowance, something like Berkeley in the sixties.

Those were the early Roosevelt days, and the country was floundering in deep depression. In Europe, Hitler loomed in menace. Nevertheless, the university continued in session. The farmers were still there in the Ag School, scientists (did we know any?) were still in their labs—unperturbed worlds, alien worlds. Most of my older friends were in, or trying to get into, medical school or law school. Not for me. I was repelled by the organic intimacy of the one and frightened by the close-argued heavy-tomed intricacy of the other. What else was there? Some were edging into the chaotic world of government and economics, but I never seemed to understand what they were doing when they did "research" (I still don't). John Gaus was making public administration exciting to a generation of solid young men. I did not feel solid. And there was the Department of Economics. A center of intellectual energy, it was home to something called Institutional Economics. Its great figure, John R. Commons, still lived, faded, on the edge of the campus, and homage was paid to Thorstein Veblen. Younger economists wore the halo of commuters to Washington. But for me, as for many, the dominant force in the university was Selig Perlman.

Perlman, to those who encountered him in those days, was an unforgettable figure. Swarthy, a nose that was a caricature of itself, a high-pitched squeaky voice, an agonizing stutter, a heavy accent enhancing the impeccable English that painfully emerged, his eyes always fixed on an invisible spot on the ceiling as he excitedly roamed the aisles, he fought adamantly against the popular Marxism of the day, fought it on its own ground with devastating effectiveness.

I was a cradle socialist, fairly familiar with Marx, not a Bolshevik, virtually represented, I suppose, by Norman Thomas. Perlman was the first adult I met who knew all about it and, incredibly, did not believe in it. I sat in his classes stunned, fascinated, destroyed, robbed bit by bit of my faith, all certainties dissolved, all direction lost. This is not an attempt to recreate the intellectual ferment of the thirties in a vigorous university. I mention Perlman, as I could mention others, to indicate that Meiklejohn did not appear as a solitary candle in a dim world, a lone mind in a world of clods. The scene was one of vigorous controversy about urgent issues, of powerful assertive teaching. And Meiklejohn, beaten in battle, stripped of his Experimental College, strode into an expectant classroom not quite in the center of things.

What he offered us was the figure of Socrates. That is an interesting selection from among the possible offerings to the young facing a time of troubles. What thirst could Socrates slake? Of course the man sentenced to death by the Athenians on the charge of subversion, of misleading the young, must be with us on the side of the angels. That he refused the invitation to escape the death penalty out of respect for the law that had so unfairly condemned him, out of commitment to the city, was a troubling complication. We were being introduced to the loyal questioner when it seemed obvious that questioning was called for and loyalty was suspect—a fault, not a virtue. No, Socrates was not an unflawed hero. He did go, with dignity, into that dark night. But his reasons!

Nor was it easy to accept the Socratic profession of ignorance. It takes time to realize that life is lived in a deep fog lit fitfully by the glitter of illusions, and we thought that he must know what he denied that he knew, and found his denial affected, insincere.

And even the questioning! How many generations of students have thought that Thrasymachus, the unabashed realist, is merely tricked into silence, outwitted but not fairly refuted. And poor Euthyphro, rushing off, in an early civil-rights case, to report his father for mistreating a slave, waylaid by Socrates and drawn into a diversionary argument about whether the gods love what is right because it is right or whether their loving something makes it right—about whether, as we might put it, public opinion is the measure of rightness. When the injustice is so obvious why must we be stopped to question? There is a kind of impatience with Socrates; in a mood of practical urgency we brush aside the Socratic web and rush into the pit, muttering at Socrates for trying to delay us. Question, yes; but what about action!

So, Meiklejohn brought Socrates to class and introduced him to us. Avoid the unexamined life! Matthew Arnold, offering "culture" in a Socratic mood to his busy world, wryly reports the criticism: "Death, sin, cruelty stalk among us, filling their maws with innocence and youth, and me in the midst of the general tribulation, handing out my pouncet-box." Well, I have come to love Socrates, but it may not have been love at first sight.

Meiklejohn also brought us, newly published, his book, *What Does America Mean? (WDAM)*. To reread it after almost half a century is a bittersweet experience. Ideas long appropriated appear like forgotten old friends, evoking a flood of sharp images, the passions, the doubts, the agonies of youth. To remember Alexander Meiklejohn is to re-examine oneself, to recall painfully the ways of self-defeat, to retrace journeys, to feel the mind begin to stir again over questions never answered but somehow put aside.

WDAM, deeply characteristic as it is, has a special quality of intimacy almost unique among his writings. This is due, I think, to its being written for his college students. It is not condescending, but it has that special unguarded quality of working classroom discourse; it is a teacher's working revelation. It has an air of vulnerability, and now, as then, I feel protective about it. I don't think I want everyone to read it; I would recommend it to only a few of my friends. I do not want to hear what Callicles has to say about it, nor the scoffing of Thrasymachus. I shrink from the burden of defending it, although it is all true.

We are spirits as well as bodies; we have obligations and commitments as well as interests and desires; significance is more than satisfaction; excellence is more than happiness. The pervasive human tragedy is the self-defeat in which the higher is confused with, betrayed to, the lower. Every attempt I make to describe the "doctrine" strikes me as a hopeless caricature. It is, I think, the most personally revealing of Meiklejohn's books, the unshaken base from which he, all his life, conducted his sorties against the materialism he detested.

How did we take all this? In a way, I think, that seemed a part of Meiklejohn's special fate. Generally, we loved where he came out, but we could not accept or understand the philosophy that led him there. Spirit? Whatever is solid. We were, on the whole, confident materialists. We felt in our bones that interests were real and obligations snares for the unwary, part of a pernicious ideological superstructure. Happiness made sense. Excellence? Quite all right if it contributed to happiness; but preferable even if it did not? We overlooked his philosophical oddities because he warmed us by his criticism of the society we lived in, of exploitation, by his scornful rejection of the marketplace as the center of life, of selling as a human transaction, of the competitive success that destroys us. He seemed a prophet crying in the marketplace. He thrilled with sympathy for the notion of a people undertaking, together, to plan for justice and for beauty; with scorn for the idea that each should simply seek his own good. He laughed—and it comforted us—at the idea that the business of America was business. Oddly enough, I cannot remember ever really thinking of him as a Socialist or, if the thought crossed my mind, taking it seriously as having anything to do with the core of Alexander Meiklejohn. The issue was deeper; he was an idealist.

As I have said, we found the talk about spirit and obligation to be unreal, something to be treated with polite scepticism. (Perhaps I should not speak of "we" so casually. There were some young Meiklejohnians who eagerly adopted the language of "spirit," but I thought, I must confess, that they simply didn't understand anything. Sometimes "we" shrinks to "I.") But there was another point about which we fought with impolite vigor. What Does America Mean? The very title was an irritation. What do you mean, "What Does America Mean? A country doesn't mean anything! It is just spread out there, sometimes where it shouldn't be. It has just grown. Individuals have interests and purposes, Americans have them like everyone else. But "America" is a seething mass of individuals, special interests, classes; it has no special purpose of its own, no unifying transcending common purpose uniting its diverse members. Years later a classmate unmet for decades shouted in greeting across a room, "common purpose!" and it all came flooding back—the excited class, Meiklejohn smiling, nodding, not arguing as we raged against political piety and superstition. Common purpose, indeed!

It was a great stumbling block. Individuals and their interests seemed real enough. Radical enlightenment expressed itself in the view that classes were even realer. It did not seem strange to assert that Jones was a member of the working class whether he realized it or not. It was a fact about him. He needed to be brought to see that he had interests he was not aware of, that he shared a common class destiny, a common purpose—something given by the situation, not chosen, to which he could, if morally asleep, be oblivious, but which, if he awoke, gave his life significance. It is obvious that the movement from individual to class consciousness has something in common with a movement from individual to community consciousness. But the awareness of class conflict, of class war, made it difficult to assume a unity that transcended the class struggle. Classes seemed real; the broader "community" did not.

I should say, rather, that the broader community seemed real enough to Meiklejohn but not to some of his devoted followers. And it made him an easy target. Who, after all, was talking about the political community, the state, those days? Not the phalanx of left intellectuals; not the individualistic liberal. Fascists? Simple-minded patriots? And, oblivious of his bedfellows, Alexander Meiklejohn? Obligations, duty, the general will—clearly the language of the enemy. And we could not cure our master of his habit of using that language. We had to try to defend him. He seemed to be attracted to dangerous ideas.

Looking back, it seems to me that I was not converted to anything by *WDAM*. When I remember being shaken, it is by Perlman and his persistent argument. To lose one's socialist faith is one thing; to embrace idealism was quite another matter, and I was not prepared to do that. But the special quality of the situation was that we loved Meiklejohn, loved the quality of his human sympathy and social perception, the hard integrity of his mind and wit, but viewed with suspicion, even embarrassment, the idealistic philosophy he seemed to believe in. I believed in Meiklejohn, but not in what Meiklejohn believed in.

So it is odd to reread *WDAM* after all these years. The philosophy that seemed to me then to be so unsubstantial now seems to have the irresistible weight of common sense. The argument does not seem new; it is somehow heavier, right. But to my chagrin, the fervor of my accord with the criticism of the marketplace and all that seems to have abated a bit. How can the student, the disciple of Alexander Meiklejohn, explain the depressing drift into the reasonableness of the editorial page of the *Wall Street Journal*? The God that failed, to be sure, but is that really enough? And why, unlike years ago, when I read "We must take the social order in our hands and set it right," do I shy like a frightened horse or shudder like Burke presented with an interesting new proposal? I will, of course, postpone any attempt to answer these depressingly interesting questions.

So there was the figure of Socrates, and there was *What Does America Mean?* There was also a faint expectation of philosophical conflict in the air. Max Carl Otto was a popular figure in the university—an exponent of a variety of pragmatism, a follower of James and Dewey. Since Meiklejohn was an idealist, the stage was set for a Wisconsin variation on Harvard's earlier James-Royce encounter. It did not quite come off. I had always liked William James and had, therefore, tried to study Dewey and was disposed to be a pragmatist. I was also prepared to like Otto, who was iconoclastic about the gods and derisive about Kant and that sort of thing. But Otto tended, I thought, to ridicule what he disagreed with and was quite unfair in his characterization of Meiklejohn. At any rate, there was no great feast of argument between them. Still, I tried to show Meiklejohn that he and Dewey really agreed about everything. He smiled and shook his head; I didn't convince him.

In my last year at the University of Wisconsin, still at loose ends, Meiklejohn suggested that I take up graduate work in philosophy. That, he said, meant either Harvard or Berkeley. Since his home was now in Berkeley, I did not consider Harvard, and one fall day in 1937 I trudged up the hill to the house, about a half mile from the Berkeley campus, that was to be Meiklejohn's home for the next quarter of a century.

I was rescued from the miseries of life as a graduate student in philosophy by World War II, but not before I had endured some four years of it, living most of the time within a few blocks of the Meiklejohn home on La Loma. His chief activity during that period was in connection with the San Francisco School of Social Studies, which he founded and struggled to maintain. It was a venture in Adult Education, something very close to Meiklejohn's heart. I was drawn in to the edge of the work of the school, asked to teach several classes. There was a lively faculty group. Alexander Meiklejohn took a hand, Helen (Mrs. Meiklejohn) was enthusiastically engaged, John Powell from the Experimental College faculty acted as director (was director I should say, but John never seemed quite like a director to me), and there was the sparkling team of Hogan and Cohen. And several others I never got to know very well. John Powell has written interesting accounts of the school. I did not witness the throes of its creation, nor was I there when, during the war, it closed its doors.

It was an attempt to create an institution within which a persistent effort to develop the political and social understanding necessary for the life of a democratic citizen could be sustained. It was not concerned with credit towards a degree, nor with vocational retooling or promotion, nor even with cultivating the enjoyment of leisure. It was to be a place for adults to study their common concerns as members of the polis. "School," I suppose, is the inevitable name, although it is a name laden with doom. But we seem to have no better name for what, in any case, we hardly have at all. Still, there is a not unreasonable dream that adult members of a democratic community will, as a normal part of their lives, read and gather to discuss materials out of which a common understanding will grow, a school that need never come to an end, a habit from which there is no graduation, a community made by taking thought together. Amherst, Wisconsin, San Francisco—a story with the same golden thread. Not, this time, on a green New England college campus, not in an enclave by the shore of a lake on a middle western university campus, but in a part of an office building in downtown San Francisco or in the rooms of a Santa Rosa Junior College in their deserted evenings.

My memory of those days, little as I trust it, is of a Meiklejohn slightly withdrawn from the battle. He was in it, and his presence was clearly indispensable, but he was more like Moses raising his arms over the battlefield than like the commander in the field. A bit remote; a good part of his mind otherwise occupied. That, at least, is my impression, although I'm sure it understates the degree of his devotion to the school, to adult education.

He was also engaged with the American Civil Liberties Union. I had not yet awakened to the delights of constitutional law, and I wondered why he was so interested in something as unimportant as civil liberties. The northern California branch was in a running dispute with the national office about the inclusion of Communists on the ACLU board—something like that. Meiklejohn, of course, argued against the exclusion of Communists—as he was also to argue brilliantly against the exclusion of Communists from university faculties. But apart from this particular controversy, his concern with civil liberties and with the ACLU was deep and persistent. And it had that odd quality I have already mentioned. Civil libertarians hailed him as their champion. Few have matched his enlightened passion about the First Amendment, his defense of freedom of speech. But, of course, while they loved where he came out they did not, generally, understand or agree with how he got there. Most thought of civil liberties as belonging to individuals "against" the state; Meiklejohn thought of them as the powers of citizens implied by their public function (a point I hope to make clearer when I speak of Free Speech). Puzzled by his reasons, enthusiastic about his conclusions. Even, perhaps, forgiven his reasons for the sake of his conclusions.

Eventually, there were consequences. Meiklejohn always insisted on the crucial distinction between the powers or civil liberties of the citizen as ruler and the civil rights of the citizen as subject. He considered the ACLU as primarily dedicated to the former, to the protection of the integrity of the mind of the sovereign people. In the end, if I may pass lightly over intervening years, he became increasingly unhappy with the tendency of the ACLU to move away from his conception of its proper role. Finally, he withdrew from the ACLU. He withdrew quietly. He did not, he told me, want to resign with a public statement of disagreement. But, with disappointment and regret, he left the organization he had cared for so many years. In the 1960s I had actually joined the ACLU and was, for a time, on the board of the Berkeley branch. I left in a huff, in disgust, over what I thought was the ACLU's utter failure to understand academic freedom and its stupid tolerance of disorder on the campus. I felt quite Meiklejohnian, but I must stop short of tarring him by association.

So, in those prewar years Meiklejohn was busy with the San Francisco School of Social Studies, with the ACLU, and with what seemed to me to be a booming social life. He and Helen had many friends on the faculty and in the area, and visitors from the East were always dropping in. Lunches, teas, dinners, social evenings seemed to besiege the carefully protected mornings in the study. The study in which, at that time, he was writing *Education Between Two Worlds (EBTW)*.

EBTW is a sustained, impassioned attack on the competitive individualism which he calls "Protestant capitalism" or, when he warms up, "Anglo-Saxon Protestant capitalism." Not exactly, for Meiklejohn, a newly discovered villain. In fact, from start to finish, grappling with life as a teacher, what seems to unmask itself everywhere as the enemy is, on the one hand, the adamant assertion of the private or "selfish" interest—however enlightened the self—as the proper aim of all action and the companion view that on the intellectual plane the mind was to rest content with "the way it seems to me" as the final view of things, polished with the politeness of a tolerance for the regrettably different views of other minds. We each have desires; we each have opinions; and if we have good manners we can live with the unavoidable conflicts without the futile struggle to impose a common "good" on the teeming world of desire, or a common "truth" on the mad and blind world of opinion. Some such view, encountered everywhere, was, to Meiklejohn, the denial of the possibility of human fellowship and human sanity, a rejection of Jesus and Socrates.

The book has a dramatic form. Something has broken down and we need to rebuild, but we stand baffled amidst the rubble. Surprising studies of key figures trace the story. Comenius, the frustrated hero of the old religious order; Locke, the destructive compromiser; Matthew Arnold, the yearning victim; Rousseau, the incoherent prophet of a new order. The individual

148

studies are gems in themselves, fresh, perceptive, controversial interpretations, made, as they are put together, to carry the story line. The story is really simple, stark, central. The old religious order with God and the conception of men as his children, a human family under a single moral law—that conception of the world is shattered, gone, not really believed in. And even when not explicitly renounced, we have learned to put religion to one side, to separate it from the prudential world, banish it to a private realm. And, generally, the church has been replaced by the state as the central public institution. The public school, under the aegis of the state, has become our chief teacher. Can it, how can it, what can it, teach? The intellectual basis of the old order is gone; we are left with the competitive individualism of an essentially warring world, fundamentally inadequate; we seem not to have developed the understanding that would do for the state what religion had done for the church. We are, as Arnold mourned, between two worlds—one dead, the other powerless to be born.

1 must pause over the relation of Meiklejohn to religion. It must have seemed to me that anyone who was "idealistic," who spoke of duty and obligation, of brotherhood, of unity, was religious. Meiklejohn even looked a bit clerical; he had bishops and rabbis among his friends; he spoke lovingly of the culture of Burns and the bible; he wrote tenderly of Comenius. And yet he was not a churchgoer, he was not pious, he was not devout. He did not believe the religious story in the terms in which it was told, and he did not pretend he did, or act as if he did, or ever use a religious prop to support an argument, or ever wrap anything in religious mystery. Risking all sorts of misunderstanding, I will assert that in all the years I knew him, he was absolutely unreligious. Unreligious. "Atheist" does not describe it, since what we usually think of as atheism is merely a form of fundamentalism; and to deny the literal truth of a parable is as misguided as to affirm it. His position, made explicit in *EBTW* is that some deep intuitions were once expressed in religious form and language, that the religious form no longer served; but that the insights are still valid and need to find adequate expression—"political" (in a proper sense) rather than religious.

The difficulty with this analysis is that it is both undeniable and unpalatable. Religion has become for us an essentially private matter; church and state have become "separate"; and the state, moving into the space left by the shrinking church, has become the instrument through which we seek the public good. Through which, especially, we seek to educate. At the same time, we can hardly be said to have a view of the "state" that would lead us to trust it with the care and nurture of the soul. We would need to think better of the state. But that "thinking better of the state" seemed almost to be the distinctive mark of the enemy—of the authoritarians or totalitarians against whose exaltation of the state we were being driven to a defiant affirmation of "individualism." Meiklejohn seemed all too willing to think sympathetically about the state, about government which, more deeply understood, might be made a worthy servant of the community's aspirations. But he was swimming against the tide. The liberal mind found "pluralism" more safely congenial; conservatives, when not drifting into a libertarian folly, wanted, at least, to shrink the public sector. Government, however much we depend upon it, was in disrepute, and public education, therefore, in serious disarray.

I read parts of *EBTW* in manuscript, but I was not able, at that time, to get a sense of the work as a whole. I agreed with the formulation of the problem. A long section in which Meiklejohn dealt with Dewey seemed to me to be right, but to be too polemical and somehow not very satisfactory. I found it hard to disagree with what he offered as the way out, but I also felt unmoved by it, and a bit let down. I suppose I expected, as a friend of mine said, that he would pull a rabbit out of the hat, and I didn't see a rabbit—although I don't suppose I would have recognized one if it had been, as perhaps it was, produced. But I was a bit preoccupied with exams and the approaching war. I was an isolationist in those days, reluctant, as we were saying, to pull the chestnuts of the British Empire out of the fire, horrified by Hitler, appalled by the power of the Axis, raised on the futility of war, the injustice of Versailles, a stranger to the culture of guns. Meiklejohn was not an isolationist, but I cannot remember arguing with him. When, some months before Pearl Harbor, I was drafted, Meiklejohn said only "You will not want to miss the formative experience of your generation." I was startled by the unexpected remark, but it seemed to make sense; and in any case, Pearl Harbor overrode doubts.

Sometime in 1942, just out of Officer Candidate School, I had a few days in the New York area and went to Annapolis for a day to visit Meiklejohn who was spending some time as a friendly observer at St. John's College. It was the only glimpse I had of him on a small eastern college campus, and I don't think I ever saw him happier and more at home. It was also the first glimpse I ever had of that lovely world. Meiklejohn belonged there as, I suppose, he did not belong in Madison, as he did not belong in San Francisco, as he really did not belong in Berkeley. When the roll is called, it will be Meiklejohn of Amherst. It was that day, I think, that he told me of his visit to Woodrow Wilson, still in the White House "Ah, Meiklejohn," sitting up in his sickbed, the Scot president of Princeton greeted the Scot president of Amherst, "when I get out of here we must start a college together!"

That day at St. John's remains in memory. Green, quiet, sunny. Meiklejohn smiling, loitering at the tennis courts, alert at the back of a classroom, jesting with Scott Buchanan about something Scott was brooding over. A Meiklejohn absorbed, springy-stepped, happy, in a world he knew to the core and loved.

After the war I returned to Berkeley and soon settled into teaching at the university. Meiklejohn was there on La Loma. The San Francisco School of Social Studies was gone. *Education Between Two Worlds* had been quietly received by the world. And Meiklejohn was launching his career as expounder of the meaning of the First Amendment. Berkeley had lost its bucolic air and seemed quite in the center of things. We were excited about big issues—the United Nations, the bomb, hopes for peace and a new order, growing tensions with Russia as the Cold War developed, Senator McCarthy and the hunt for subversives. Against this background, the great dramatic episode for the university, and for Meiklejohn, was the faculty loyalty oath fight of 1949-1950.

It was a bitter, heartbreaking fight, and in spite of some ultimate judicial triumph and the vindication and recall of the nonsigners, in spite, even, of the amazing persistence of a determined but divided faculty, the feeling I now have as I try to recapture the memories of those days is a deep sense of defeat—a defeat that tormented me even then and from which I have probably never really recovered.

Faculty members were required to sign a statement disavowing membership in (or belief in the principles of) the Communist Party, as a condition of continuing employment. There were, of course, all sort of issues, motives, pressures, questions, variations in formulation, but I think a crude formulation that ignores vanished contextual subtleties will serve best. Should a Communist be allowed to teach in the university?

There was a simple common sense view that Communists did not believe in democracy, would destroy it if they could, and that it made no sense to give them the chance to undermine the democratic educational system. (How do you convince the man in the street that you should hire your enemy to corrupt your children?) At the level of academic, not "man in the street" or the "people out in the state" common sense, the view was that a full-fledged Communist had a disciplined commitment to a dogma as interpreted by the Party, expressed as the party-line, and was not, therefore, committed to the free pursuit of truth, did not have the open-mindedness essential to the community of scholars. The regents, in requiring the disclaimer, were standing on popular ground. Nevertheless, the faculty found itself drawn into a bitter, prolonged fight.

In a simpler world, one of our respected colleagues would have simply announced, truly, that he was a member of the Party, that he believed its program was best for America, that he wanted to continue his scholarly work and teaching, that he could not take the oath without lying and he wouldn't do that, and that he didn't see why he should be fired. Alas, no one stepped forward to give us a concrete case to fight about. We were not to know, made it a point of honor not to try to find out, if there were real live Communist Party members on the faculty. The matter was to be fought out on "principle."

But what principle? Many, if not most, thought that a dedicated Communist was as unfit to teach as a dedicated Fascist, as (a bit *sotto voce*) a dedicated Catholic (the pope, infallibility and all that . . .), as in fact a "dedicated" anything—if the dedication was to anything but the unbiased pursuit of truth. And in any case the faculty in its "practical" mood (an amusing madness that sometimes seizes it) did not think a defense of Communists would sell in the provinces. So the basic question, involving the difficulties of the relation between commitment and truth or between passion and cognition, was avoided so far as was possible. Instead, we retreated to such things as: party membership involves guilt by association; actions are punishable, not beliefs; oaths are silly and don't work because liars take them routinely; singling out a group like professors was discriminatory and insulting; the regents had no business meddling with hiring and firing, which were governed by faculty procedures; "academic freedom" was being violated; and so on. Early in the struggle, tragically, I thought, the faculty—the Academic Senate—abandoning the heartland, formally endorsed the Regents' anti-Communist policy—while the fight continued on a variety of the other grounds.

Meiklejohn had published the clearest defense of the position of the Communist teacher and scholar in the university world. If the person was otherwise qualified, the fact that he believed in communism and joined the Party was an exercise of judgment and a matter of intellectual freedom—not a ground for disqualification. Beyond the question of "rights," he also argued the educational advisability of having convinced Communists in the educational institution. And, of course, he was highly sensitive to the procedural matters that lie at the heart of academic freedom. It was a brilliant argument, and I agreed (and still agree) with it completely.

During the long struggle, Meiklejohn was in a delicate position. He cared passionately about the issue and thought it was the most significant crisis of the modern American university. He had close friends on the faculty, yet he was not a member of the university; it was his battle, but he could not take a direct part in it. The leader of the embattled faculty, of those who fought against the oath requirement, was Edward Tolman, shy, courageous, sensitive, intelligent, a man of utter integrity. Tolman lived on La Loma also, his home just across the way from Meiklejohn's. They were old friends. Tolman was a scientist, a psychologist, and not a constitutional or political theorist. He did not formulate the issues or elaborate defenses of abstract positions. He acted out of a sense of responsibility for more vulnerable colleagues, out of an instinct for freedom and decency as well as a conviction that there was something improper about the demand for an oath, for a disclaimer of belief. Close as he was to Meiklejohn, I do not think he found his ideas, his theories, congenial. Nor did many who were taking part in the fight. Meiklejohn was, after all, the spokesman for the "absolutist" position, the defender of the right of Communists to teach. That was a position that, as I said, was abandoned by the Academic Senate, which, after endorsing the regents' anti-Communist policy, could no longer continue the fight on those grounds. But the play ran on, without Hamlet, for a bitter year—the grounds of opposition constantly narrowing as the faculty, involved heavily in negotiation, lost one piece of ground after another.

Meiklejohn, uninvolved in the day to day struggle, not a party to deals and concessions, had no need to change his position or to drop the main issue. He continued to follow the battle closely. I, and others, dropped in frequently to discuss the situation with him. He was especially concerned about the position of the left-wing junior faculty members, not by this time, it must be said, the center of the faculty's general concern. Meiklejohn seldom asked me to do anything, but once, as I was going off to some meeting to plan the next move, he asked me to raise a question about the general indifference to the fate of a young "radical." I intended, because he asked me, to do so. But I found that when the moment came, I shrank from doing it. I was being practical that week, and I could not bring myself to do something so quixotic. I still remember the bitter taste of failing to do one of the few things Meiklejohn ever asked me to do.

So, throughout the oath fight Meiklejohn was on the sidelines, never inciting others to fight, sympathetic, clear headed, and at times, I think, almost heartsick. Perhaps not heartsick; he was used to being with a losing minority and never seemed to lose his verve. And always, he was surprisingly realistic. Above all, in all the turmoil he never seemed to lose sight of the fundamental issues, never seemed to lose his appreciation of the quality of human action. Had he been on the faculty, I cannot imagine him signing the oath.

More than a decade later, during the student unrest, the so-called "free speech movement," Meiklejohn was still on the sidelines, living a bit more quietly on La Loma. He was, of course, deeply interested in what was going on, and many of the student leaders found their way to his home. And I would drop in frequently while he was lingering over the paper at breakfast and bring him up to date with what I thought was going on. (I was moving steadily from Young Turk to Old Guard.) He was, by this time, the Grand Old Man of Free Speech. And it was assumed that he would be in sympathy with a movement that unfurled the flag of free speech—a movement of students in a university that was large and impersonal and generally criticized as being indifferent to the educational fate of its undergraduates. Meiklejohn liked students and he listened to them and understood them. But while in the faculty oath fight he had provided active intellectual support for the position opposed to that of the regents, on the "free speech movement" he was, I believe, publicly silent. His position, as I remember it: So far as students were objecting to a fragmented undergraduate education, he agreed that much of undergraduate education was a shambles. He did not think that students knew how to remedy the situation and did not think that student participation in the running of the institution made any sense. This may perhaps surprise some who misunderstood his deep sympathy for students. But educational matters were, in fact, a very small part of the student revolt in any case.

As for the so-called free speech issue—the right of students to pursue their politics on campus—Meiklejohn's position was clear. Students had no "right," not even a First Amendment right, to engage in political activity on campus. "The issue," he once said to me, "should not be put in terms of rights. It is entirely one of educational policy. If in the judgment of university authorities it is conducive to the educational purposes of the

university to permit political activity, then it should permit it; if not, not."
I do not think that, as an administrator, he would have compromised on this
fundamental point. So, while sympathetic to the students, he did not agree
with their position. On the other hand, it would have been very difficult for
him to come to the aid of an administration whose exercise of its authority
he regarded as an educational disgrace. So, he listened to everyone, nodded,
asked gentle questions, did not argue, did not incite, did not make public
declarations.

When we think of his first 70 years, it is Meiklejohn the Educator. For
the two decades after that he is, of course, Meiklejohn of the First Amendment. Even earlier he had been interested in law and the constitution. I
remember being surprised at Wisconsin by his defense of the Supreme Court
against Roosevelt's attack; a packed auditorium, Meiklejohn cheerfully
taking the unpopular side. A single sentence of his floats intact out of
memory's haze: "It was a greater mind than Justice Holmes' that said 'Only
the Permanent changes!'" Meiklejohn had been close to Walton Hamilton
and Malcolm Sharp, two great teachers of the Constitution and had seen the
fertility of the Constitution and law as teaching material. And, of course,
there was his long involvement with the ACLU. But it was with the
publication of *Free Speech* in 1948 that he emerged as a great interpreter of
the First Amendment.

The First Amendment is, as every lawyer knows, a complicated and
treacherous swamp—a simple statement overlaid by a thick and perplexing
gloss. A modern landmark was the work of Oliver W. Holmes, Jr., who had
mitigated the apparently unqualified character of "no law abridging the
freedom of speech" by, to put it crudely, adding "except when there is a
'clear and present danger'" of something or other. How clear, how present,
how great a danger of what to what are questions that have engaged a great
deal of legal ingenuity. The upshot is that there is to be no abridging of the
freedom of speech except, of course, to avoid "danger," and history and
practice have worked out details. It has been worked out in such a way,
moreover, that, on the whole, we do not complain of too little freedom of
speech. To take "no law" as actually meaning "no law" is an affront to our
practical sense, hopelessly "absolute"; and Holmes and clear and present
danger have set it all right.

Meiklejohn, if I may dare to oversimplify, did two things. He narrowed
the scope of the First Amendment by reading "freedom of speech" to mean
the freedom of "political" speech; and, thus narrowed, gave it a preferred

position among forms of communication. So that government may not abridge the freedom of political discussion, even on the ground that the government thinks the discussion is dangerous; "nonpolitical" speech—commercial speech, for example—does not enjoy that degree of protection and may be, as are other activities, governed by "due process of law." In short, one kind of speech is given more protection and the other kinds of speech are given less protection.

This interpretation—narrowing and deepening the First Amendment's protection—is supported by a rather surprising move. I remember the day I first heard it. Professor Jacobus tenBroek and I were sitting in Meiklejohn's study while he read to us an argument against the power of congressional committees to probe the political beliefs of citizens. As the issue had been put, there were said to be three branches of government, each with its necessary powers, and, posed against these, the private individual with his desire to express himself and his desire for privacy—a private desire that must give way to public necessity. But, Meiklejohn pointed out, there are really four branches of government—the fourth branch being the electorate, a branch of government with special functions to perform and with powers that must be protected if that function is to be properly performed. Each citizen is a member of the electorate and in that capacity has the powers of a public office, quite apart from his private interests and rights. The First Amendment, Meiklejohn argued, should be read not as referring to the private right of expression, but as a statement of the powers of the electorate and the assurance that these powers—assembly, speech, publication—are not to be interfered with by another, an inferior, branch of government. The amendment is the fundamental guarantee of the political power of the people, acting as the electorate, a power so fundamental as to be properly taken as relatively absolute. To relate the meaning of the First Amendment to the theory of self-government through the fourth branch is, I think, a stunning stroke of genius.

Free Speech, reissued with some added papers as *Political Freedom*, is probably now the most readable of Meiklejohn's books. And it has some characteristic Meiklejohnian features. It is both crisply written and full of passion—as usual; it is, also, as usual, immoderate and defiantly iconoclastic; it is an analysis, but it is also an attack. It is an attack on a great popular hero and a related attack on the popular principle for which the hero is honored as creator—on Justice Holmes and on "clear and present danger."

Holmes is surely one of the most popular of American legal giants, and to attack him is to ask for trouble. But Meiklejohn finds the combination of hard-headed "realism" or cynicism eked out by sheer sentimentality an example of the quality of mind that marks the failure of education. So, with some preliminary gestures of respect he launches a powerful attack on the mind of Holmes. But, of course, the worshipers of Holmes will simply set their dented idol back on its feet and continue the idolatry. And, as I have indicated, Meiklejohn rejects the position that the meaning of the First Amendment is adequately expressed by the view that there is a personal right (a natural right?) of free expression limited only by the need to avert a clear and present danger. But his own position involves a rejection of competitive individualism and a troublesome view of the state that seems both innocent and dangerous. Clear and present danger seems good enough to many warriors in the civil liberties struggle. To reject it is impractical, but it is nice to have someone around (like Meiklejohn) to take an "absolutist" position that, dangerous or not, freedom of speech should never be abridged. So, without being understood, Meiklejohn was hailed as the great First Amendment Absolutist—stirring, but, as a philosopher, naturally a bit idealistic.

Meiklejohn's central preoccupation during the last decades of his life was with the First Amendment and with the claims upon his time and attention flowing from his stature as the defender of the absolute right of freedom of speech. In this connection I must speak of a month-long session held at the Center for the Study of Democratic Institutions in Santa Barbara. The Center had been established and was presided over by Robert M. Hutchins who, after a brief and stormy time with the Ford Foundation, went off to create a serious nonacademic intellectual center. A month, one summer, was to be devoted entirely to a consideration of the First Amendment and, in addition to the resident members of the center, a number of others were invited—Meiklejohn, of course, and Harry Kalven of the University of Chicago Law School, and I, among them.

It was an interesting ramble through some of the thickets in that field of constitutional law. Meiklejohn's ideas had been published, so that they were part of the background, familiar to us. We went through a number of papers without unusual enthusiasm. I took up four days with the first presentation I ever made of what, some years later, was to be developed and published as *Government and the Mind.* Kalven, full of wit and knowledge, was, I think, the star of the show. Lots of indecisive meandering, mostly enjoyable.

157

Meiklejohn sat there quiet and attentive, saying very little but, as usual, everyone seemed to be speaking primarily to him, vying to impress him. His ideas, as I said, were familiar and, on this occasion, not being presented as having to be argued for. I remember only a growing sense of regret that the negative form of the First Amendment might obscure the possible responsibility of government for cultivating and enhancing the life of the public mind. But on the whole, the conference left matters about where they had been. What else should one expect?

What was memorable to me about that month with Meiklejohn at Santa Barbara was not the free speech discussion; it was education. Assembled there, almost accidentally, were some of the leading figures in the modern history of American higher education. There was Hutchins of the University of Chicago; there were Scott Buchanan and Stringfellow Barr of St. John's; there was Meiklejohn of Amherst and Wisconsin. (The missing voice was Dewey's, perhaps, but Dewey—or his followers in the stronghold of the Teacher's College—had never really hurled himself against the formidable institutional structure of the American college or university.)

Hutchins was an impressive figure. He presided with intelligence, grace, courtesy, and beyond presiding, he had a mind of his own. He worked hard, still getting to his desk by 5 or so every morning, winding up a fair day's work by 10 a.m. He had lived at the center of conversation and argument for years, had heard everything, read widely, listened patiently, assimilating what came to him to a strong structure of convictions. Striking, courtly, formidable. He was, as I said, trying to create a new kind of intellectual center, beyond the gates of the university. He was devoted to the attempt, but the center did not, I think, live up to his hopes. Still, it was a gallant attempt, and Hutchins seemed relatively untouched by the bitter infighting that swirled around him—small stuff, no doubt, compared with what he had endured in his attempts to launch and protect his college at the University of Chicago. What little I knew of the Chicago enterprise I did not find terribly congenial. I did not like its metaphysical basis, and I had resented Hutchins' articulate visibility. He had, as spokesman for reform in higher education, stood in the place I thought should have been Meiklejohn's. I thought the Experimental College was a better idea than the Chicago plan, that Meiklejohn had a deeper mind than Hutchins', that Hutchins had a better public-relations flair. But all that was long ago. Both shared a common experience of defeat in the educational wars, and the relation between the two of them was warm and friendly. It was a delight to see them at the same long table.

And there was Scott Buchanan. He was one of the permanent members of the center and, to my mind, one of the most powerful and interesting influences there—learned, broodingly thoughtful, a ranging irreverent imagination, a patient gentle wit. His presence was, I thought, comforting and reassuring to Hutchins. Scott had been an undergraduate at Amherst during Meiklejohn's presidency and Meiklejohn always remembered that when he was "fired" from the presidency Scott had said to him, "You have been Socrates; now it is time for you to be Plato." Buchanan sketches part of his own intellectual history in the Introduction to *Poetry and Mathematics*, but I don't remember him telling the story of St. John's in detail. Meiklejohn was close to St. John's as he was never close to Chicago, although he may have had reservations about the conception of liberal education as defined by the trivium and the quadrivium. Still, St. John's was the embodiment of a serious conception, and Meiklejohn enjoyed his times in friendly residence there. Buchanan and Barr had left St. John's some time before this meeting in Santa Barbara. Scott mentioned wryly that when he wrote the description of the program in the first catalogue he thought it would be changed every year; he had not expected it to become a bible. Buchanan was close to Meiklejohn and close to Hutchins and, as we sat there, the only one of the three whose institutional efforts still had a concrete expression. The Experimental College was gone; Chicago had dismantled the college after Hutchins had left; but St. John's abandoned by Buchanan and Barr, had survived, still living, I think, on Scott's inspiration. But they were all retired from the struggle, assembled now to discuss the problems of intellectual freedom under the First Amendment.

In those two postwar decades Meiklejohn lived, as I have said, on the edge of the campus, with many faculty friends but nevertheless at arm's length from the university. He often appeared on campus. Every Friday a group of a dozen or so faculty from different departments met for lunch in a room in the Faculty Club. Meiklejohn was a member of this group and often on Friday I would walk down the hill with him to the club. It was a relaxed, loud, jesting lunch—the pursuit of truth adjourned for the moment—seldom serious, gossipy, full of confident self-assertion. Meiklejohn sat there, well-liked, one of the group, joining in laughter but seldom evoking it, quiet and observant, not in the least interfering with the unabashed display of unharnessed faculty wit. But I would wonder what he thought of it all, coming down from his study in anticipation of intellectual fellowship, a foray into the world that was essentially hostile to all he believed in about college education—hard-headed successful scholars, teachers of disciplines, rugged individualists of the mind, personally very friendly, but professionally hostile to almost everything Meiklejohn as an educator had always stood for, not only hostile toward but triumphant over—Meiklejohn the teacher in the midst of the successful professoriate. It could really only be a luncheon truce although the group, I think, was unaware of how deeply he was at odds with them. They were professors; he was an educational reformer—enemies by nature. Strangely, of all the years of talk I remember only one exchange: "Alec, it's amazing that at 90 you can polish off that strawberry ice cream! How do you do it?" "Oh" came the reply, "I've always followed a rule: anything I want; but never a second helping."

I had long been restless about the nature of lower-division education and when I returned to teach at Berkeley in 1963, I began an effort to establish a version of the Experimental College on the Berkeley campus. The program did not go into operation until 1965 and Meiklejohn was not there to see it, but I had discussed my plan with him before he died. It was, as I said, based on what I understood, or perhaps fantasized, of the Wisconsin experiment; but I was hesitant to discuss it in detail with Meiklejohn or to involve him in it in any way. I felt that there was something presumptuous in my trying to do what he had done, and I did not want to ask his approval or involve him in criticism. But I told him about it and about the progress of the enterprise as it made its way through the obstacle course of committee approval. He listened patiently. He made no suggestions; I don't think he even asked any questions. He was, now that I think of it, utterly unexcited by the prospect. I was, and I knew it, and he knew it, no Alexander Meiklejohn. He could have stopped me with a word, but he did not utter it, so I went ahead stubbornly. At one point he asked, firmly, that I not call it the Experimental College. But by that time there was a budget line for an Experimental Collegiate Program (not a title of my choosing) and the program became known as the Experimental Program—close enough to make me uneasy. It did not occur to me then, but he must have had deep misgivings. It does occur to me now, but I am far from regretting the adventure—part of which I have recounted in *Experiment at Berkeley*. Nothing remains of it at Berkeley, but oddly enough there is a program at the University of Wisconsin that claims lineal descent from the original Experimental College.

Meiklejohn continued the pattern of life he had established until the end. The intensity of his social life abated; his daily walks in the hills were a bit less brisk; he lingered a bit longer over his breakfast coffee, chatting leisurely with me when I dropped in to see him on my way to the campus, less anxious to get to his study to write. He told me one day, a bit upset, that he was having trouble writing—that he seemed to be writing in circles. He allowed me to dissuade him from publishing a short review that I thought was uncharacteristically personal in its polemics. And then, one day, neatly, without fuss, he took a deep breath and died.

How can I describe the special quality of Meiklejohn's presence? Beyond the crisp alertness, the sense that everything was being enjoyed, that every moment was a special occasion, beyond the flashing wit, the friendly invitation to combat, the unpretentious formality, the encouraging smile that seemed to tempt everyone into putting his best foot forward or to live for a while on tiptoe. Most deeply, I think, it was a matter of awareness, a consciousness of significance, the sense that the world contained more things than one ordinarily supposed. Meiklejohn seemed to see more. Some of his responses—a smile of appreciation, a quick flare of indignation—came unexpectedly, so that you became aware, at least, that you were missing something. I remember an experience I had in a plane while a movie was being shown on a screen. I watched idly, not wearing the headset for sound. I saw lips moving, arms waving; it was strange and dull. But once in a while those around me burst into laughter, and I realized that I was missing something that was going on before my uncomprehending eyes. They were aware of something there that made the situation comic; I was blind, or deaf, to it. Meiklejohn always seemed to be tuned in to a richer world—one in which more things were going on than met the ordinary casual eye. In his contagious presence you became aware of stories, plots, dramas you would not have noticed on your own and which, when you left his presence, seemed to fade out of mind, persisting only like the memory of a dream. As his student, evoking the aid of his memory, I do not find myself asking "What would Meiklejohn say" but rather "What am I missing that Meiklejohn would see?"

As for "What would Meiklejohn say?," I must say something about how he said things. In a classroom, or in the midst of a group engaged in discussion, he said, in fact, very little. It is not that he would not take part in the exchange; but what he said always had the quality of an intervention. A question, a quick short sentence. I cannot remember him making anything like a sustained argument, or pressing a point, or loosing a barrage of words. His interventions were often startling and would send the discussion off on a fresh tack or recall it from a diversion; but they were brief, friendly, good humored, often witty. The unit of discourse was, for him, the single short sentence set off by an encouraging nod, a smile, or even a defiant thrust of the chin.

But his speeches were quite another matter. I heard him speak in public many times, but I do not remember him ever speaking extemporaneously. He read what he had to say; it was prepared in advance. He read well, as such things went, but he did not make it up as he went along. And it was quite a different Meiklejohn. I was often shocked by it; it did not seem in character. Or rather it was, since he spoke often enough, another side of his character. He was nervous beforehand and he began calmly enough, but soon his voice rang out, he almost shouted—sometimes did—and there was very little diffidence at the heart of the argument. Full of fervor, full even of denunciation, hurling gauntlets all over the place. I hasten to add that this was not always the case. There were short graceful speeches, often of a ceremonial type, done gently and elegantly, also written out. But I mostly remember the Meiklejohn fighting speech, and it was far removed from the conversational Meiklejohn. He was well received, admired in his oratorical role, but it was the side of him I liked least. I was uneasy, I think, at the change in the familiar voice, the almost strident insistence of tone. Perhaps I was simply unfamiliar with the vanishing tradition of oratory. Still. . . . Once, after one of his longer speeches, I remarked that I thought that it had ended anticlimactically, that I had noticed this about several of his speeches—a considerable letdown toward the end. "Of course," he said, "of course. I have an obligation to return the listener to the condition in which I found him." A characteristically surprising remark evoking the image of Meiklejohn taking his passengers on a wild roller-coaster ride, tapering off at the end, smiling and straightening their ties as they file out, handing their destinies, like transfers, back into their own hands.

Remembering Alexander Meiklejohn! It is unlikely that there will be a 75th reunion of the Experimental College. Soon enough there will be no one left who will remember the lifting of the spirits at the sight of his spare figure entering the room. I am filled with a regret that he would laugh at. Have I not heard of mortality? Are we to be concerned about the persistence of fame? The accidents upon which that rests? Meiklejohn was a great man and, I admit, I do not want him to join the anonymous ranks of forgotten great men. Every generation must have them—men who stand out among their contemporaries by virtue of character, integrity, intelligence, vitality, who leave a deep mark on those whose lives they have touched and then are known no more, who have not left a permanent monument behind to reinvoke their presence. They are the fresh incarnations of the great human archetypes, as Alexander Meiklejohn was a great incarnation of the type of which Socrates was also an instance—the teacher who seems never to be off duty.

CHAPTER 5

GOVERNMENT AND THE
TEACHING POWER

The art of government, in as far as it concerns the direction of actions of persons in a non-adult state, may be termed the art of education.

JEREMY BENTHAM

Consider for example the case of education. Is it not almost a self-evident axiom, that the state should require and compel the education, up to a certain standard, of every human being who is born its citizen? Yet who is there that is not afraid to recognize and assert this truth?

J. S. MILL

The social "present" is generationally thick. Although we may think of child, parent, and grandparent as representing the future, the present, and the past, they are all here now. And while each is at a particular stage and may, in his self-centeredness reinforced by peer-group consciousness, think of himself as the moving center, to the dispassionate observer peer groups come in stacks, and the here and now is many-layered. Lost or isolated generations hold a special interest—as when the Pied Piper removes a layer, or when a retirement village cuts itself off, or when a horde of children rediscover Beelzebub on an island or campus—but, normally, the social present is thick with generations.

This excerpt is taken from Tussman's book *Government and the Mind* (New York: Oxford University Press, 1977).

This circumstance—that the individual lives through stages and is always at a particular place, while the society at any particular time has all stages present—has a profound bearing upon political theory and especially that part of political theory that concerns the relation of government to the mind. It means, I believe, that no single set of principles is adequate to the governing of the entire range of stages and that the basis and scope of authority within a single society may vary drastically over its different stages. Let me elaborate a bit.

There is a strange passage in the *Republic* in which Plato with deceptive diffidence offers us a myth which, he says, everyone should, if possible, be brought to believe. It is, apparently, a ridiculous tale, and it is greeted as such and may seem so to us, until we realize that it is among the deepest accounts of our creation. I quote a relevant part. Everyone is to be convinced, when he reaches adulthood,

> that all our training and education of them, all those things which they thought they experienced were only dreams. In reality, all that time they were under the earth, being fashioned and trained, and they themselves, their arms and all their possessions were being manufactured, and when they had been made quite ready, this earth, their mother, sent them up to the surface. Now, therefore, they must watch over the land in which they dwell, as their mother and nurse, and defend her against all invaders, and look upon the other citizens as their brothers and children of the same soil. . . .

The proposal is, of course, that we be brought to understand ourselves as children of the polis, as the political animals that we are; that we understand our nonage or childhood as part of the process of the birth of a person, a fetal stage during which we receive our equipment—the language, habits, culture—without which we cannot emerge from underground, from limbo, from the social womb, from the childhood that, when we recall it later, seems like a strange prenatal dream. We are born in stages and, for the crucial stage, the polis is parental. We are, accordingly, siblings, brothers and sisters, children of the polis, polis-animated. The ridiculous tale is utterly true.

But generation is painful, and the generations may forget the traumas of birth. In a familiar crisis of identity a generation may deny its generator and deny that it was generated at all. "Nonsense!" says Satan when the faithful Abdiel reminds him of his creator; "As long as I can remember I was there."

Surely, no one who endured life in the American incubator of the sixties can forget the sophomoric cry of generational revolt: "We are a self-created angelic generation, immaculate, untainted by parental sin, and we will remake the world [Ah, Pandemonium!] in our own image." Nature, when she is bored, imitates art.

The point of all this is so obvious that we need constantly to be reminded of it. A society is not an undifferentiated heap of individuals, equal, at the same level of "authority" and "right." It is a continuing entity, continuously regenerating itself, always pregnant, always with a generation in limbo, always with a part of itself in a condition of tutelage. The distinction between minor and adult—however much we may be baffled by borderline problems, by demands for adequate criteria, by administrative difficulties—is fundamental and inescapable. There is no society that does not recognize the distinction or mark, by some rite of passage, the movement from one condition to the other—the achievement, as we would say, of the age of consent. No single set of principles can adequately govern both minor and adult; we need both caterpillar principles and butterfly principles. *Republic* is a discussion of the raising of children; *On Liberty* is a discussion of the governing of adults. They are complementary works about different generations. John Stuart Mill would have been horrified by the application of the principles of *On Liberty* to children.

The special authority of a community over its emerging generation grows naturally out of the minor-adult aspect of the human situation. The conception of the community as the womb of the person puts the matter beyond the question of merely formal political authority and into the domain of parental function. The nurturing of children is to be seen, on the one hand, as the developing of persons and, on the other hand, as the process of social self-preservation and renewal—the re-embodiment, the reincarnation of the parental culture through the creation of the individual in its own image.

The natural right of self-preservation lies behind not only the traditionally asserted powers of war or defense, but also the universally claimed right of the community to shape its children. More fundamental and inalienable than even the war power stands the tutelary power of the state, or, as I shall call it, the teaching power.

The teaching power is the inherent constitutional authority of the state to establish and direct the teaching activity and institutions needed to ensure its continuity and further its legitimate general and special purposes. It is rather strange that a governmental power so visible in its operation and so pervasive in effect should lack a familiar name. The Supreme Court refers to the power of the state "to prescribe regulations to promote peace, morals, education, and good order of the people. . ."—a power, it adds casually, "sometimes termed its 'police power'. . . ." But it will prove useful if we separate out the school and call the power of government that comes to focus there by its own appropriate name. The teaching power is a peer to the legislative, the executive, and the judicial powers, if it is not, indeed, first among them.

In a federal system we may have questions about the location of the teaching power. It is generally assumed, in the United States system, that powers not delegated to the federal government are reserved or retained by the states and, accordingly, that education is primarily a state matter, although subject, as are other state matters, to federal constitutional constraints and enjoying, under a variety of pretexts, federal support.

The teaching power is not limited in its scope to children or minors, although I stress that aspect. To exercise the teaching power is to make claims upon attention and to subject mental and physical energies to discipline. This is done in various ways. We may, as with minors, enforce attendance in accredited schools with required curricular elements for a number of years. But beyond compulsory schooling we may provide for general, professional, and vocational education. And here the idea of compulsion gives way to competitive claims to opportunities as we scramble for places in schools of medicine, law, engineering, etc., provided, in part at least, by the state. Beyond this voluntary relation to the teaching power by adults there may even be compulsory or quasi-compulsory relations in corrective, penal, or therapeutic situations. Thus the teaching power ranges over minor and adult, in voluntary and involuntary ways, for purposes ranging from the sheer necessities of survival and continuity to the enhancement of the quality of social services and individual lives.[1]

The state's claim to the teaching power may be asserted in a strong or a weak form. The strong claim is that the teaching power is vested fully in the state and is to be exercised exclusively by agencies of government or, in a variation, by licensed, authorized, supervised nongovernmental institutions that operate within governmentally determined policy. In the strong view, nongovernmental institutions—religious, commercial, private—in the domain of education exist not by inherent right but on tolerance or out of considerations of policy.

In its weak form the assertion is that the state is one of the legitimate claimants to a teaching power; it does not enjoy monopoly or even priority; but it may enter the field. This view would support an extensive proliferation of public education institutions, but governmental exercise of the teaching power would have to accommodate itself to the equal legitimacy and even independence of other teaching institutions. The weak assertion might carry us to the requirement that all be educated to a certain level; but not that we necessarily struggle in government classrooms.

The strong and weak versions pose, in this context, the bitter controversy between unitary sovereignty and pluralistic theories of the state.[2] Fortunately, it is not necessary to resolve this dispute at a theoretical level in order to explicate or develop the notion of the teaching power. Nor need I, nor do I, assume the burden of defending the assertion of the teaching power in its strong form as appropriate for contemporary America. (But see endnote 2.) We are deeply involved in the problems and politics of education and, I believe, the missing or neglected conception of the teaching power will clarify and aid our understanding. But it may well be the weak version that is implied in our theory and practice. In any case, that is a version more likely to be hospitably received; is compatible if it should prove necessary in the end, with the strong form; and is sufficient to establish government's legitimate involvement with the mind. There is, even on a grudging view of our constitutional system, a teaching power, exercised by government, sustaining a public school system, whose existence or legitimacy is virtually beyond challenge.[3] That is not to say, of course, that the teaching power is boundless in scope or untrammeled in its exercise. Government is permitted, in its exercise, much that goes beyond what it is permitted in the governing, as we shall see, of the forum. But it is, like any governmental power, subject to the general and particular constraints that are the conditions of constitutional legitimacy.

The teaching power is vested in a structure of offices and institutions. The constitution of the state of California, for example, states (Article IX) that "A general diffusion of knowledge and intelligence being essential to the preservation of the rights and liberties of the people, the Legislature shall encourage by all suitable means the promotion of intellectual, scientific, moral, and agricultural improvement." (I love that statement for its sheer sanity, its uncomplicated directness, its casual profundity. It deserves a place, in our reflections about government, beside the First Amendment.) The California Constitution proceeds to provide for educational officials and institutions, and what evolves, here as elsewhere, is a formidable array of state or public schools—primary through university—ranks of administrative officials—principals, superintendents, chairmen, deans, provosts, chancellors, presidents, boards, councils, regents, trustees—and masses of teachers or "officers of instruction."

There are charts for everyone's taste, and the normal habits, tensions, and problems of bureaucratic life—hierarchy and autonomy, centralization and delegation, expansion and retrenchment, tradition and innovation—all bearing, although sometimes remotely, on who teaches what and to whom. But the politics of the teaching power is not confined to its internal organizational dimension. The past decades have brought into unusual prominence the surprising range of problems that haunt the exercise of the teaching power. Taxpayers, politicians, and courts struggle over the level and distribution of support; parental, ethnic, and neighborhood organizations press claims for equality and dignity; students present demands; teachers struggle to respond to new expectations and claims and to preserve their professional integrity; theorists and ideologues rush in with advice. Everyone organizes to parley or to fight as the society, uncertain about itself and its future, places heavier burdens on the school. It is not that the school has suddenly and improperly become "political," but rather that the natural, inevitable, and legitimate politics of the school has become more urgent and more visible. The political struggle over education in all its aspects is, without exaggeration, among the most significant of our time. It is a bitter conflict over unavoidable issues, and the stakes are high.

It is within this prosaic but turbulent framework that it becomes possible to understand the otherwise exotic conception of academic freedom. Immersed as it is in a sea of pressure the teaching branch of government claims the power and discretion it must have if it is to do its work. The legislature has its privilege, the executive has its prerogative, and the judiciary has its independence. Each branch claims, within a system of due process, the freedom, in its own domain, necessary for the integrity of its function. Academic freedom is simply the extension of the principles of separation of powers and due process to the teaching power. A violation of academic freedom is a breaching of the constitutional structure of the academic branch of government.

If it is not that, it is difficult to make sense out of it at all. The academy is not a subsidized enclave within which teacher or student may do as he pleases. Teachers are not ambassadors from another country enjoying extraterritorial privileges; they are not licensed to steal children. But the absence of a working conception of the teaching power encourages misconception and makes academic freedom difficult to understand and explain. Teachers are, after all, hired, and sometimes fired; texts are selected and rejected; courses are approved or discontinued; curricula and requirements are established and changed; teaching methods are authorized or disallowed; students are admitted or turned away. When controversy develops at any of these points and flares into an academic freedom case, what is the case? Surely not that such things are done at all, but that something has been done by the wrong person or tribunal, or by a flawed process, or in violation of the relevant criteria and rules. The teaching power as a branch of government has, and is part of, a constitutional structure. Its integrity, its place as a power in a system of powers subject to the separation of powers, is defended under the banner of "academic freedom," which claims for it what "judicial independence" claims for the judicial branch.

The scope of the teaching power is so formidable that the problem may appear, in the end, to be less how to protect it than how to limit it. It is not always diffident in asserting itself. Consider a classroom in a public primary school in a typical American community: a captive audience, involuntary reading, involuntary writing, involuntary reciting, involuntary revelation of guilty ignorance, all backed by the power to classify, grade, promote, fail, and expel—sanctions which, in terms of consequences for one's life, make pale indeed the transient chidings of the judicial power.[4]

The teaching power has its share of the general problem of government; it is another institutional setting for the study of politics and public administration. But it has as well the peculiar problems native to its special character. Its function is teaching; its unique functionary is the teacher.

Teaching must be seen both as an art and as an office. That teaching is an art is generally granted, although it works so mysteriously and assumes so many guises that we often attribute its fruits to luck or simply to not interfering with the inherent powers of the learner (forgetting that teaching is partly a strategy of noninterference). Teaching activity is so pervasive that much, perhaps most, of it escapes self-consciousness or identification with the teaching role. But it rises, at some points, to awareness of itself, finds its heroes and masters, cultivates its lore, and achieves the status of art and profession. As a profession it is properly seen as a fellowship entrusted with guardianship over a social function. And, in due course, as the function

171

is provided for by the politically organized community, the profession finds itself enjoying and chafing at public office.

In this sweep from activity through art and profession to public office there is tension and confusion at every point. Much teaching, as is much that is called cooking, is over-dignified in being called an art, and seems in the one case to spoil learning as in the other to spoil food. Much of the art is, in novel and creative modes, denied the imprimatur of the guild or profession. Some of the profession escape or seek escape from the constraints of the formal teaching office. And some of the holders of the teaching office, notably university professors, deny flatly that they are really officeholders or public agents at all. The art is restless in office and resists the curb. Even Socrates is enigmatic. He was, of course, a master of the teaching art to which, he believed, he was called; but he thought of his teaching as the exercise of an office in the service of the polis. His suggestion, when challenged, was that he be appointed and even paid. Athens declined the opportunity. An unwise decision, Socrates thought, but one whose authority he acknowledged. The nuances of that episode still puzzle us and the message can be misread. But the teaching power, at any rate, brings the art into office.

The office is a sensitive one and involves, as do medicine and law, close and confidential relations. There is dependence and there are frightening possibilities of misdirection, exploitation, and betrayal. The teacher is an agent in a position of trust, and it follows naturally that access to the teaching office is quite properly restricted. Merely "wanting to teach" is not enough and is often, in my experience, a surprising sign of unfitness.[5] One must be admitted to a profession that maintains itself by co-option. There are systems of candidacy and apprenticeship. Fitness must be established. There are not only technical qualifications but a broader range of considerations having to do with the ethos of the role. The latter are very important, very "obvious," and yet very difficult to translate into administrative criteria. So difficult, in fact, that the basic principle tends, too easily, to get discredited. The argument is that technical competence in "the subject" is all that is required. Because, presumably, the teacher will just teach that (mathematics, geography) and will not bring his private ideology or philosophy into the classroom. When, however, the obstreperous teacher, insisting on "wholeness," "integrity," and "conscience" does bring all that in, his "right" to do so is defended (unless, of course, he is a racist) in the name of free speech and the marketplace of ideas. The utter inappropriateness of these notions applied to a captive audience of minors in a school is so obvious to any sane person that the existence of this syndrome is believable only because it can be observed. In response, the simple-minded (but sane) fall back on notions of loyalty and orthodoxy as the appropriate spiritual complement to the teacher's technical competence, and in times of crisis we suffer populist demands for loyalty oaths and the purging of subversive teachers. This program is not pursued with the zeal and thoroughness displayed by "revolutionary" regimes, which do not fool around with idiosyncratic teachers, but some martyrs may be created. And, among the academic freedom issues, the question of the autonomy of the profession may be tentatively raised.

Whether the profession governs and polices itself or shares with laymen the authority to judge qualifications, to appoint, to discipline, and to exclude is a matter of some importance. The profession by instinct is against lay intrusion into the heart of its affairs. It is, it says, the best judge of fitness and it can, it claims, best handle its own disciplinary problems. The first is generally conceded; the second is treated as a joke or a scandal. Whether we consider the legal, medical, law enforcement, or teaching professions, the professional capacity to tolerate marginal freebooters often seems excessive. But while autonomy claims receive some deference even in the case of teaching, where a profession works largely within a public institutional setting lay influence looms larger. The teacher may be a member of a profession; but he is also, in the usual case, working in a school—a public agent subject to a measure of political control. The teacher, as a wielder of the teaching power is ultimately answerable to the polity.

Life within the orbit of the teaching power shares the quandaries of life within any great bureau—the struggle to preserve the central vision against the corrosive effects of institutional inertia, habit, sloth, ambition, and time-serving cynicism; to preserve integrity against the pressures of institutional necessity, external and internal politics, colleagues, clients, and critics—whether seen from the point of view of the lower-echelon maverick or the senior establishment guardian. It has, additionally, the problems of a profession asserting, in its pride, the claim to autonomy while working within and subject to the constraints of public office. All, we must now consider, to what end?

The teaching power is primarily responsible for those institutional processes through which individuals are developed, recruited, and prepared for social functions or, more broadly, for life in a particular society. To the already familiar Platonic images of womb and cave let us add that of the great ladder, accessible to all, which each person climbs to the height of his powers, to the social and functional level suitably his. The teacher governs the ladder which, in its full Platonic or Jeffersonian reach, involves universal schooling and careers open to talent, with mobility, regardless of parental status, determined only by ability and character. Societies fall short of this ideal in characteristic ways, but it is surprising how rarely present-day societies repudiate the ideal itself—democracy and dictatorship alike. All seek continuity through the developing, husbanding, and directing of the energies of the mind. All, that is to say, must engage in education.

This is not a treatise on education but rather a squint at it from a particular perspective; not that of the individual learner but that of the teaching power itself, considering its task. That task, in its most general terms can be seen as development in a context of initiation. It is the combination of "development" and "initiation" that is crucial and it is the failure to temper the one by the other that breeds both individual and social monstrosities.

Development is a familiar educational idea and its very use is a protection against the errors of cruder notions—the potter's shaping of clay, the filling of bottles, the stuffing with input, the conditioning of responses. Its attendant notions are more organic—cultivating, nourishing, unfolding, growing, strengthening, ripening—and, as any teacher recognizes, fundamentally appropriate. But development is only part of the story and, on its own, may generate anarchic or individualistic aberrations—the worship of the purely inner light, eccentricity, self-centeredness, solipsism. Development, yes; but in a context of initiation. For education is also the initiation into the ongoing activities of a culture, its arts and enterprises, its fellowships and pursuits. The great and universally applicable example is language: the development of one's linguistic powers is an ever-deepening initiation into a particular set of cultural habits. And what is so obviously true of language is true of every human art, activity, power.

The teaching power has, so to speak, a double focus. One eye is on the particular student—his special bent, his character, his talents, his potentialities, and even, for what it signals, his likes, dislikes, desires. The other eye is on the needs, the tasks, the opportunities, the practices to which the student must, in his development, be led, to which his energies must be yoked. Teaching is not only developing; it is recruiting and initiating as well. The teaching power's task is not so much to transmit culture as to continue it.

Thus, the teaching power, deployed at a crucial front, deals routinely with the generational crisis. Or rather, normal generational tension becomes a crisis when, for one reason or another, the teaching power is unable to take the inevitable challenge in its stride. Initiation into an ongoing enterprise involves, to some degree, a confrontation or encounter with the given. Recalcitrance, rejection, rebellion are, as we know, normal aspects of the complex response. The desired outcome is a well-tempered involvement, even commitment; failure, for the teaching power, for the society, and, most disastrously, for the individual, appears as alienation or estrangement—the deepest, although sometimes fashionable, of social diseases.

While it is obvious that the state acting through its teaching power is necessarily and legitimately involved with the mind, special features of that involvement are not always appreciated. The school is not a public forum and it is not governed by the same principles; children are not adults and are not governed by the same principles. If we grasp this we can begin to understand the distinctive exercise of the teaching power and not gape in foolish horror at the discovery that the school is neither a town hall nor an intellectual fair. It has its own version of due process. But it has unusual power to create and protect a special intellectual environment within which it may determine the mind's agenda and cultivate its proper manners.

To begin to understand the school and the teaching power, therefore, requires that we begin by taking two simple steps; the first takes us over the cliché that marks off the realm of intellect and spirit, the second takes us deeper into the "forbidden" realm, beyond the forum-governing principles of freedom of speech. To make this a bit clearer let us consider, briefly, some aspects of liberty and dissent—of "doing as one pleases" and "criticizing"—as they apply to the school or appear to the teaching power.

An adult may, generally, have a choice about whether to submit himself to the disciplines of the teaching power. He need not go to the university or to a professional school. He may choose to live his life without more formal schooling if he is willing to pay the price. The choice (unless, perhaps, he is in the army or in a prison) is his. The child has no such choice. He may be compelled, for a time, to attend a public, or accredited, school; for him, to be at liberty is to be at large, to be a truant. Why do we not give him a choice? Because, although there are other reasons as well, it would be too cruel to condemn a person to a mode of life "chosen," if we can even use the term here, in a condition of innocence, ignorance, and immaturity; he is, as yet, an incompetent guardian of his own future interests. He can, to be sure, frustrate and defeat us—himself—in many ways, but at least he must report in to the teaching power.

But the principle of voluntarism reappears beyond the threshold of the school because students may feel (I believe "feel" is the accepted locution for "assert without sufficient thought") that they should have more choice about what to do or should even be governed entirely by the principle of student choice; and there are usually some teachers around, and youth-sycophant ideologues, who feel the same way.

In the world of development, however, below the age of consent, the choice or consent of the undeveloped cannot claim full sway. For mind, as for body, growth has its requirements, and what is required is not always obvious to those in need. Thus, the school has curricular responsibilities that it is not constitutionally free to abandon or to delegate unduly.[6] This is required, or this and that, or this first then that, like it or not. The teaching power must take account of liking and disliking as presenting problems and opportunities, not as limiting its authority. The student may be granted some elective options, but he must be led to whatever, in its place and season, is appropriate. It is not merely a case of formal exposure to required subjects. Habits must be formed and powers developed. The school is the kind of place where that goes on. It has a habituating mission and the necessary disciplinary power. The state, acting through its teaching power, confronts the mind in circumstances in which its authority is not defined by impulse and inclination. Here it can demand the attention and application for which, in the life of the forum, it can only plead.

The principle of liberty or of student-centered voluntarism is, nevertheless, persistently asserted. The argument, although varied, takes two main forms that I shall characterize as, first, a romantic view of pedagogy and, second, an infantile view of reality.

First, it is held that one learns (or learns best?) only when one has a desire to learn. Children, it is said, are naturally curious, and this curiosity should be encouraged as the motive for learning. It is encouraged when given free rein and deadened when one is forced to learn what one is not curious about or interested in. Learning should be a self-directed form of play, and we are offered the vision of a society of addicted learners driven by unquenched curiosity, probing, examining, uprooting, creating, vanquishing ignorance, and bursting into the promised land—if only we don't interfere with the game and if we get rid of requirements and structure.

This view of learning has deep roots and has all the power of a caricature. It cannot easily be refuted, and it deserves appreciation and sympathy. Curiosity is important; enjoyment does attend learning. One would have to be a fool or worse to deliberately strip education of their support. But, but, but.... It is simply not the case that we learn only when we want to learn or that curiosity and cognitive pleasure are sufficient to guide and sustain us. There are some, no doubt, for whom knowledge is an end in itself, in whom curiosity or a desire to learn is the master passion. But for most, and I do not say this with regret or in derogation, learning is simply a part of life. We learn in the process of doing, developing, making, failing, experiencing, judging. We learn in stride, as we cope with situations in which we find ourselves or in which we are placed. Curiosity flashes on and off, opens up or diverts; enjoyment comes and goes, encouraging, rewarding, deserting, betraying. No, it is not the aim of the school to turn us into cognitive hedonists living to satisfy the demands of curiosity; the love of knowledge is not quite the love of wisdom. Curiosity can be an asset; but it does not deserve autonomy. The enjoyment of learning is to be encouraged; but it cannot determine or govern the curriculum. The teaching power must utilize these forces; it cannot abdicate to them. The conception of the school as an autonomous playground is a disaster.

Second, student-centered voluntarism is sometimes defended simply in the name of the autonomous child. The child, it is said, is a person, and his rights and dignity as a person should be respected. He has beliefs, desires, and needs and knows himself better than others know him. He is, of course, weak and dependent, but that does not justify overriding his beliefs, ignoring his desires, or deciding for him what he needs—subjecting him, in short, to a tyrannical regime, denying him his proper liberty.[7]

I cannot undertake to present fairly or adequately the variety of views that develop this theme. Sometimes the child-adult dichotomy is rejected in toto; sometimes it is accepted, guardedly, and the dispute is over where to draw the line. Sometimes it is granted that parents may, for a time, stand in *loco parentis*, but that no one else may. In some versions skepticism and relativism are pushed to the point of denying the parental claim to know better. In others, parents and the adult society are said to know worse. The child and the culture of the young may be seen as the embodiment of the virtues—innocence, goodness, spontaneity, honesty, generosity, love—

which are corroded and corrupted by death-enamored adult culture. In many variations, "leave them alone and they will save us" is the underlying theme.

In spite of all this charming (in small doses) childishness, society, all unregenerate, declines to regard the child as the tribunal to which it submits for judgment, or even as a proper claimant to an equal voice. It asserts over its children a measure of control that it does not claim over adults. It comforts itself, in doing so, with J. S. Mill's observation in *On Liberty* that a society has only itself to blame "if it lets any considerable number of its members grow up mere children" since it has, he adds, "the whole period of childhood and nonage in which to try whether it could make them capable of rational conduct in life." So we interfere with the liberty of children and impose our culture upon them—our language and arts, our sciences and crafts, our categories and creeds—preparing them for the processes of adult life and the rights, the liberties, and the dignities of that condition.

Is it not obvious, in this controversy, who has the deeper regard for the person who is, as yet, a child and under tutelage? The teacher, it seems, is torn between the role of nanny and the role of guardian. As nanny, one is allied with the child against the world—comforts, soothes, shields, indulges, interposes—and lets him play. As guardian, one scans the generation with a recruiter's eye, aware of the world's tasks, seeking to fit talents to roles and to harness and realize potentialities. The teaching power, in the end, is more than nanny. It cannot be completely child centered or bound by a claim of the right—not yet inherited—to do as one pleases.

A glance at "criticism" also reveals significant differences between life under the teaching power and life in the adult forum. Central to our view of the normal political process is the conception of a stream of criticism playing heavily and relentlessly over all that we are and do. It is, we believe, essential; it reveals our problems and moves us to improvement in a continuous process. Criticism as a way of life is seen as the cultural alternative to a life of dogmatic slumber punctuated by nightmare.

The principles of freedom of speech in the forum are, in good part, designed to encourage and protect the dissenter and critic. But, in many ways, the forum presupposes the school; it assumes and needs a general condition of forum-worthiness, the ingrained habits of discussion, disagreement, cooperation. In short, the institutions of criticism rest upon the art of criticism. We expect—demand—that the school prepare us for the forum. It is not enough to turn out acquiescent schoolboy patriots; we want a constant supply of fresh, critical minds. If we are to live with "*caveat*

178

emptor" in the marketplace of ideas, we must do our best, in the school, to make ourselves capable of rational conduct.

The teaching power must, therefore, approach criticism as an art to be cultivated. It must understand criticism. It must, to begin with, understand that it is closer to appreciation than to hostility. To criticize is not simply—although long experience with the "critical essay" of students fresh from high school is sobering—to "find something wrong with" or "say something bad about"; it is to exercise intelligent judgment. It is easy to find something bad to say about a book, a person, an institution, a society; but to allow that to pass as "being critical" is to confuse hostility with understanding—to confuse, as we tend so easily to do, the loud expression of innocent (ignorant) hostility with the announcement of the arrival of the new age of critical consciousness.

Criticism is more difficult. We expect a music critic to understand music, a literary critic to understand literature. Must not a critic of society understand something? Is every ignorant carper to be dignified into social critic? Significant criticism is a form of appreciation; appreciation requires understanding. The teaching power, therefore, as it seeks to cultivate critical minds, does not merely encourage and protect irreverent outspokenness. It prods the impulsive mind into the discipline of understanding, into deeper comprehension, into sympathy, objectivity, fairness.

But the critical art may require more, even, than perceptiveness and understanding. Just as there is something strange about an art critic who does not love art, so there is something strange—and even fraudulent—about the critic of society, of politics, of government, who does not love the object of his critical attention. Burke says somewhere that one must approach the flaws in his society as one would approach the wounds of a parent. It may be difficult, these days, to know how to do either, but what is required are understanding and love.

The task of the teaching power is, with respect to criticism, not an easy one. It cannot simply supply rashness with a few tricks and pride itself on the critics it then unleashes and sends into the world. It must cultivate carefully, presiding over a process of growth that has its own seasons. It must take account of timeliness, of due course, of the stages out of which critical intelligence ultimately emerges.

Consider, for example, the relation of habits to questions. Early education is largely the formation of habits, and questioning is one habit among others. To properly acquire the questioning habit is to learn when and how to question and when and how not to question; it is not simply to increase the proportion of our sentences ending in question marks. Questions can be premature or belated, relevant or irrelevant, superficial or profound, helpful or destructive, pointed or distracting, proper or improper. Questioning which can be an aggressive verbal habit, must be developed into a deeper irenic art. Socrates is the patron saint of questions. He stands for the examined life. Not for indiscriminate questioning, not for eristic games, but for the right question at the right time and in the right way. And he held, it should be remembered, that virtue must be habitual before it is to be questioned or criticized. Thus, when the teaching power addresses itself to the task of developing the art of questioning, it may appear, to the unenlightened, that it is engaged in taming questioners.

The well-tempered questioning attitude is haunted by skepticism, cynicism, and iconoclasm, and the teaching power is badly vexed by these seductive spirits. It is, as has been stressed, concerned with initiation into the life of the community. It seeks participation and commitment to processes and ends that must be characterized normatively. But where there are methods there are always botchings; where there are goals there are failures; where there is faith and trust there is betrayal. The introduction to shoulds, oughts, and goods is also an introduction to evil. This can be bewildering and complex where the need may be for something clear and simple. So we evoke—every culture evokes—its special parables and myths, its exemplary world. Here purposes are clearer and purer, devotion more unwavering, arts more potent than in the more prosaic world. And we begin the inevitable shuffling between two worlds—the ideal and the actual, the immaculate and the soiled, archetype and copy, normative and descriptive.

This aspect of education is, I believe, an inevitable feature of growth, and it is full of hazards for everyone. Ideals can suddenly seem illusions, and the disillusioned idealist falls easy prey to self-destructive cynicism. Myths and parables can be foolishly rejected as lies instead of being cherished as perpetual invitations to interpretation and reinterpretation, lifelong touchstones. There is a need for enchantment; without it, nothing much happens. But it is shadowed by disenchantment. Or rather, there is a rhythm of enchantment, disenchantment, and enlightenment, which education must respect. There is a time for myth and a time to be literal, a time to accept and a time to examine, a time to be soft and a time to be tough. Confusion in timing can be disastrous, and even what is timely can be misunderstood. A quick glimpse of enchanting—Ah! Brainwashing, indoctrination; a glimpse at disenchanting—Ah! Subversion. A cross section of a process may not be very illuminating. But the confused outsider is more than matched by the confused insider—the ever-present educator-idiot who shouts "It's up his sleeve" in the middle of the act; the professional iconoclast who doesn't understand icons or, for that matter, truth; the teacher who applauds when the child says "The king is naked," not realizing that a "king" is never naked and that it takes imagination, understanding, and discipline to see the otherwise invisible but real clothing—not the child's half-opened eye. Problems such as this, alien to the public forum, are native to the teaching power.

A last comment on the cultivation of criticism. The critic, we say, must be independent minded, with courage to stand alone, with confidence in his own judgment. He must speak his mind, like Abdiel, "unshaken, unseduced, unterrified" by any serpentine chorus. But even here vices lurk in the shadow of virtue, waiting to pounce. Independence, yes. But not the incipient idiocy of the loner, stubborn, hard-core adamancy. Self-confidence, perhaps, if warranted. But pride is still, although this seems hard to remember, a terrible vice. In the healthy critic, independence must be tempered by modesty and humility, by the awareness of other minds, by the occasional recollection that the common herd contains one more member than each of us supposes. The critical independence we seek to cultivate is that of a partner, not of a crank.

This cursory glance at the shape of liberty and criticism in the domain of the teaching power should remind us that the school cannot be essentially understood as marketplace or forum and that the teaching power must wield routinely powers that are frightening in scope and implication and that are, perhaps, uniquely its own. The legislature, we say, cannot legislate morality. Can that be said of the teaching power? Not if we understand development in the context of initiation. The school seems inevitably to moralize. It is a dangerous place. We are concerned, therefore, to control the teaching power and prevent its misuse. We embed the school in a context of political controls and constitutional constraints. We insist on due process. We may encourage competitive and alternative schools. But this is not enough. We can hardly add—although some are tempted to—the principle that the school should leave the mind alone. But we do attempt to make distinctions and develop principles that clarify the proper function of the teaching power and which, if observed, would keep us safe. Some of these principles are better than others; some are misleading; all, I am sure, invite interpretation and require that we reflect upon important questions of educational and political theory. I turn now to a brief consideration of some principles proffered in the hope of fending off threats to freedom posed by the undeniable presence of government, in the guise of the teaching power, in the realm of the intellect and spirit.

The School Should Stick to Facts

Threatened by controversy it may seem wise for the school to retreat and take its stand on information. Here is the community torn by conflict over race, religion, sex, and politics. What is the school to do? It cannot altogether avoid everything that is controversial. But can it not, at least, eschew judgment and confine itself to dealing in information and to sticking to the hard facts? Let the school teach, it is said, the facts about religion, the facts about sex, the facts about race, the facts about capitalism and communism, the facts about history. Then the student can make up his own mind, or someone else can make it up for him—parents, priests, scout-masters—as long as it is not the school. Education then takes its stand on the acquiring of knowledge, on information, on getting the facts. Facts may be presented or, better still, the student can be taught to dig them out for himself. He is taught to demand them, to respect them, to gaze at them unflinchingly, to accept their verdict.

Respect for facts is not a negligible virtue, and I do not mean to disparage it when I suggest that it is not central in the educational drama. It supports, but it does not lead. The facts do not present themselves to be served up in passive heaps, nor in complete collections, nor stripped bare, nor underlined for significance. They simply cannot be doled out, or gathered and assimilated first, without guidance by nonfactual considerations.

Facts are digestible or significant only in context. When we are entertaining a belief, an hypothesis, a theory, then facts come into play. They are relevant or beside the point, they support or shake, they are insufficient or decisive, convenient or inconvenient, they help explain or need to be explained away. But the significant context is more than a context of belief. It is a context of actions, of enterprises, of purposes that, in turn, lend significance to belief and theory. In this broader practical context, facts, as they bear on action, can be upsetting, discouraging, destructive—one man's triumph, another's defeat.

To the teaching power, "just stick to the facts," is advice that is easier to give than to follow. It cannot really strip education of its context of significance or values; it cannot organize itself around the bare facts. There are, for example, facts about sex. What is to be done with them? Are they to be dumped helter-skelter before schoolchildren? Or are they to be placed carefully in a context of love, family, society, cosmos? Clearly, facts must be handled with tact. (If the sex example doesn't move you, try race.) They must be placed in context, seen in context, understood. There are educational tactics about facts—conditions of readiness which must be respected, questions of emphasis and focus, preparation and postponement, discretion and revelation. Facts are to come in time and season, not in an indiscriminate flood. But the flood is controlled by policy, and policy is controversial, and we are back, almost, to where we began. We cannot find permanent educational peace under the aegis of fact.

Nor is it clear that, if we could, we should. The teaching power, I have argued, is concerned with development in the context of initiation, with induction into ways of life, into modes of action which are purposive and value laden. Do we really mean—separating "fact" and "value"—that the schools should inform about honesty but not cultivate it? Inform about race but not affect racism? Here are the quests for truth, justice, beauty—take it or leave it. This is proper usage, should you ever care to use it. Are we running a gigantic department store, displaying all the options, teachers attending every counter, careful, in the name of free choice, not to influence the customers? Utter nonsense! The school is not a store. Students are not customers.

The relation of fact to context and the necessities of initiation defeat simplistic attempts to erect the fact-value distinction—itself rather tattered, by the way—into a basis for the limiting of the authority of the teaching power. The school cannot just stick to the facts.

The School Should Just Teach "Methods"

The school, if it cannot simply stick to the facts should, it is said, teach not what to think but how to think. Learning is seen as learning how, as acquiring skills—reading, writing, calculating, arguing, proving, deciding. There are methods of inquiry, of disputation, of decision making supported by methodologies. The school is to transform these methods into habits; the method of inquiry, understood by the teacher, becomes, in due course, Johnny's habit of inquiring. Since we do not know, and therefore cannot teach him what he will need to know, we teach him how to find out; since we cannot teach him what to do we must teach him how to decide for himself. The school, in short, is not to stuff students with information but is to train them as enquirers; it is not to supply them with opinions but is to prepare them for controversy. Not "what," but "how" is all.

The power and appeal of this educational methodism is obvious. First, it celebrates the centrality of habit and, icon for icon, habit is better than fact as the object of educational adoration. (Mind is better seen as muscle than as bottle.) The teacher understands that skills are central and that imparting skills is forming habits, accustoming.

Second, teaching "how to" seems to respect and enhance the active independence of the student. Learning how is acquiring the ability, the power, to do something. The more we learn how, the greater our power, the greater our freedom to do or not to do. There is a real sense of liberation that one experiences as he learns how to do it himself. Who cannot recall the feeling of freedom and power that grew upon him as, learning to read, he found he could conquer libraries alone. Learning how frees us from dependence, from the transient fashions of teachers, from narrow, limiting context. We become empowered.

And finally, in teaching "method" the school seems to serve the community without becoming embroiled in its quarrels. Is there conflict over tradition and change, liberty and equality, left and right? Certainly. But the school need not decide who or what is right; it need not declare for Yin or for Yang. It tries to teach how to behave in the midst of controversy, how to solve problems and resolve disputes. It is everyone's coach.

This attractive view of education seems to promise the avoidance of partisanship through a deeper commitment to methodology.. It deserves respect. But, of course, it has its problems. To begin with, faith in "method" may be a misplaced faith. There are some areas in which we speak with confidence—"the scientific method," for example; but even here, while there are zealots who regard its teaching as the panacea for all ills, there is an undercurrent of professional skepticism that provides a derisive undertone to naive enthusiasm. And when we get beyond the hard and triumphant sciences and look around for methods of decision making, conflict resolving, of dealing with moral or value questions, the faith in methodology gets stretched to the breaking point. To teach methods in these areas seems less to teach how problems are to be solved than to teach how to blunder, stumble, cope, suffer, and endure. There is, at any rate, some allowable doubt about the efficacy of faith in method. It sometimes seems that the farther one gets from the genuinely creative or productive master-worker the more one hears eulogies to method.

Nevertheless, teaching is largely teaching how. But teaching "how" is more fundamentally teaching "how we . . . " rather than "how to. . . ." Teaching a child to speak is, after all, teaching him to speak as we do, with some marginal play between how we do and how we should speak. Teaching how is always teaching something in particular. That is, we teach (and learn) English, not language: tennis, not game; democratic politics, not governance. In learning something general we learn something particular first.

Teaching "how" it turns out, is initiating into a particular, active fellowship. Someone is to get involved in what is going on; he is to get into the habit of doing something, to share in, participate in an institution. The habits, the methods, the ways, which the teaching power cultivates in its special environment prefigure, reflect, and prepare for the institutions, the culture of which the teaching power is the agent. The more we learn "how" the more we become involved, the more fully our habits incorporate our institutions, the more inevitably our character exemplifies our culture, the more deeply we become part of the going system.

And there, for some, is the rub. It is difficult, if not impossible, to habituate to what is not institutionalized, to teach a habit not supported by the environment, to shape a utopian character in an imperfect world. The Tao is the way; the way is the method; the method is the habit; the habit is wedded to the established fact. To those who do not realize that all our trips begin from where we are, it all sounds too much like a conservative plot.

The School Should Be Neutral

Besides being urged to stick to the facts and to teach how, not what, the teaching power, in order to serve the whole community, is urged or required to embrace neutrality as a guiding principle. This is a valid enough principle where it is applicable, but its scope is narrower than is often supposed and it can, when its limitation is not realized, cause serious confusion.

185

Neutrality is called for in the face of the partisanship of others; one is neutral as between combatants. I stress "as between." Neutral "against" is a familiar joke. Neutral "about" is a locution suggesting indifference, "not caring," lukewarmness rather than impartiality; and that is not the sense in which neutrality is recommended to the teaching power. Neutral *as between* . . . and, moreover, as between alternatives *on the same level.* That is, a referee is called on to be neutral between Ohio State and Michigan, not between Ohio State and Football. Or, to take another example, a judge is to be neutral as between the defense and the prosecution in a case before him. That does not mean that he is neutral in any sense about law. He is not—it hardly makes sense to talk this way—neutral as between the accused and lawfulness. He is not required to be lukewarm or indifferent about, or uncommitted to, legality.

The familiar American educational example has to do with religion. "No establishment" at least requires, almost everyone agrees, neutrality as between religions in the public schools. There is to be no favoring of Protestant over Catholic or Jew. But this, of course, should not be taken as implying that the school must be indifferent to religion or even that it is to be neutral as between parties to *another* dispute between the religious and unreligious views of life. Perhaps it should be, but that is another question, and it should not be settled by momentum borrowed from the requirement of neutrality as between religious sects. We have drifted into such confusion about the implications of neutrality for education and religion as to evoke from Justice Douglas the remark: "We are a religious people whose institutions presuppose a Supreme Being"—a heresy for which, as a reward for his many other deeds, he may be forgiven.

Much the same problem appears in connection with the proper demand for political nonpartisanship. When we say that the school should stay out of politics, we intend that its operation should not reflect partisan bias. It is not for this party or that, for Republican or Democrat; it is neutral as between parties. But this does not mean, as it is sometimes taken to mean, that the school is to be indifferent about politics in general or about the political system. Nonpartisanship serves a deeper commitment to politics. The school is, among other things, to prepare people for political life, to develop the capacity, the understanding, the attitudes necessary for the operation of the society's political institutions. It is indifferent to the fate of this or that party, but it is deeply concerned with the health of the political or constitutional structure. It educates members, agents, critics; it furnishes the establishment; it supports the system. This is not an accusation; it is a statement of its function.

The danger in the careless use of the notions of neutrality and non-partisanship is that the concern for fairness may be taken as requiring the relinquishing of commitment. Or, on the other hand, the obvious commitments of the school may be taken as reducing any claims to fairness to mere pretense and hypocrisy. These are foolish views and result, I repeat, from confusion; but this is a point around which fools, impatient with distinctions, seem to swarm and buzz. "Neutral" and "nonpartisan" are necessary conceptions. There is a narrow sense of these terms suitably applied in limited contexts. But if we take them out of these contexts and attempt to apply them more broadly, we do not adequately express the relation of the teaching power to the community and, in confusion about fairness, become confused about commitment as well. "Neutral" does not express the fundamental relation of the school to the society it serves.

Seeing the teaching power as an inherent power of the polity we have considered ways in which its frightening power might be checked. Decentralization, the proliferation of private and parochial alternatives to government schools, attempts to define and limit the teaching role may, together, be quite effective. But there is something chilling about the very conception of the teaching power itself, about the conception of the teacher as the agent of the state. Can we somehow get out of *that*? I do not think so. We can ignore it or pretend it isn't so, but there is no salvation in the averted gaze. Can we defiantly place the teaching power elsewhere? In the hands of the (a) church? The family? Can we simply renounce it or relinquish it? No such mere institutional moves will solve the problem any more effectively than will the principles of separation and distribution of powers, of decentralization and delegation of authority within the state. The teaching power inheres in the state as clearly and inevitably as does the judicial power.

Can we, in that case, at least formulate the function of the teaching power in such a way as to keep the agent from servility, to keep the schools from becoming the instrument of the sins of the fathers, to aid the teacher in an attempt to shield the generation in its care from the influence of a sick or evil social order?

As we approach this question let us note that the same range of problems exists also in the comparable case of the judicial power. The judiciary practices its art within the structure of the judicial office. It is clearly a branch of government. Judges are officials of the state. Their functions can be described in different ways, but two things are centrally involved. First, judges decide certain disputes in a context of, with reference to, and in accordance with the positive law of a particular society. This law varies from society to society and is subject to judgment as foolish, harsh, or unenlightened or worse. Nevertheless the positive law has a strong initial claim to judicial deference whatever the private views of the judge may be. It is his job to apply it, to interpret it, to say what it requires. He is sometimes called the servant of the law. But second, the judicial concern is also for "justice," and in its name, in many guises, the judge subjects the positive law to some higher-law influence, checking, frustrating, mitigating, reinterpreting the apparent will of the law-maker. It would be a naive mistake to dismiss justice or constitutionalism, or the higher law, as a mere "brooding omnipresence in the sky." It is a fundamental feature of the legal order that keeps the service of legality distinct from mere subservience. Popular judgment, with a healthy instinct, has little difficulty with the dual conception of the judicial function as "enforcing the law" and "promoting justice," is perfectly aware of the possible divergence between law and justice, and accepts "judicial independence" as necessary if the judiciary is to be able to do its job properly. It does not occur to anyone that because a law may be unjust our judges, in order to promote justice, should not be agents of the state or public officials.

I find the parallel between the judicial and the teaching power very striking in many respects, but the similarity relevant here is this: just as the judicial power has a commitment to the "given" in the form of the society's positive law, so the teaching power has a commitment to the given expressed as the function of initiation into the ongoing society. And just as the judicial power cherishes and insists on a commitment to a normative higher-law or justice, so the teaching power in the midst of its mundane initiatory tasks insists that it must also keep its commitment to the logos, or rationality, or virtue, or objectivity, or perhaps, the free mind—some transcendent, culture-critical higher-law ideal. I will consider this in a moment, but let me note again that to preserve the "higher-law" aspect of the teaching power's function it is not necessary, anymore than in the case of the judiciary, to free the teacher from his role as agent of the state. Academic independence—the separation of powers—is enough.

What, then, do we want when we are dissatisfied with a merely initiatory role for the teaching power? What do we fear? We want the teaching power to protect our children from our errors, our follies, our vices, our shortcomings. We fear that a teaching power too timid, too uncritical, too responsive, will only perpetuate our betrayals of the ideal. And we fear, in the extreme case, that, if and when the state falls victim to tyranny, to the dictatorship of the zealot, a docile teaching power will dutifully warp the mind to its decrees.

In the context of these anxieties it is understandable that there is reluctance to accept the commitment of the teaching power to initiation into what is going on, and that there are recurring attempts to get around that commitment. One attempt, of course, is to deny that initiation is, in any sense, part of the teaching power's function. Stress is placed on helping the learner develop himself as he sees fit and leaving him free, so to speak, to attach his energies to stars of his own choosing. I will not linger over this plausible view that produces, from time to time, child-centered schools with administrators who see their tasks as pandering to kids and keeping the adult culture off their backs. If, at this stage of the game, it is necessary to explain what is wrong with this to anyone, he is probably incapable of understanding the answer.

But the other attempt is more interesting. It accepts initiation as an educational necessity but claims, in a utopian spirit, the mission of initiating into a higher order of life than is exemplified by the imperfect existing culture. It attempts to shape an ideal character fit for an ideal culture, for the brotherhood of man, for a rational cosmopolis, for a "perfect" democracy, for the good life—whatever that may be. In this attempt it may find the existing culture of the community an obstacle to be swept aside or surmounted, and it may come to regard the alienation of the student from that as a preliminary triumph.

The elevated tone of all this is, no doubt, appealing. It captivates the idealistic teacher disillusioned with a society that espouses competition for material goods—and all that. But I cannot really end on a note of acquiescence in a self-righteous declaration of independence by the teaching power in the name of its service to a higher morality. First, there is always the question to be put to the self-appointed guardians of the higher goods: Who are you? Where did you get your special insights? On what road did you find illumination? The local School of Education? The Teachers' Union? A meeting of the committee on the curriculum? Who appointed you to veto the culture?

But, second, there are profound difficulties in the path of any attempt to derive from the contemplation of an "ideal"specific prescription for conduct. Thus, we cannot derive from the idea of justice a proper or ideal code of positive law; we cannot derive from the idea of a good society any particular set of social institutions; we cannot derive from an understanding of rationality the particular beliefs we ought to hold. We cannot, to add an odder example, determine from the most profound understanding of "language" what language the ideally educated person should speak, nor create the ideal language to supplant the poor excuses for language that people happen to use. The higher law, the higher ideal is critical, not creative; it may improve a way of life, but it cannot bypass it or provide another in its place. The road to paradise lies through and not around the here and now; if we are to get there, we must get there from here.

Teaching-power utopianism ignores these truisms and produces, from time to time, an other-worldly school with its strangely victimized students, or a gaggle of counter-culture gurus leading sullen children in circles, but on the whole the teaching power is saved, perhaps by lack of imagination, from messianic delusions. Its basic style is more Sancho Panza than Quixote, more Sam Weller than Mr. Pickwick, more Jeeves than Bertie Wooster. Its strength is in its pedestrian sanity, and if it seems, at times, to lead its master a bit, it leads, nevertheless, in the master's direction, in his terms, under his banners. It teaches English, if that is the going tongue, as she is spoke, perhaps, a bit, as she should be. And it does not harbor the illusion that all the errors made, lamentably, in English, would disappear if only we could be induced to speak in French.

Keeping the public school in the center of the stage, in principle undeniably legitimate, I have argued that it is an institutional expression of the teaching power, understood as a fundamental constitutional power of the state. The scope of the teaching power is enormous, and the danger in its exercise, no less than the dangers of leaving it unexercised, requires the constant attempt to clarify and safeguard its proper goals. We need to see the school as a primary agency of the state exercising its authority over those who are still below the threshold of consent; we need to understand the special powers implied by the related tasks of development and initiation and the very limited assurance against misuse provided by oversimple theoretical attempts to disengage the school from politics. Education must be understood as an enterprise that places government fully within the sphere of the intellect and spirit and that requires, as a part of pedagogic theory, an understanding of the political aspects of the habitual structure of the mind.

NOTES

1. I realize that, in what follows, I devote most of my attention to the teaching power as it comes to bear upon the minor and where it operates, when challenged with the powers of compulsion. That is its most difficult and controversial sphere and the one in which the challenge to its legitimacy, when its claims are pushed to the limit, is most familiar. But I do not mean, by this emphasis, to decry the importance of the teaching power as it exercises itself in the world of adults where, as I suggest, the issue is not the scope and nature of compulsory schooling but rather the access to special opportunities. The competition for places in professional and graduate schools has become quite fierce and the politics of opportunity quite bitter. Traditional admission criteria—grades, scores, recommendations—are challenged as racially, or sexually, or economically biased, and there is a push toward quotas and "affirmative" admission procedures that, in some cases, are being challenged as "reverse discrimination." An implicit assumption is that an "unbiased" distribution of professional schooling opportunity would produce professions that are both "representative" and maximally competent. But even if this were not the case some difficult questions would remain. For example, if the ideal criteria filled our medical schools entirely with white women, there would be legitimate political questions about departing from the "ideal result"—the "most skilled" medical profession—in order to provide for existence of some male and some nonwhite doctors for reasons of social policy. There is a growing body of literature on such fascinating questions, and my bypassing them does not mean that I do not consider them important.

There are other questions as well as these more familiar ones. Most of our teaching energy is directed at the young and even our graduate and professional schools are inhabited largely by those within a decade of adolescence. But as we become affluent and live longer and entertain possibilities of mid-career vocational changes and become accustomed to early retirement, the redirection of the attention of the teaching power, in various ways, to the adult population becomes an interesting question of policy. Adult education may cease, someday, to be an oddity.

Nor do I deal here with the questions of "re-education," compulsory or voluntary, that really deserve some attention. Some regimes are determined to "re-educate" significant portions of their populations in concentration-campuses. Others limit compulsory re-education attempts to the rehabilitation of those in reformatories or to those whose mental health leaves something to be desired.

There are, in short, a great many aspects of the exercise of the teaching power of the state, broadly conceived, that I mention only in passing. I cannot really defend this as a complete account. My lame excuse is that "Government and the Mind" does not mean "Everything that should be said about Government and the Mind."

2. The question is, "Who shapes the young?" And the initial response inevitably puts the family in the center of the picture. But the family is not autonomous. It is constrained by the law of the broader community. It may drift in the mainstream of religious life or may be caught up more strenuously in a sectarian enclave; it may dwell in social and political orthodoxy or stamp itself with the deep mark of a dissenting or heretical movement. It brings up its children not merely for family life but for something more. But its control over the situation seems to have diminished drastically. The family may no longer control the significant educational environment of its children. The movies, the news and magazine rack, radio, television, the neighborhood are competing influences almost impossible to overcome. And the children are yielded up earlier. The remorseless pushing up of the home-leaving date—kindergarten, nursery school, prenursery school, day-care center—interposes ever earlier between parent and child another set of adults serving it is not always clear whom and equipped with God knows what sort of weird notions. In relatively free situations the parent may stand bewildered, reduced to insignificance by a seething Babel; in dictatorships he may be rudely elbowed out of the picture, reduced to subservience by children who have been taught to report on backward tendencies. The condition of the family in the contemporary world does not really permit us to rest with "the family" as a conclusive answer to "Who shapes the young?" or even to "Who should?" Still, the family, and its condition, must be kept in mind as we consider the claim of the state to the teaching power in its strong or in its weaker form.

I begin with a reminder of the stark simplicity of the strong claim as it is asserted, for example, in states like the Soviet Union or Cuba or China. Where the problem of education is seen in terms of raising a new kind of person, of creating a fresh or correct consciousness free of the corruption of an old system, the triumphant revolutionary power simply takes over the incubator and rules it with a jealous eye. We hear little there of "private" schools, of alternative schools as counter-cultural enclaves, of old-style or deviant adult values interposed legitimately by parents between the child and the ministers of education. The teaching power, wielded exclusively by government, brooks no challenge (although it may sometimes condescend to explain to awed gapers from abroad, whose children are safe in alternative private schools back home, that someday in the happy future . . .).

The assertion of a direct governmental monopoly of the teaching power is hardly familiar on the American scene and is not advocated by left, right, or center. Compulsory schooling, yes; with some marginal dissent—generally not, it should be noted, by the "disadvantaged." There are disputes about substance and standards and duration. But there is general agreement that compulsory education in America does not mean compulsory public school education. Our educational establishment has three parts: a massive public system, nursery school through graduate or professional school; a large, almost massive parochial or church-related sector that, under our "no establishment" commitment, is broadly hospitable to almost all claimants, is without formal distinction between orthodoxy and dissent, and is largely, in principle, without public funds; and a large private sector, neither church-controlled nor public, also ranging from nursery school through the graduate and professional school. Clearly, the arrangement is not one in which the government's claim to authority to teach is asserted in a monopolistic form.

But even this proliferation of teaching institutions does not lay the possibly overriding claims of government to rest. We require "schooling" up to a certain age. we undertake to provide a place in a public school for everyone subject to compulsory attendance. The parent may decline the public school option. Truancy is avoided by the provision of equivalent schooling, and equivalence requires governmental certification. The certification or accreditation of schools as equivalent may, in practice, be quite lax, but the principle of the authority of government to set standards is preserved. The parent is permitted to offer attendance at an accredited school as satisfying the compulsory schooling requirement. It is not quite the case that no school may exist without the permission of the government; it is the case, however, that no school can offer itself as satisfying the attendance requirement unless it has been authorized, by government accreditation, to do so. Something of the "strong" assertion of the teaching power is preserved in this form, even though there is no public school monopoly.

The point of our arrangement lies in the choice and variety it offers. Since we are dealing with children or minors the choice is exercised on their behalf by parent or guardian. It may be an exaggeration to characterize as "choice" what may be so much a result of circumstance and family habit but, within limits, the choice is real. It may be based on anything from considerations of class size and curricular richness to pedagogic style and religious orientation. The value of the arrangement is not only that it does satisfy deep and differing convictions about how children should be educated but also that, by providing alternatives, it removes from the public school an insupportable burden of controversy that, if there were no alternatives, would rage bitterly within it. And, for those who are neither substantively partisan nor impressed with the avoidance of trouble, a complex, varied system of schools can be seen as insurance against serious error, as a way to avoid putting all our educational eggs in one basket.

In spite of alternatives and variety there are, however, two points at which the authority of government asserts itself. First, there is the question of a government-ally insisted-on minimal core that all schools must provide; and, second, there is the question of governmentally declared and enforced limits to what may be taught in any school. There are some things that all schools must do; there are some things that some may do that others need not or may not; and there are some things that no school may do. In spite of efforts to restrict the teaching power to a weak form—in which government merely operates its public schools as one element among others—the authority of government inevitably asserts itself in guarding both the essential educational core and the bounds of educational legitimacy.

Consider, first, the problem of the essential core. Since this is normally a minimal requirement the argument for it is more likely to be based on the needs of the child, if he is to have his fair chance, than on what is essential to the society, although that may also be involved. Thus, a polity may have a mandatory universal language requirement: everyone, let us say, must be taught English as the primary language, whatever other language he may be taught; or, perhaps, everyone must be taught both English and French if the polity adopts a policy of cultural bilingualism. The core may include the elements of calculation or mathematics and some history and social studies deemed essential for life in the community. And we may, as John Stuart Mill suggested, require the cultivation of competence up to a certain level. All this seems unobjectionable enough. The public schools provide at least the minimal core and a nonpublic school alternative must be certified as doing so as well. But there are objections. Some parents may consider some part of the core as not necessary at all and even as harmful, and some may consider that it does not include what is really essential. There may be some attempts to reshape the public requirements to these views before taking refuge in private or parochial schools. Thus, we have had battles over the inclusion in the public school of a religious element considered, by some, an essential part of any sound education. And, in the case of the Amish, the required level of education was regarded as producing a worldliness that threatened their way of life. The core included too much; it might enable a boy to leave the farm and the community. It may seem odd that the Supreme Court heeded this plea and acquiesced in the parental demand for a lower minimal core for their children to deprive them of mobility, but in any case it took an action by the Supreme Court to sanction this anomaly.

A core requirement the polity insists upon is something that all schools, public or private, must do. Where that is not considered enough, the parent may seek to supplement it in various ways; but where that is considered too much, the process of certification of alternative schools makes the requirement, in principle, inescapable. *What* shall be required is a part of the politics of education.

There are times when the intervention of the government with its insistence on what is required appears as a rescuing of the child from parental tyranny, from a pattern of hereditary ignorance, from a narrow, limiting irrationality, from a depressingly benighted pattern of culture—the parent grimly following the child to school with "I don't want him reading this. I don't want him hearing about that. . . ." Or taking him out of public school to put him in his own safe special culture-preserving school to evade, if possible, even the minimal demands of the general culture. But soft! Do we believe in pluralism? In real differences, not merely trivial variations? Are we serious when we assert our belief in the value of different styles of life? How different? Can some differences be beyond the pale? The answer is, "Some differences are intolerable."

That is to say, the principle of pluralism, like the principle of toleration, has its limits. I cannot understand why this should be treated as a scandal. When we learn that more than a single way will serve, we open up to a range of acceptable alternatives. Not to everything. The prohibition of some "alternatives" is compatible with pluralism. If we give up the principle of a single religious establishment and recognize, pluralistically, Catholicism, Judaism, and Protestantism, it does not follow that we must also recognize atheism as an alternative on an equal footing. The principle of pluralism does not require universal hospitality. Some things may be out of bounds.

So, also, with educational pluralism seeking scope in our complex system of public, parochial, and private schools. I have already argued that a common core can be required. I now suggest that some things, some culture patterns, may be educationally out of bounds. I will not parade horrible possibilities. Let me refer, instead, to the growing political quandary over "school busing" and let me put it as a question.

What is the real issue over busing? Not a ride in a vehicle. Not even equal or "quality" education. The real issue is over the determination of government to interpose itself between the child and the parent who, in his bones, wants to bring up his child in his environment and his culture—white, middle class, ethnocentric, color proud—the culture of his home, his neighborhood, his mores, his traditions, his ethnic jokes and foibles—the way of his fathers. What are we to say? "That's pluralism!" or "Not *that* culture; it's against public policy." We can ban it, let us say, in the public schools. But suppose it moves massively to the private school system. Will we still want to say, or be able to say, "*That* culture pattern in the schools is beyond the bounds of American pluralism?" If there is to be the exclusion of an educational pattern from the sphere of legitimacy—whether we take the above example or other examples—the only effective exclusionary agency is government. It is the only possible guardian of the limits.

Thus, I believe it is apparent that the teaching power of the state, even when it is asserted in its weak form, even when it eschews the right of monopoly, retains, in the power to require and in the power to exclude, something of the final power that, ordinarily, we associate with the right of sovereignty.

3. There are, of course, challenges to the public school establishment that direct themselves not so much to the legitimacy as to the desirability of the system. The hysterical critics who would abolish the schools that they see as warehouses or prisons for the young do not deserve notice. The faddish vogue of "de-schooling" would, if anyone listened, merely doom the "disadvantaged" to permanent hopelessness. The attack on the privileged claim of the public school to tax support expressed in the "voucher" movement is more interesting and does raise a significant issue about fairness in support of educational variety. It also offers the benefit of genuine competition to a complacent institution. And, in various ways, the growth of private schools as an escape from the turmoil and inadequacy of the public school, challenges the dominant status of the public school. In many ways the public school comes under increasing criticism. Much of the criticism is well deserved, but it

should not obscure the fact that the public school is an amazing institution, relatively recent in its massiveness, brilliantly successful in giving a concrete form to the ideal of free (relatively) education for all as far as ability, energy, character, and luck will carry. In the midst of our frustration over its disarray and its obvious shortcomings we should pause, from time to time, to acknowledge the incredible success with which it performs its impossible task.

4.   The ultimate sanction of the teaching power, expulsion, is really too drastic to be used freely. It can relieve the school of the burden of dealing with a troublesome and intractable youngster, but it dooms him to a life with limitations of which he is not yet really aware. The school, it should be noted, really loses nothing by expelling the hard case; it puts up with him for his own good. If we didn't care about him the school could restore order with relative ease. Expulsion is like spiritual abortion.

But the consequences of the exercise of teaching power authority are drastic in other than disciplinary contexts. Tracking and guiding into roles may have decisive and permanent effects. The certification of competence or fitness for higher educational opportunities is the modern substitute for the accident of birth as the determiner of the quality of life.

It is, I believe, no exaggeration to say that the consequences of the exercise of the teaching power outweigh the sanctions of the judicial power.

5.   What Plato says about politics seems to me at times—although I hesitate to say so—applicable to teaching as well: that eagerness for the role is more likely to be a sign of unfitness than of fitness. (My hesitation is due to the fact that this runs counter to the normal pieties of my profession, and I am growing suspicious of heresies even when they are my own.) I have in mind less the teacher of a particular craft or art who, as part of his practice, initiates others into its mysteries than the person less concerned to teach something in particular than just "to teach" or to teach "students, not subjects." That suggests to me a dangerous disposition to impose oneself upon others, an eagerness to shape the malleable, a confident egoism, far removed from the spiritual condition of the true teacher. Preacher, perhaps, but that is quite another thing.

Nor do I consider that wanting to teach creates in any remote way the right to do so. Adults, of course, are presumably able to take care of themselves. But children are not fair game for spiritual pitchmen. It is odd that anyone should think otherwise; to think that he has a right to try to shape them or influence them or awaken them or lead them anywhere. Unless he is a parent exercising responsibility for his own children. Or unless he is appointed to the office of teacher by the proper authorities. The self-appointed teacher of the young is almost always a menace to everyone.

6.   That the school cannot properly delegate or abdicate its curricular responsibilities should be obvious, but apparently this is not always the case. We have traditionally been alert to pressure from this or that interest group seeking

curricular influence, and, when it works its way through school boards and educational authority generally it may be said to be a part of curricular politics and not necessarily illegitimate or, as going beyond proper politics, a case of educational irresponsibility. The responsibility most pervasive recently has been in connection with the demand for student determination of the curriculum—either individually, as in the abolition of requirements so that each student can elect what to study; or collectively, as when student representatives claim or are granted an equal or even preponderant voice in the establishment of educational policy. In either case to turn the shaping of a student's education over to the student himself or to his peers is so deep a betrayal of the student's interests and so complete an abdication of educational responsibility as to leave one speechless. The smug, uncomprehending, "democratic" spirit in which this is done is, to my mind, more unbearable than the cynical indifference that simply bows to student pressure for the sake of peace and quiet.

7.   Defenders of the liberty and the "rights" of children spring up everywhere. It begins with the clear case of the battered, mistreated, or neglected child, surely an object of proper concern, and goes on from there. Soon we hear of ministers who offer themselves as negotiators between parent and child who have "differences" over questions of lifestyle; we hear of schools or teachers arranging for services for minors, bypassing parental knowledge or consent; of legal organizations for the defense of children's rights. There is a lovely aura of goodness about all this—the gallant rescue and defense of the weak and helpless. And yet. . . . First, in spite of everything we say about the family, we systematically weaken its essential structure by diminishing the authority of parent over child. Second, we systematically weaken the tutelary power of public authority—as, for example, in the really ridiculous flag-salute opinion in the Barnette case and the more recent monstrosity, the Tinker case, that denied school authorities the power to ban a peaceful political demonstration in the classroom.

So we rescue the children. From their parents; from the state. Then what? Then we complain about alienation and pointlessness. We visit China and swoon in ecstasy at the sight of regiments of children pledging undying allegiance to their leader in schools from which no Supreme Court has banished a flag salute as an invasion of the rights of children.

There are other ways of battering children than by mistreating them physically—intolerable and inexcusable as that is. We can treat them as if they were adults and pretend that since "persons" have rights they all have the same rights. To treat those below the age of consent as if they have the rights of a consent-based status is not merely silly. It is suicidal.